Reflection and Doubt in the Thought of Paul Tillich

Reflection and Doubt

in the Thought of Paul Tillich

Robert P. Scharlemann

Yale University Press   New Haven and London

1969

Contents

Introduction

What certainty is left for thought after men have become conscious that thinking itself is historical? If thinking is historically conditioned, can ontological thought ever achieve objective certainty and can theological thought ever achieve religious certainty? If thinking cannot reach ontological or religious certainties, can the claims of truth on the part of theology and philosophy be taken seriously? Before men were conscious that thinking is as historical as man's existence, philosophy and theology could claim to provide the certainty which science and history lacked, because metaphysics reached beyond the changing world to unchangeable being and theology beyond the flux of history to the eternal God. But after men have become historically conscious, is there any objective reality that cannot be dislodged by critical thought or any religious presence that does not fade when it is doubted? If so, what is that reality and where is that presence?

These questions express the crisis which theological and philosophical thinking have faced since the death of Hegel. Nietzsche's atheism and nihilism were only the celebration—if one may call it that—of the triumph of the questions over any possible answers. No systematic thinker can avoid them once he has felt their impact, for without answering them his thinking can never find footing in a historically conscious world. Paul Tillich, like many of his great contemporaries in theology and philosophy, was profoundly affected by the problem these questions pose in a historically conscious age. But how did he answer them? And does his answer surmount the difficulties, seemingly insurmountable, which were created by the grand failure of Hegel's "absolute" system? Does it succeed in being systematic without being totalitarian, and does it disclose an objective reality that cannot be dislodged or a religious presence that cannot be made to fade?

I think that Tillich did find an answer, which does, within the limits given in my concluding chapter, surmount the difficul-

ties. Therefore I have endeavored to show in the present work
how he constructs his answer with two basic ideas, that of "correlation" and that of a "paradoxical reality and presence." The
first is used to connect religious symbols with ontological concepts,
and the second is used to formulate the meaning of the event of
Christ. In addition to constituting his answer to the problems of
historical thought, these ideas show to what extent Tillich is continuous with, and to what extent he breaks with, speculative idealism of the nineteenth century. Few theologians of his generation
were as sympathetic to speculative idealism as he was. Yet, though
he had a clear insight into its positive contribution, he also saw its
fundamental weakness; and, especially in his writings from the
1920s, he worked its problems through.

The way in which Tillich used these two ideas to answer the
questions which historical consciousness raises for serious systematic thought has rarely been noticed and never expounded. In the
present study I have undertaken to provide such an exposition in
the form of a "constructive analysis" of the themes of reflection
and doubt (or response) in his thought.

Before explaining how these themes are related to the questions
with which I began, I want to define what is meant by a "constructive analysis." Except for the concluding chapter, this study
is mainly concerned with analyzing Tillich's own thought, showing how its pieces fit together and where its limits become visible.
In that sense the exposition is an analysis. But the point of view
from which this is carried out as well as the concepts used are
somewhat different from those of Tillich himself. In that sense the
analysis is "constructive." The aim of such a constructive analysis is to find an approach to another man's thought which is
close enough to how he understands himself that it can interpret
him fairly but at the same time is far enough removed that it allows one to transform the material and take it into a new systematic construction. A constructive analysis prevents the interpreter
from exercising an arbitrary criticism (as much of the criticism of
Tillich's thought over the decades has been). It provides an in-

termediate step for transposing the substance of the thought from one systematic whole into another.

This approach is also suggested by the nature of the existing studies of Tillich, which fall roughly into two classes. In one class are those works critical of Tillich from a standpoint that is never explicitly justified and that, so far as one can piece it together indirectly, seems to be more vulnerable than Tillich's own. While such exercises in criticism may be important and significant for those who are committed in advance to that alternate standpoint, they disclose nothing about the tenability of Tillich's thought and only the extent to which it coincides or fails to coincide with the position implied in the critics' objections. Generally speaking the positions which have led to this kind of approach have been two forms of positivism, biblical or theological and linguistic or logical. In the second class of existing works are those which have provided an exposition of Tillich's thought by using his own position and conceptual equipment with the aim of making clearer certain phases which he expressed only obscurely or indirectly.

Within each of these classes some of the productions are, of course, better than others. But taken together they have already accomplished as much as can be accomplished by these methods. The expository studies have clarified as much of Tillich's thought as can be clarified by remaining within his own thought structure and vocabulary, and the critical studies have fairly well defined the extent to which Tillich is not a biblical positivist and the extent to which, measured by the narrower canons of logical positivism, he does or does not talk nonsense and confuse categories. The three most recent full-length studies of Tillich, therefore, have adopted a somewhat different approach.[1] Kelsey's *The Fabric of Paul Tillich's Thought* develops a critical theme but tries expressly to make

1. Carl J. Armbruster, S.J., *The Vision of Paul Tillich* (New York, Sheed and Ward, 1967). David Kelsey, *The Fabric of Paul Tillich's Theology* (New Haven, Yale University Press, 1967). William L. Rowe, *Religious Symbols and God* (Chicago, University of Chicago Press, 1968).

it an immanent criticism. William Rowe's *Religious Symbols and God* represents the concern of a logician but does not adopt the narrow canons of logical positivism a priori in order to measure Tillich by them. Armbruster's *The Vision of Paul Tillich* is an exposition from a Roman Catholic point of view, but it is more receptive and succeeds in catching Tillich's vision much more than would be allowed by one who wanted only to offer a Roman Catholic reinterpretation of the man.

The present study continues the line of these recent works. My thesis is a critical one, though it happens to be affirmative: I shall try to show that Tillich resolves the problem I have defined, and how he does it. The standpoint from which the thesis is developed is explicitly set forth in the terms defined in this introduction, which set up a structure intended to enable one both to interpret Tillich fairly and to take a step away toward a full transposition into another system which might stand on its own. In developing the main, affirmative thesis I have uncovered a number of points at which a negative critique is suggested, but I have refrained from elaborating them until the final chapter because their significance cannot be measured fully by a constructively analytical approach alone. There is, of course, a critique built into the analysis because of its constructive character; but since the critical stance in this case is an affirmative judgment concerning Tillich's accomplishment, the casual reader or the reader who has only a passing acquaintance with Tillich's writings may receive the impression that the first seven chapters are purely expository.

In order to define the connection between the themes of reflection and doubt and the questions posed at the beginning, it will be helpful to introduce here several terms which are used throughout this book in a technical sense. One set of terms has to do with the two poles that are involved when I think anything at all. In current parlance these are usually called "subject" and "object." It is necessary, however, to make some distinctions within these two terms. Accordingly, instead of "subject" and "object" I shall speak of the *subjectival* and the *objectival* poles or elements of thought. What is meant by "subjectival" is anything that is on the "I" side of the relation implied when I think something. What is meant by "objectival" is anything on the other side of the relation. By using these terms and making the distinction in this way, we can allow for the fact that there are *"objectival subjects"* as well as *"subjectival objects"* and thus avoid the confusion that comes from using only "subject" and "object."

For example, a relation between me and another person involves a *subjectival subject,* which is myself, and an *objectival subject,* which is the other person. This is different from a relation in which there is a *subjectival subject* on one side and an *objectival object* on the other. The difference is the same one Buber formulated in his two "primary words" of I-Thou and I-It. Again, in cases where I am simply the dead recipient of something's or someone's action upon me, I am a subjectival object and what is over against me is an objectival subject. (In cases where the question of whether a given subject or object is subjectival or objectival has no bearing on the matter under discussion, I shall use the terms "subject" and "object," with their corresponding adjectives "subjective" and "objective," without further specification.) Synonyms for "objectival subject" are "power" and "presence." In certain contexts—which will be obvious in the exposition—"form" is a synonym for "subject" and "content" a synonym for "object."

A second set of terms defines the kinds of acts through which the subjectival and objectival are related to each other. There are basically two, which I call critical reflection and doubting response. In critical reflection I endeavor to grasp the objectivity of whatever I am dealing with in thought; I endeavor to understand what it is. By contrast, in doubting response I reply to the power (the subjectivity) acting upon me. Critical reflection endeavors to grasp the objectivity of the objectival, and doubting response replies to its subjectivity. This is to say that by reflecting I ultimately grasp *being* and by doubting I respond to *God*. *Being* is the objectivity of the objectival sphere, and *God* is its subjectivity.[2]

2. The two terms are to be distinguished from Tillich's "being-itself" and "God" as the ground of being, since these two terms are both subjectival and objectival in their reference. See n. 5, below.

Thus, a word used as a concept is a means of grasping objectivity through acts of reflection. Used as a symbol, it is a means of responding to the power acting upon me.

Some synonyms for reflection and response will be used in the following chapters, partly for variety and partly for introducing other connotations into these activities. For doubting response I also use distancing doubt, doubting, and religious response; for critical reflection, critical understanding, reflective understanding, questioning, criticizing, grasping. Justification for these substitutions is provided along the way, mostly by the context itself. (In order to keep the meaning of "reflection" distinct from something like "self-reflection" or "reflexivity," I use its verbal form without a preposition and with a direct object: "reflect something" rather than "reflect upon something.")

These terms now permit me to state the connection of reflection and response to my opening questions. Reflection is the process in which I understand what is real or what an object really is. What is objectively real is distinguished from what is illusory by the fact that it is not changed by my act of reflection. The one objectively certain reality is the one which can never be changed by my reflection or anyone's reflection of it. But here an apparently insoluble problem presents itself. In order to tell whether my here-and-now reflection changes the reality I reflect, I should be able to say what my here-and-now reflection itself is. Is it or is it not an act that changes the reality? It is no great problem to answer that question—to think my act of thinking—if one ignores or is not conscious of the temporality, or historical character, of the act. But once I take into account this temporality, I am conscious that each act, each here-and-now, is new. And if each here-and-now act is a new reflection, I can never "catch" it, I can never think my present act because it has already gone when I think it.

Doubting response ends in the same perplexity. Response is the act in which I reply to an objectival presence. If reflection answers the question of what is real, then response shows where or who the true presence is. A true presence is distinguished from a false one by the fact that it does not fade when I doubt it; its power is not diminished by my response. The one certain presence is the one which my response can never remove. But how can I tell whether my response diminishes the power of the presence or confirms it? Again, this problem is not acute if one ignores the temporality of every response. But if each here-and-now act of response is new, then I can never "catch" my present response to know what presence is eliciting it; what I "catch" in my present response is always something past.

To historically conscious thinking the only certainty seems to be my temporality itself, that continuing "now" from which all my acts emerge. But what is this temporality? Where is it present to me as a power? If thinking could answer these questions, it could reach at least one objective certainty and one unfading presence. But that is precisely what thinking seems incapable of doing. It cannot say what temporality is or where its power is present to me because thinking cannot catch its own act; what I think is never identical with the here-and-now act of thinking it; the act is always gone before it becomes content. The restless "now" is the one certainty for historically conscious thinking, but I cannot grasp it in reflection to know what it *is,* nor can I discover where it is objectively *present.* If "thinking is being" (*Denken ist Sein*), as Hegel said, and if God is my responding, as Schleiermacher seemed to imply, then I can never understand being or know what it is, and I can never respond to God or encounter his presence. For every understanding of being is dislodged by my here-and-now reflecting and every god is made to vanish by my here-and-now response. Then, as Nietzsche saw, being is nothing and God is dead; there is no certain objectivity and no certain presence, only temporality which can neither be understood nor responded to.

With this consideration we come back to the questions with which I began. The one certainty for historically conscious thinking always eludes reflection and response; it can never be objectively present. This is the same as saying that there is no objectively certain reality or a religiously certain presence left, since every reality is dislodged by a new act of reflection and every presence is diminished by a new act of response—unless there is some way of making temporality objective and present.

The grandest attempt to do just this in the nineteenth century was Hegel's "absolute" system, and we can best see the nature of Tillich's solution by noticing how it contrasts with that system. Hegel saw only one way out of the predicament. If it were possible to construct a whole of such a kind that it could not be further reflected, the whole itself would be the embodiment of temporality, the one certainty for historical thinking; the whole of temporality would be the eternal. Of course, men would continue to think; acts of thinking would still go on. But if the whole succeeded in its aim, these further acts of reflection would never alter the whole, even though they would be chronologically distinct from former acts of reflection. They would repeat reflections already made, but they would never introduce anything new. The whole would be reality and truth itself because it always anticipated, and was never changed by, acts of reflection. But in the nature of the case, the structure of such a whole had to be a system in which thinking had traversed all objectival relations, logically and historically, and had done so from all possible perspectives—that is, with all possible kinds of reflective acts; only then would every act and every content already be included in the whole. This is exactly what Hegel believed he had accomplished, though the cost of it was to deny that any new perspectives upon the whole were possible, a denial which in turn gave the "absolute" system its totalitarian character.

Tillich saw this weakness in the foundation of a Hegelian system. He recognized that thinking continues to be historical rather than absolute even in Hegel's whole. But if one cannot make the character of temporality objectival even in a whole system of thought, isn't this fact itself an irrefutable confirmation of nihilism? Tillich saw another solution, which avoided that apparently inevitable conclusion. This solution is contained, as I stated earlier, in the two ideas of correlation and paradox. My next task, accordingly, will be to show how these two ideas provide the kind of solution which the idea of an absolute whole misses.

First the idea of correlation. Instead of defining the fundamental relation of the subjectival to the objectival from one direction only —that in which the self reflects the whole of reality—Tillich defines it from two directions, neither of which is reduced to the other. Since the self has two relations to the objectival sphere, that of response and that of reflection, the truth of a system of reflection does not rest solely upon the possibility of an absolute reflection because it can be checked against a system of response correlated with it. The understanding of being which is given by a systematic whole cannot be corrected by another reflection; it is already a whole and can only be accepted and repeated. If there were no other way of correcting it, it could not be corrected at all.

Yet there *is* another way. A systematic understanding of being can be corrected by a *response* to "God" because this arises from the second, and correlative, relation of the subjectival to the objectival. A system of reflection is true if its understanding of being is confirmed by a response to God in a system of response. What being is is answered by God, to whom response is made; and the God to whom total response is made is present as being. This sort of control over the truth of a systematic whole is missing if either of the two relations is subordinated to the other. If one is subordinate, there is no way of evaluating the whole system apart from the vigor or seriousness of the one who asserts it, and its implicit totalitarianism is kept in check only by an equally vigorous or serious assertion of an opposing position. A system of correlation, however, is capable of being both systematic and open because it has a self-corrective embedded in it. It is systematic, but it is never completed.[3]

3. I am omitting here a formulation of the further question, What kind of activity is it when I carry out (as we are doing now) a second-order thinking of the (first-order) reflection of being and the (first-order) response to God? As will become clearer in the next paragraphs, I think the systematic problems of second-order thinking are no different from those of first-order reflection of being and response to God. In other words, what I have been speaking of as the problem of "catching" my here-and-now act of reflection or response is in fact a problem of second-order thinking. But this problem is identical with that of reflecting being and responding to God—i.e. of reflecting the one objectivity which is not altered by my reflection and responding to the one presence which is not absented by my response—for if I "catch" it, I can either compare it with what it reflects or use it as a response to the presence that elicits it.

Although this correlation makes it possible for systematic thinking to be whole and yet never complete, it does not solve the problem of temporality in reflection and response. It keeps both of them from being totalitarian, but it does not provide an ontological or theological embodiment of temporality itself. Here a second consideration must be brought to bear. Temporality cannot be presented to me or objectivally embodied as a finished *whole* but only as a *paradoxical* reality and a *paradoxical* presence —a content which is objectival but is not changed by reflection or response even for historically conscious thinking. We can best see how this is possible if we proceed step by step.

We are concerned here with two activities, reflection and response, and the special significance of a paradoxical reality for them. Let us first notice what such a paradox would be in relation to reflection, and then what it would be in relation to response. A paradoxical reality for critical reflection would be something objectival which I can understand only by thinking my act of reflection—that is to say, the very endeavor and failure of this undertaking is itself the way of critically reflecting a paradoxical reality. If I ask, "What do I grasp when I think my reflecting (and discover the split between my act and its intended content)?" the answer can be provided objectively only by a reality which embodies this double reflection itself—its impossibility as well as its endeavor. If I ask the same question in another way, "What *is* temporality itself—that is, what *is* this one certainty for historical thinking?" the answer is a paradoxical reality. Temporality *is* that paradox. In the case of all other objectival realities, I understand them objectively by critically reflecting *them*. In the case of a paradoxical reality, I understand it only by trying to "catch" *my act of critically reflecting*.[4] Tillich finds there is such a real para-

4. One might also note that this notion of a paradoxical thing and its role for reflection differs from the notion that one can pass beyond a critical attitude simply by criticizing the criticism, or that one can overcome skepticism by becoming skeptical of one's skepticism, or transcend radical questioning by questioning one's own questioning. Tillich has seen clearly on this point and has recognized the fact that skepticism, criticism, and questioning are not self-transcending *unless they come into view of a content* which is objectively a

dox, for the cross of the Christ Jesus is an object that can be understood only paradoxically, that is to say, only by the endeavor and failure included in my here-and-now act of double reflection.

A parallel state of affairs exists with regard to a paradoxical presence, which is a presence, or power, to which I am responding when I try to "catch" my here-and-now act of response. If I ask, "To what or to whom am I responding in this kind of act?" or "Where is temporality itself present for my response?" the answer is provided only by the kind of objectival subject who embodies that self-negating activity in himself. In the case of other presences, my response is made directly to *them;* in the case of a paradoxical presence, I respond by relating to *my act of responding.* In other words, the act in which I respond appropriately to such a subject is one in which I try to catch my own act of response; it is a double response, parallel to an act of double reflection. Again, Tillich finds there is such a paradoxical presence. The "Jesus who sacrifices himself as Jesus to himself as Christ" is present for our response paradoxically.[5]

It is with this conception of a paradoxical reality and presence that Tillich shows the possibility of a reflective and responsive reasoning that is at once historical and capable of achieving a certainty. Being is given to reflection as a self-negating being, a paradox; and God is present for response as a self-removing presence, a paradox. These are knowable certainties for historically conscious reflection and response because they embody temporality in an object and a presence. What such paradoxes embody is precisely the temporality of my acts which I can never catch. They are an objectival presentation of my subjectivity in its temporality, the manifestation of God and being to temporal being.

If we put Tillich's two ideas together—correlation and paradox

---

paradox. I cannot escape radical doubt simply by doubting my doubt; but I can escape it if I come upon an objective presence which, paradoxically, is not removed but established by my doubting of my doubt.

5. In Tillich's terms, this is the point at which being (the objective) is also being-itself (the depth of the subjectival and the objectival) and God (objectival presence) is also God himself (depth). See n. 2, above.

—we can summarize his solution of the problem of systematic thought in a historically conscious period by saying that the totalitarian character of absolute systems is replaced by the self-correcting character of a system of correlation, and that the certainty of an absolute whole is replaced by the certainty of a paradoxical reality and presence. This leaves us with only one more task to carry out in explicating the full solution. This task is to show how a paradoxical presence and a paradoxical reality are related to each other. The relation is this: the reflection of a paradoxical object and the response to a paradoxical presence are *one and the same* act. In other words, here is the point at which the juncture of the two activities is effected and which therefore makes the whole correlation of the two possible. Here the two lines converge.

Thus, although response and reflection reach the paradoxical point from two different directions, they come together at this point. The act of reflecting a paradoxical object and the act of responding to a paradoxical presence are one and the same act. In both cases I am "catching" the temporality, or historical character, of all thinking. Temporality pervades responsive as well as reflective thinking, and whether I catch that temporality at the end of my response or at the end of my reflection makes no difference in the structure of the act itself.

The problem of certainty for reflection is not radical so long as reflective thinking is directed immediately toward what the world provides as content. At least the whole world itself is a certainty, even if no items in it are. Similarly, this problem is not radical for responsive thinking so long as the powers, the mythological gods, immediately elicit a response. The characteristic of historically conscious thinking, however, is its loss of the immediacy of its reflection or its response. It knows that even the whole world is not given but is reflected, and it knows that even the one God is not an immediate presence but a presence as responded to. Tillich's solution is that historical thinking reaches a certainty of some reality or some presence *not by constructing an "absolute" whole, not by subordinating reflection to response, or conversely; but by a cor-*

*relation of reflection and response that is made possible when
thinking grasps or responds to a paradox.*

In the following chapters I present various contexts and aspects
of this one answer. The chapters have been arranged in part as
divisions of the subjectival-objectival structure used for the analysis
and in part by historical considerations. On the whole they present
successive contexts in which the basic pattern of Tillich's solution
is always rediscovered.

Chapter 1 presents the historical development leading up to the
problem of absolute reflection and response in the nineteenth
century. Like all such historical sketches it is a schematization
which ignores many historical details, and it suggests an orderli-
ness about the history of thought which one does not find so neatly
present in the historical material. Besides that, it is rather tightly
written since it must cover a great span of time and ideas.

Chapter 2 brings, from Tillich's early writings, an elaboration
of his conception of God and the method appropriate to theology.
The context here is the ontological structure of self, world, and
God. Chapter 3 is concerned with a discussion of the relation between subject and object objectively—the ultimate presence (the
symbol of God) and the ultimate object (the concept of being-
itself), while Chapter 4 is addressed to the relation between the
subject on the subjectival side and the subject on the objectival
side of the polar structure. Since in Chapters 3 and 4 the various
terms of the structure are related to each other, in Chapter 5 the
relation between this whole structure and the depth it expresses is
discussed.

Chapter 6 connects the framework of reflection and response to
the more familiar terms which Tillich uses to describe correlation:
question and answer. Here the basic forms of question and answer,
as found in the *Systematic Theology,* are put into the contexts of
the methods of reflection and response.

Chapter 7 undertakes to do the same thing with the problem
posed in the first chapter. Here we follow the way Tillich himself
used to address the problem rather than our analysis of what he

was actually doing, but we connect it with our posing of the problem.

The analysis is completed with Chapter 7, in which we return to the starting point. But, just as Chapter 1 provided a broad historical background leading into the analysis, it is appropriate that an additional chapter, Chapter 8, provide observations which summarize and lead out of the constructive analysis into an independent construction. That construction is not, however, part of the present work, which is intended to be a study of Tillich's solution to the problem of certainty for historically conscious thought.

Some readers may find it advisable to read Chapter 8 first, then Chapters 3 to 7, and finally Chapters 1 and 2.

I should like to thank Mr. Gary Davis for assistance in preparation of the index and Mr. James Bross for assistance in reading page proofs.

Reflection and Doubt in the Thought of Paul Tillich

CHAPTER 1

Critical Reflection and Doubting Response

In the famous last chapter of *The Courage To Be* Tillich introduces the conception of God beyond the God of theism, "the God
who appears when God has disappeared in the anxiety of doubt."[1]
According to Christoph Rhein's report,[2] Tillich thought it possible to use the conclusion of this book as a transition to an outline
of a theological system. Rightly so, for this conception does indeed
serve as a foundation for Tillich's systematic thinking and contains
his solution to the problem of the presence of God for historically
conscious thinking. How can such thinking know the presence of
God? Does the rise of historical consciousness itself make God
obsolete? Tillich pursued such questions relentlessly, and his
quest resulted in a theological system which gives expression to
the God of historical thinking beyond the God of theistic thinking.

The purpose of this chapter is to set forth the development of
the problem of God and being by means of a historical sketch
that culminates in the "absolute" reflection of Hegel and the "absolute" response of Schleiermacher. The chapter concludes with
a three-step description of the way in which Tillich reached a
solution to it.

The human self (the subjectival) is constituted by a double
relation to the objectival. On the one hand it grasps the objectivity
of the objectival, and on the other it responds to the subjectivity
of the objectival.[3] These two relations define the fundamental ac-

1. *The Courage To Be* (New Haven, Yale University Press, 1952), p. 190.
2. *Paul Tillich: Philosoph und Theologe* (Stuttgart, Evangelisches Verlagswerk, 1957), p. 111, n. 27.
3. Either of these relations is possible. A self-destructive relation appears
only when the subjectival character of the self is endangered. Thus, if "God"
is a subject for whom the self is nothing but an object (cf. *Courage To Be,* p.
185), the self is reduced to an objectival object and God to a subjectival sub-

tivities in which the human self is continuously engaged. It is always grasping the objectivity or responding to the power of the objectival sphere to which it is related. Two systems of thought arise from these two activities, ontology and theology. In asking the question of being, the self is laying hold upon objectivity, and the result of its activity is philosophy. In receiving the answer of God, it is responding to subjectivity, and the result of its activity is theology.

Though these are fundamental activities, continuous movements, in which the human self is always engaged, it is not self-evident that either of them is salutary. It is possible that their meaning is negative, both as they are directly experienced and as they are ultimately judged. The profoundest question about the meaning of being human is raised by the ambiguity of objectively grasping being and religiously responding to God. Perhaps they both spell self-destruction. In a historically conscious age this possibility is not only a theoretical question but an actual threat for thinking and being. Nowhere is this more visible than in the modern era, especially in the work of Hegel and Schleiermacher, and especially if their work is seen at the end of the various stages through which *critical reflection* and *doubting response*[4] passed before reaching their "absolute" forms.

Critical reflection removes the immediacy or the self-evidence of objects that appear to the self, and doubting response removes the immediate impact of the religious powers that act upon it. By

---

ject. Both of these are destructive because they are inherently self-contradictory. The self is inescapably subjectival because it is the originator of its actions, whether they are actions of grasping or actions of responding.

4. Neither of these terms is found in Tillich's writings in the technical sense given them here, but I use them to draw together the various formulations he does use, chiefly "existential (ontological) analysis" in the first half and "critical phenomenology" in the second half of his correlations in the *Systematic Theology,* and "Form" and *"Gehalt"* in his *System der Wissenschaften* of 1923. Cf. my "Der Begriff der Systematik bei Paul Tillich," *Neue Zeitschrift für systematische Theologie und Religionsphilosophie* (Berlin), 8 (1966), 242–54; "The Scope of Systematics: An Analysis of Tillich's Two Systems," *Journal of Religion, 48* (April 1968), 136–49.

doing so, reflection establishes the real objectivity of the objectival and response establishes the religious character of the power to which the subjectival responds. But they both become gravely problematic when they turn upon their own acts—when reflection and response try to grasp their own here-and-now acts of reflecting and responding. This is the point at which thinking is historically conscious, and the objectivity which reflection establishes or the power which response establishes seems to disappear in an omnivorous temporality.

The stages through which reflection goes are determined by what it is directed at. The self can reflect things or groups of things within the whole objectival sphere; the whole objectival sphere; subjectivity; the relation between subjectivity and objectivity—the presuppositions of the subject-object relation; and the self's here-and-now act of reflecting.

Critical reflection[5] establishes objectivity by introducing a form of the negative. It can lay hold upon objectivity when it can distinguish an object from everything that contrasts with it. Thus the form of objectivity and the related form of negativity which are achieved depend upon the sort of object to which critical reflection is directed, and this determines its several stages.

In the first place, reflection can be directed toward anything or

5. On the problem of critical reflection see Gotthard Günther, *Idee und Grundriss einer nicht-aristotelischen Logik* (Hamburg, Felix Meiner, 1959). Gerhard Krüger, *Die Herkunft des philosophischen Selbstbewusstseins* (Darmstadt, Wissenschaftliche Buchgesellschaft, 1962). Walter Schulz, *Die Vollendung des deutschen Idealismus in der Spätphilosophie Schellings* (Stuttgart, W. Kohlhammer Verlag, 1955); "Der Gott der modernen Metaphysik," in *Der Gottesgedanke im Abendland,* ed. Albert Schaefer (Stuttgart, Kohlhammer Verlag, 1964), pp. 89–108; "Das Problem der absoluten Reflexion," in *Einsichten: Gerhard Krüger zum 60. Geburtstag,* ed. Klaus Oehler and Richard Schaeffler (Frankfurt am Main, Vittorio Klostermann, 1962), pp. 334–60; "Hegel und das Problem der Aufhebung der Metaphysik," in *Martin Heidegger zum 70. Geburtstag,* ed. Günther Neske (Pfullingen, Verlag Günther Neske, 1959), pp. 67–92. Karl Heinz Volkmann-Schluck, "Der Satz vom Widerspruch als Anfang der Philosophie," in *Martin Heidegger zum 70. Geburtstag,* pp. 134 ff.

any groups of things within the whole objectival sphere. This form of reflection is characteristic of Greek thought, in which "being" meant the whole of *ta onta,* the things that are. By means of the negative which it introduces, reflection distinguishes between what is and what is not, or between the things that are and the things that are not. The negative is everything that contrasts with what is. Thus, the objectivity of anything is established when the object is set off from everything that in any way contrasts with it. It is what it is and nothing else. The philosophical axiom related to this distinction was first[6] formulated by Aristotle as the rule of noncontradiction, which in one of its variations reads thus: "It is impossible for the same thing both to be present and not to be present in the same subject and in the same respect."[7] In a philosophical understanding which is directed toward everything that is insofar as it is, this axiom is fundamental. What does not come into consideration at this stage is the objectivity of the whole itself. To the Greek mind, and to any mind at this stage of reflection, the whole is a given. However doubtful certain objects may be, the objectivity of the whole is self-evident, immediately given. No contrast is yet thought between the objectival and the subjectival or between objectivity as such and the sum total of objects, but only between the different beings and kinds of beings.

However, at the second stage reflection is directed toward the whole itself. In this case even the law of contradiction, which Aristotle knew one must *use* in thinking but which he did not make an object of reflection, is drawn into the scope of thought. That is to say, in the Greek *on* (being)[8] the distinction between being and beings, *Sein* and *Seiendes, esse* and *essentia,* is still unthought and undeveloped. Only when critical reflection is directed toward the whole does it develop that distinction. For then the question arises: "What contrasts with the whole itself?" Beings can be contrasted with other beings, but can the whole be contrasted only with its parts? If so, the whole itself cannot be reflected. At this stage reflection recognizes the new distinction be-

6. Volkmann-Schluck, p. 139.
7. Met IV, c. 3, 1005b, 18f.
8. Volkmann-Schluck, p. 149.

tween the universe of beings and being-as-such. The quality of being at all—or, to employ the metaphor Tillich uses, the power to be—is found in all beings as that which makes them be but which is not identical with any one or any group or even the whole of them. The quality of objectivity as such is established in contrast to sheer not-being. One example of reflection at this level is the early Christian doctrine of *creatio ex nihilo* and the difference between God the creator and the world as created. The *ex nihilo* identifies the negative as sheer not-being, and the doctrine of God as the almighty creator distinguishes between everything that is (the created universe) and its power to be at all (the creative activity). This doctrine was philosophically formulated by Avicenna and Thomas as the difference between *esse* (being-itself) and *entia* or *essentiae* (beings or essences).[9]

One should also notice that the medieval distinction between the natural and the supernatural was a form of reflection, which introduced a modification of this second stage. What role, after all, did the conception of a supernatural reality play, if not to reflect the naturally given world? Supernatural thinking was a way of critically reflecting the natural world in detail. This in turn meant that the objectival sphere was divided into two parts, natural and supernatural, which together constituted one whole. The relation between the two parts of the one whole was the relation of reality as given and reality as reflected. The supernatural world was the real world which contrasted with the unreflected or only rationally reflected reality of the natural world; fully (i.e. by reason and faith) reflected naturalness was equivalent to supernaturalness. But both natural being and supernatural being were distinguished from God as not only the first cause but the *esse* of everything natural and supernatural.

In the natural–supernatural scheme, accordingly, objectivity

9. A. M. Goichon, *La philosophie d'Avicenne et son influence en Europe médiévale* (Paris, 1944), pp. 23 and 43ff. Johannes Hegyi, *Die Bedeutung des Seins bei den klassischen Kommentatoren des heiligen Thomas von Aquin: Capreolus-Silvester von Ferrara-Cajetan* (Pullach bei München, Verlag Berchmannskolleg, 1959). W. Pannenberg, "Akt und Sein im Mittelalter," *Kerygma und Dogma*, 7 (1961), 202–11.

was established at two different levels and by two different capacities, reason and faith. What could be established objectively by the reflection of reason was in turn critically reflected by faith, and faith rested upon authority. The objectivity of the supernatural as established by faith was not in turn critically reflected, except that it was subordinated to its first cause, which was also its *esse*. In other words, the whole of natural objectivity could be critically reflected in each of its details by the supernatural, and the supernatural could be critically reflected only by faith in God himself.

But why was the supernatural world needed at all? Why was the contrast between creation and the creator not enough? What additional purpose did something intermediate between the given world and being-itself serve? The explanation is that this intermediate reality allowed a reflection of all the details of the natural world; it represented the reemergence of an appreciative understanding of nature and natural man. Medieval supernaturalism took the concrete richness of the world into the reflection of the supernatural world and graced it.[10] In other words, this sort of supernatural thinking was not the fanciful construction of an invisible second-story to the visible world, but a detailed reflection of the world that reached appreciatively into its manifold particulars.

At the first two stages, reflection establishes objectivity by contrasting it with two kinds of negative—things are differentiated from other things, and the objectivity of each thing is distinguished from the sum total of things. At the third stage, the negative is identified with subjectivity,[11] as the connection is recognized between the negative, which is introduced in order to objectify objects, and the self who does the introducing. The basic distinction exists between subjectivity and objectivity, rather than between what is and what is not or between being and not being, and the

10. Cf. Friedrich Gogarten, *The Reality of Faith,* tr. Carl Michalson and others (Philadelphia, Westminster Press, 1959), pp. 12–15.

11. As in Descartes especially, but also in Duns Scotus and Suarez. See K. Oehler, "Subjekt und Objekt," in *Religion in Geschichte und Gegenwart* (3d ed. Tübingen, J. C. B. Mohr, 1962), 6, col. 448–51.

objectivity of the objectival depends upon its being distinguished from the subjectivity of the one who is reflecting it. It is the subjectival which reflects the world. The difference between objective and non-objective is not just a difference between ways of being but a difference in how the self is related to the objectival. Things are objective because I can grasp them as over against me and fix them in relation to other forms of objectivity.

One should note, however, that the subjectivity we are dealing with here is not yet the here-and-now act of reflection that is the main problem of the modern age. Rather it is the reflecting subject itself, in disregard of the temporality of its act. This stage of reflection is associated with Descartes, for it was he who uncovered the "split" between subjects and objects. Moreover, both the supernatural realm, as it existed for medieval theology, and the notion of God's knowledge of the world, which was contained in the supernatural, were dislodged by this Cartesian split. If the source of the negative which reflects objectivity is the subjectival, then the supernatural and God are only ways in which a subject reflects the objectival.

This fact has been noted by Gerhard Krüger and Walter Schulz, among others, who have called attention to the difference between Descartes' and Augustine's meditations upon the self.[12] For Augustine and the Middle Ages God was a power that called the world into question. By contrast, for Descartes God was the guarantor of the reality of the world, the one that makes it possible for me to bridge the gap from the immediate certainty of myself to the certainty of the world. From here it is a small step to saying that God is only the concept I use in order to grasp the objectivity of the world. For Descartes himself the relation is still mediated. The objectivity of the world is established by God, who exists outside of man; the idea of God is in the subjectival subject.[13]

12. Krüger, *Die Herkunft,* pp. 9–12; Schulz, "Hegel und das Problem der Aufhebung der Metaphysik."

13. In Descartes, however, subjectivity, although reflected and distinguished from objectivity, is not yet reflected in itself. That is to say, no distinction is made between what I as one self might establish objectively and what another self might establish. Subjectivity is differentiated from objectivity, but one concrete subject is not distinguished from any other one.

In other words, there is a reversal of positions between the Augustinian and the Cartesian reflections. Augustine's God removes the self-evident givenness of the whole world; Descartes' God gives back the objectivity of the world to the subject who has removed its givenness by reflection. For Augustine the being of God is presupposed in the self's activity; for Descartes it is inferred from an idea present in the mind. The difference between these two mirrors the fact that Descartes' God, even though he still exists independently, is being drawn into the subject–object structure, and that the basic contrast with the objective world is not God or being but the reflecting subject. For Augustine the true objectivity of the world is known in its contrast with the creator God, who has made it; for Descartes the objectivity of the world is known in its contrast with the subjectivity of the self.

The fourth stage is entered when reflection is directed toward what is *presupposed* in the fact that subjectivity reflects objectivity, or toward what Kant called the "conditions" of knowing at all. Here the basic distinction is made between objectivity for subjectivity—that is, objects as thought by subjects—and the presuppositions, or conditions, implied in the fact that objects can be thought by subjects at all. Objectivity is thus established at two levels, first as objectivity for subjectivity (which is Kant's *Verstand*) and second as an objectification of the conditions of thinking at all—the transcendental objectivity which is related to Kant's *Vernunft*.

The difference between the fourth and fifth stages is the difference between Kant and Fichte or Hegel. At the fifth stage reflection is directed to its own here-and-now act of critically reflecting, and this is the point at which its temporality is a decisive problem. Reflection at this stage is historically conscious. Its object is no longer just the objectivity of things or transcendental objectivity but the act of critically reflecting here-and-now. Now an additional distinction is made, between the conditions of thinking at all, on one hand, and the *act* of thinking even those conditions, on the other hand.

Here reflection has reached the apparently insuperable barrier of temporality. If the subjectival engages only in trying to reflect its own act, it loses objectival content because it can never catch the here-and-now act. If on the other hand it does introduce content, the content is ultimately arbitrary and unfounded; it is posited but not confirmed as objective content, because the act which posits it has not in turn been reflected. How can any objectivity finally be established if critical reflection cannot reflect the act by which objectivity is established? Yet how can reflection establish itself since there is nothing with which it can be contrasted in the act of reflection? The choice seems to be this. Either I halt reflection at the point where it tries to grasp its own act and simply *assume* that it does establish objectivity, and then I defeat the purpose for engaging in it in the first place and fail to achieve what it had promised; or I continue trying to reflect the act of reflecting and lose all content because of the interminable character of self-reflection.

Hegel, who took this problem most seriously, saw a solution if one could traverse all possible content and all possible kinds of reflections which culminate in an absolute whole, a system of thought whose content could not be, and need not be, further reflected because it already included the here-and-now act of reflecting. The construction of this absolute had a double consequence. First, Hegel's own act of reflecting the whole, once it was constructed, could not be considered a new act but only a repetition of some act already done; otherwise the whole, upon his completion of it, would not be whole because it did not include his act of critically reflecting it.[14] Second, he had to treat history as having ended. No further acts of reflection could bring anything new because all possible objectivity had already manifested itself, and thinking was fully reconciled with being. In retrospect this may seem to be an astounding presumption on Hegel's part, but it was the only way in which he believed it was possible to solve the problem of absolute reflection—that is, re-

14. See Ernst Bloch, *Subjekt-Objekt: Erläuterungen zu Hegel* (rev. and exp. ed. Frankfurt am Main, Suhrkamp Verlag, 1962), pp. 361–65. Paul Tillich, "Kairos und Logos," in *GW, 4,* 54, 62.

flection which has turned upon its own act. Moreover, we might remember that, however astounding Hegel's presumption might seem to be, the merciless attacks to which it was subsequently subjected were no less astounding. One can explain both the presumption and the attacks by the fact that the problem of absolute reflection was felt by all sides to be radically serious.[15]

Thus far we have described the stages through which reflection moves on its way toward the absolute reflection of Hegel, with all of the problems then exposed. The picture needs to be completed, however, by a sketch of the decline of an *absolute object*—an objectival reality that can resist being reflected. The process in which reflection moves toward an absolute stage is attended by the decline of an absolute object, either as a *first principle* or as a *highest being*. This process of dissolution is visible in Descartes, as we noted, when God begins to be thought of as dependent upon the self or the world. It is completed by Kant's analysis of the antinomies of reason and the idealist thinking founded on it. Kant's analysis ends a long tradition, for the history of such a first or highest reality goes back philosophically to Aristotle; it was accepted by medieval theology as well as classical Protestant theology, even though in each case it was somewhat modified. Our sketch here will present just the outlines of the origin and decline of the first principle and supreme being.

The conception arises in Aristotle in connection with definitions and judgments. The proper object of scientific knowledge, he says, is something which cannot be other than it is. But to know it in its necessity, we must know how to define it, to distinguish it from the "other" and to relate it to the cause upon which it depends. "We suppose ourselves to possess unqualified scientific knowledge of a thing, as opposed to knowing it in the accidental way in which the sophist knows, when we think that we know the cause on which the fact depends, as the cause of that fact and of

15. See Robert Heiss, *Die grossen Dialektiker des 19. Jahrhunderts: Hegel, Kierkegaard, Marx* (Köln & Berlin, Kiepenheuer & Witsch, 1963), p. 199.

no other, and, further, that the fact could not be other than it is."[16]

We define an object by relating it to the genus under which it falls and by distinguishing it from other objects in the same genus. To relate it to its genus and to distinguish it from other things in the same genus is to fix it in its objectivity, to know it as the object which it is. A genus, in turn, is defined when we relate it to a yet higher genus and distinguish it from the other genera in that yet higher genus. For the whole series of definitions to be established we must at some point reach a highest genus, to which all others are related and within which they are found. Yet if we establish objects by relating them to their genus, how do we establish the highest genus which, in the nature of the case, cannot be referred to anything else? The same question is reached by the causal or judgmental series. If we found a particular judgment by relating it to a judgment more inclusive (Socrates is mortal because Socrates is a man and all men are mortal), we found the more inclusive judgment upon one that is still more inclusive. How then do we found the judgment which is most inclusive, upon which the others depend but which itself cannot, in the nature of the case, be made to depend on any others?[17]

Aristotle's solution was to distinguish two kinds of knowledge, two ways of establishing objectivity. He acknowledged that the series had to be terminable if there was to be knowledge of objects at all and that the first in any series could not be known "demonstratively" as the others in the series. This could only mean that our knowledge of first principles or of universals is intuitive, in contrast to our knowledge of subordinate judgments or particular things, which is demonstrative. Both are knowledge, but one is immediate and the other is mediate. The difference be-

16. *Anal. post.* I 2 and 3, II 10, II 19; *De anima* III 6. See also Hans Wagner, *Philosophie und Reflexion* (München and Basel, Ernst Reinhardt Verlag, 1959), pp. 119ff.

17. I am leaving aside the question whether there are many series, each of which arrives at a relative "first," or whether there is but one universal series and one absolute first. Only in the latter case does the problem emerge in a radical form. If it can be solved, the former case presents no problem.

tween them is like the difference between seeing an object and judging what the object is.[18]

Medieval theology—and in a limited way classical Protestant theology—accepted Aristotle's solution but modified it according to its conception of the whole as consisting of a natural and a supernatural aspect. The first modification included recognition of a facet of the case that does not come out clearly in Aristotle's discussion. He concluded that the series must be terminable since knowledge would be impossible otherwise. The other half of this issue is the fact that nowhere do we find an object that is absolutely the first. Indeed, this side of it would not emerge as long as it was thought that there was such a first—a self-sufficient deity—somewhere within the universe of beings. Medieval theology denied that there was such a first being in the natural universe. This denial partly recognizes the half of the issue which Aristotle neglected, namely, that no series is absolutely terminable because we cannot find any absolute object in the world. It retains, however, an emphasis upon the first half of the argument by locating the absolute object, God, in the supernatural realm. Thus, Thomas' five ways of proving that God is[19] depend upon the fact that any series—of movers, of causes, of contingencies, of gradations, and of ends—must be terminable in order for the series itself or any item within it to be at all. They then identify God with that terminal point. Everyone "knows" or "names" or "calls" such a first mover or first cause or final end by the name "God." If there were no first, there would be nothing at all—"quod patet esse falsum." God is the name of the first, and the content of the first premise or first judgment is that he is.

Medieval theologians therefore agreed with Aristotle that there must be a terminating point in the whole series and sets of series for there to be intelligibility. They differed from him in their recognition that no object in the world met the qualifications of such a first being. It was supernatural. That there must be a first

18. De anima III 6 430b 29f.
19. *Summa theologiae*, I, 2, 3.

could be known by reason, but what or who it was could be known only in the way we know the supernatural—by revelation.

In Kant the other side of the issue emerges fully. His analysis of the fourth antinomy of reason shows how one can argue with equal cogency that there must be a necessary being and there cannot be a necessary being. Here the antinomy is exposed—there must be a first, and there cannot be a first.[20] The implication of this antinomy for thinking is that anything posited as the first is only provisionally the first, for it in turn has to be thought in relation to something else upon which it depends. If God is then defined as the supreme being or the first principle, he cannot be thought of as an absolute object, only as a directing idea. Whatever content is used to fill out the conception of God, it is only provisional and lasts only until one asks about something prior to that content. This recognition on the part of Kant and idealism puts an end to the conception of God as a supreme being, whether in its natural or supernatural form.

By the time of Hegel, therefore, absolute reflection meant not only that reflection tried to grasp its own act but also that it found no objectival absolute. It was left alone with the ungraspable temporality of its own act, unable to restore a supreme being as an absolute object. Either temporality had to be expressible by a whole system, or it was not expressible at all, and absolute reflection was the end of God and being. The failure of Hegel's solution became evident in the nineteenth century, but no one was able to do any better than he had done. The great merit of Tillich's system, I believe, lies in the fact that it does provide a solution to the problem of the temporality of reflection in its "correlation" and "paradox." The significance of this solution becomes clearer, however, after we see that there is a development in the stages of doubting response which runs parallel to reflection.

---

20. Anselm's definition of God as *quo maius cogitari nequit* anticipates Kant's solution of "directing concepts," but the significance of the negative element in Anselm's definition was overlooked and *quo maius cogitari nequit* was treated as though it were equivalent to *ens supremum* or *ens realissimum*.

In religious response the self (subjectival subject) is related to the power that acts upon it (objectival subject). The human self is constituted by both movements toward the objectival, one in which it grasps objectivity and one in which it responds to subjectivity. Since this is the case, the development of critical reflection has a parallel in the development of the method by which power is established as religious. The character of religious power is that it engages the free response of the self by answering the doubt or bridging the distance set by the self. A power that is religious does not violate freedom but elicits it; its presence is acknowledged freely. The method by which a power acting upon the self is established as religious is one which opens the power's capacity to engage a free response. I call that method *doubting response,* or *distancing doubt.* It means that religious power establishes itself by its ability to overcome the distance, the negation, which I place between it and myself; it establishes its presence by the fact that my doubt does not remove it. If it cannot bridge the distance or reestablish its own presence, it cannot elicit a free response.

As in the case of reflection, the kind of religious power established varies with the presence to which the response is directed. Thus, where a second-stage reflection differentiates between being-as-such and any or all beings, response distinguishes between the gods and one God, between polytheism or henotheism and radical monotheism. At the monotheistic stage response is made not to any one objectival subject but to the quality of subjectivity as such in the objectival. Historically the emergence of this monotheism is usually identified with prophetic religion in the Old Testament, but the exact point at which it arrived on the scene of history is of no importance here. What is important is that, like reflection, responsive thinking is imperiled by historical consciousness, which seems to engulf even a monotheistic God.

The crisis for responsive thinking, as for reflective thinking, is reached when it turns upon its own act and discovers that its temporality always eludes its grasp. This crisis is continually impending in monotheism because a monotheistic response denies the identification of God with any particular objectival presence. In the Christian theological development, however, it became explicit at the beginning of the nineteenth century, when the sacral presences of medieval and classical Protestant theology had been lost. By a sacral presence I mean some reality—an institution, a person, an idea, or whatever else—which is present in the world in such a way as to be qualitatively different from everything else. Its identifying characteristic is the fact that when I view it I do not view it in its relation to things around it. I do not ask from what other thing it comes (since it is directly of God) or to what other things it leads or is related. It is "just there," underivable from anything around it, encompassing and sustaining all else. So long as there is such a sacral presence in the world, religious response is not turned upon itself, since the sacral presence performs for response the same service that an absolutely first principle or highest being does for critical reflection. It provides a point at which reflection or response is halted by something in the universe.

Both medieval theology and classical Protestant theology had such a sacral presence. For medieval theology it was the penitential and sacramental institution of the church, and for classical Protestant theology it was the Sacred Scriptures as the very voice of God. Both theologies could stand upon an objectival presence of the invisible God. He was the founder of the church; he was the author of the Scriptures. The sacral presence, like the bodily presence of the God of all, possessed the power to overcome the distance a subject might open by his doubt. It had the capacity to elicit man's free response. To be sure, there was a difference between the presence of the church and that of the Scriptures. The ecclesiastical institution was a visible organization, and its presence was visibly objectival. The voice of God in the Scriptures, on the other hand, was objectival audibly rather than visibly. It could be heard rather than seen. In Luther's phrase, *natura verbi est audiri* —the word is something to be heard. The holy word was not the book one could see and touch and feel but the message that could be heard in public preaching or in private devotion.[21] Nonetheless, whether for the eye or the ear, there was an objectival presence in the world which could in fact overcome doubt because of its sacral character. It was always just there, even if its ways were often incalculable.

Both sacral presences were dissolved by the beginning of the nineteenth century. Protestantism had destroyed the sacral character of the medieval church, and historical criticism had destroyed the sacral character of the Scriptures. Henceforth they were both subject to criticism and doubt. Of course, they were and are still sacral for many people, but not for theological thinking that is historically conscious. And they were not available for theological construction in the new era since their sacral character could not be restored. Anyone who either directly or by recapitulation participated in the historical development leading into the nineteenth and twentieth centuries could no longer revert to the medieval and Protestant theological stances without a loss of integrity. The disappearance of sacral realities is never a reversible process.

The dissolution of sacral presences put religious response into a difficulty parallel to that of reflective understanding. When a faith-response turns upon its own act it seems to meet the same insuperable obstacle as when objectifying thought turns upon itself. When I try to catch my here-and-now act of responding I am confronted with the same dilemma as when I try to reflect my reflecting. I arbitrarily can call a halt at this point and become prey for whatever demonic powers may move in, since there is nothing to prevent my doubting action from being stopped at any point whatsoever; I have lost the freedom of my response. Or I can continue the doubting and the religious presence vanishes; I have lost the objectival presence to which to respond. If the freedom of the response is lost, the self is defenseless against whatever demonic

21. See R. Scharlemann, *Thomas Aquinas and John Gerhard* (New Haven, Yale University Press, 1964), pp. 22–28. Gerhard Ebeling, *Luther: Einführung in sein Denken* (Tübingen, J. C. B. Mohr. 1964), esp. Chaps. 3, 5, and 14.

powers may wish to possess it. If the objectival character of the religious power is lost, the self loses its capacity to respond at all since there is nothing to respond to. Faith turned upon itself is confronted with the choice between fanaticism or fatuousness, demonization or profanization.

Schleiermacher's solution to this problem is parallel to Hegel's solution of the problem of absolute reflection. He identified the act of religious response with the content of a whole system of responsive thinking. What the self responds to and its act of responding were identical in the whole, just as for Hegel the act and the object of critical reflection were the same in the absolute system. Schleiermacher sought to establish the content of the religious power to which the self responds by examining the whole content of the feeling of absolute dependence.[22] But if the act of response and the objectival presence to which response is made are identical, the response never finds an objectival presence, because the act it catches is already past by the time it is caught. Either that, or the whole systematic response is post-historical, in the sense that it claims to include every here-and-now act of responding, as Hegel's absolute system meant to include the temporality of reflecting. If that is the case, however, then the possibility of a new response is denied in advance and the absolute system of faith is as totalitarian as the absolute system of reflection. Although later reaction to Schleiermacher's theological system was not as vigorously negative as the reaction to Hegel's absolute system, Schleiermacher did not succeed any more than his great contemporary and colleague in solving the problem of the presence of God for historically conscious responsive thinking.

Tillich, more deeply perhaps than any contemporary theologian, felt the gravity of this problem, as is evident from such early writings as "Kairos und Logos," such later writings as *The Courage*

22. Even the most sympathetic interpretation of Schleiermacher's religious thought given by Richard R. Niebuhr notes his neglect of divine transcendence: *Schleiermacher on Christ and Religion* (New York, Scribner's, 1964), p. 191.

To Be, and even one of his last writings, "Honesty and Consecration."[23] One of the fundamental purposes of his systematic thought was to take up the problem, and to correct the failure, of the nineteenth century. In the following chapters we shall be looking at the various facets of Tillich's answer to how we escape the apparently insoluble dilemma posed by absolute reflection and absolute faith.[24] In outline, however, the answer is achieved in three steps, although Tillich nowhere sets them forth as such.

First, Tillich recognized the parallel between response and reflection, between grasping objectivity by criticism and responding to subjectivity by doubt. He also recognized that there is a juncture between the two movements because the act in which faith turns upon itself and the act in which reason turns upon itself are not only parallel but identical. The action in which I doubt the religious presence and the action in which I critically reflect the ontological object are the same action when they are in their "absolute" form. The fact that they are the same act, although reached from different sides, means that the point at which philosophical thinking turns upon itself is the point at which it is opened to religious power, and the point at which religious response turns upon itself is the point at which it is opened to philosophical objectivity.[25]

Secondly, if there is a juncture of the two movements of the self toward the objectival, then—and this is Tillich's correction of Hegel and Schleiermacher—the problem raised by their absolute form can be answered if the content established by reflection can solve the problem raised by absolute doubt, and if the power which elicits faith-response can solve the problem raised

23. *Response, 8* (1967), 203–10.

24. Tillich's "absolute faith" in the last chapter of *The Courage To Be* is not faith in faith (contrary to George Tavard, *Paul Tillich and the Christian Message* [New York, Scribner's, 1962], p. 33), or faith turned upon itself for its contents, but rather faith in God who is object and power paradoxically. See Chap. 8, pp. 169ff.

25. The convergence or identity of the acts of critical reflection and distancing doubt is nowhere stated explicitly by Tillich. But it is stated in effect in "Religionsphilosophie," *GW, 1,* 297f., and is implied in the connection between the mythological gods and being-itself. See below, Chap. 3, pp. 86f.

by absolute critical reflection. This is the foundation of the method of correlation.[26]

Third, Tillich saw that there is in fact an objectival content that cannot be canceled by either reflection or response. He did not endeavor to restore the sacral presences of classical Protestantism or medieval Christianity, both of which also had an objectival content that could not be canceled. Rather, he saw the uncancelable content in a paradoxical reality and presence (which is not sacral but which can make anything sacramental). Its content cannot be canceled by reflection or doubt because it embodies the temporality of responsive and reflective thinking. This objectival paradox is the biblical picture of Jesus as the Christ or, in a shorter phrase, the symbol of the cross. The content of this picture and symbol cannot be dissolved by critical reflection because it is grasped by radical reflection, and its presence cannot be removed by doubt because the response it elicits is that of a radically doubting response. (See Chapter 7 below for an explication of this point.)

Thus Tillich does not equate the unconditional with the whole content of a system of thought or of religious response nor with a sacral presence or an absolute object, but with a paradox—one whose objective content can be grasped only in its self-cancellation and whose power is exercised by its self-negation. It is *one* object, rather than the whole, or *one* presence, rather than a whole, but it is an object or presence which cannot be removed simply because it is laid hold of and responded to in the act of canceling it by double reflection or response.

Tillich's successful resolution of this problem is, I think, his great contribution to systematic thinking. Indeed, to the extent that he has taken up the problem of modern theology in its most radical form and successfully solved it, he provides a classical and concluding expression of this stage of theological thinking.

26. "Only if God is ultimate reality can he be the object of our unconditional concern" (*Biblical Religion and the Search for Ultimate Reality* [Chicago, University of Chicago Press, 1955], p. 59). "That which can be grasped only with 'infinite passion' . . . is identical with that which appears as the criterion in every act of rational knowledge" (*ST, 1,* 154).

CHAPTER 2

Self, World, and God

God is being-itself, Tillich argues. Behind this contention there is a vast amount of work, particularly in Tillich's early writings, on the conception it expresses and the method related to thinking it systematically. If God is neither simply subjectival nor objectival, neither an idea in the self nor an object in the world, what or who is he? He is the "depth" of both of them, Tillich replies. But how does one think the depth, and how does this depth ever make itself present? These are the questions to which the present chapter addresses itself.

Expressed in ontological terms the polarity of subjectival and objectival is the "self" and the "world." This is Tillich's definition of the basic ontological structure which constitutes the being of all finite beings. It is derived from the ontological question, which when asked presupposes both an asker and something asked about. The logical structure of the question indicates the corresponding ontological structure of self and world (ST, 1, 164, 171).

Implicitly Tillich has a double usage of "self" in this polarity, to which it is important to call attention because it is not always obvious in Tillich's own exposition. On the one hand, "self" means what Tillich calls "self-relatedness," the immediately experienced I in such acts as I am and I think. Of this meaning he writes, "The question is not whether selves exist. The question is whether we are aware of self-relatedness. And this awareness can only be denied in a statement in which self-relatedness is implicitly affirmed" (ST, 1, 169)—the act of making the denial refutes the content of the denial. On the other hand, "self" refers to a kind of being, namely, a self-reflective being, or any man, a "structure of centeredness." In this sense "self" is that kind of being in which all ontological dimensions are actualized. Tillich himself makes no

systematic use of this distinction in meaning,[1] but it is implied in
two somewhat different ways he has of speaking of the being of
God.

One should also note that, contrary to Randall,[2] the designation
of the basic polarity as self and world is no evidence that Tillich
ignores the question of man's evolution from lower forms. It may
well be true that there was a time when no human beings existed
in the universe. But that fact does not refute the designation of the
ontological structure as self and world, because the point of de-
parture for thought, even in the case of a man who affirms a pre-
human past, is necessarily in the present: it is self (the speaker)
and world (that of which he speaks). The ontological structure
includes the act of saying or thinking as well as what is thought.
It is a descriptive analysis not only of what I am speaking about
but also of the fact that I am speaking about it. Accordingly, it is
no different for a person affirming an evolutionary development
than for a person denying it, since in both cases there is an agent
and an object of thought.

At least to the extent that "self" in the self–world structure
means the *I* of *I think* Tillich's analysis of this structure is unaffected by the question of evolutionary development. In the case of
the second meaning of "self"—as a centered, self-reflective being
—one would have to say that before the existence of men the
structure was not self–world in the sense of man-in-the-world but
something else. Whether this is evidence against Tillich's description of the structure, however, can be decided only by determining
the relation between the being of man and the being of other
things. On this point Tillich's position, which scarcely needs ex-

---

1. In contrast, Fritz Buri, in *Dogmatik als Selbstverständnis des christlichen
Glaubens, 1* (Bern, Paul Haupt, 1956), pp. 120–22, makes open and systematic use of this distinction. See also his "Das Problem des ungegenständlichen Denkens und Redens in der heutigen Theologie," in *Zeitschrift für
Theologie und Kirche* (Tübingen), 61 (November 1964), 353–71.

2. "The Ontology of Paul Tillich," in *The Theology of Paul Tillich,* ed.
Charles W. Kegley and Robert W. Bretall (New York, Macmillan, 1952),
p. 153. Cf. Dorothy Emmet, "Epistemology and the Idea of Revelation," in
the same work, p. 208.

tensive justification, is that man is a focus of all dimensions of being; he is that being in whom "all levels of being are united and approachable" (*ST, 1,* 168). When man first emerged in the evolutionary development, the ontological structure which was previously only implicit became explicit in the difference between man ("spirit") and the rest of the world. Viewed retrospectively the periods prior to the emergence of man were anticipations. When he came upon the scene, subjectivity and objectivity were for the first time united in one being.

Of these two meanings of "self" and "ontological structure," the first is the more important for the theme of reflection and response, though it is the less familiar to interpreters and critics of Tillich's thought. Since they provide two different explications of the meaning of God as the depth of the ontological structure, I shall discuss them separately in this chapter even though Tillich does not do so.

The double meaning of self has a substantial tradition of controversy behind it. Tillich does not enter the debate, but it will be worthwhile here to recall the main points of the medieval and nineteenth-century discussion. The nature of the duality of the self was at issue in the theological opposition to Averroism[3] as well as in the debate between Kierkegaard and Hegel. In Aristotelianism Greek philosophical thinking had succeeded in demythologizing the conception of the self in self-consciousness. But it was at a loss how to interpret the relation between the universal intellect and the intellect in individual persons. Was the universal intellect, the *nous,* a power residing accidentally in individual human beings or was it intrinsically connected with the individuality of the thinker? The Averroists took the position that the true subject was not individual but was a substantial being whose connection with an individual person was only accidental. An individual being was the accidental place in which the universal intellect carried on its activity.

Thomas Aquinas argued against this position in his *De unitate intellectus,* on the grounds that it was inherently inconsistent because

3. See Ernst Cassirer, *Individuum und Kosmos in der Philosophie der Renaissance* (Darmstadt, Wissenschaftliche Buchgesellschaft, 1963), Chap. 4.

it denied what it sought to clarify. He contended that we cannot ask what the intellect in itself is without already exercising the function of thinking. In asking about the intellect, we already presuppose the activity we are trying to clarify. In other words, we always experience the function of thinking only individually: it is always I who am thinking even when I am thinking about the subject of thinking. To explain the intellect by eradicating the individuality given with the exercise of intelligence itself is to destroy the fact upon which the theory rests. Thomas, however, encountered an insoluble difficulty in the idea of the immortality of the soul, which he was convinced was an essential part of the Christian theological tradition. For if it is true that the self is ineradicably individual—and individuality for Thomas as for Aristotle was constituted by the materiality of beings—how can one think of a nonmaterial, permanently existing self? Here was the point at which Pomponazzi later attacked the Thomistic solution, holding that the special provisions which Thomas had introduced in order to maintain the immortality of the self were as inconsistent in their way as the Averroists were in their interpretation of the universal intellect. "It seems ridiculous to say that the intellective soul . . . has two ways of knowing, one dependent upon and one independent of the body, since then it seems to be two things"; and, moreover, "a plurality of ways of knowing is not found by Aristotle in any place, nor does it accord with reason."[4] Beyond the alternative of the positions enunciated by Thomas and Pomponazzi the theology of the Middle Ages could not move. Either one had to maintain the immortality of the soul on the basis of the supports adduced only for the purpose of maintaining it, or one had to forgo the special provisions and deny the soul's immortality.

In the early nineteenth century—the names of Fichte and Schelling signal the renewal—this same question was the center of much attention. Hegel and Kierkegaard stand out as spokesmen for two positions taken. In both of them the issue is centered in the conception of man as spirit—that is, a subjectival being who is continuously engaged in the activity of relating himself to the objectival—and the

4. "Ridiculum videtur dicere animam intellectivam . . . duos habere modos intelligendi, scilicet et dependentem et independentem a corpore, sic enim duo esse videtur habere," and "neque plures modi cognoscendi ab Aristotele in aliquo loco sunt reperti, neque consonat rationi." *De immortalitate animae* (1516), Chaps. 4, 9. Quoted by Cassirer, p. 147, n. 1.

question of the relation of the human spirit to the divine. Hegel's position is represented in the following quotations. "Finite consciousness knows God only insofar as God knows Himself in it." "Only in man when he knows God does God come to consciousness."[5] The activity of the human spirit is such that in its act the self is acting and acted upon. The subject by which the self is being acted upon is the divine Spirit, who objectifies himself in man's act of objectifying an object.

By this conception Hegel, in opposition to a subjectivist idealism, sought to maintain the individual concreteness of the experienced act of thinking together with its universal aspect. Thus, the subjectival and objectival, which are polar opposites in finitude, are taken into the embracing activity of the absolute Spirit. The duality of the self is resolved as the difference between a "natural" subjectivity and a "reborn" subjectivity, between the self that is the polar opposite of its object and the self that is the arena of the absolute Spirit. "The opposition between objectivity and subjectivity is in itself overcome, and our task is to make ourselves participants of this redemption by letting go of our immediate subjectivity and becoming conscious of God as our true and essential self."[6] Thus, the divine Spirit is not an objectival subject but the depth of finite spirit—the depth of the subjectival and the objectival in their active interrelation.

In vigorous opposition to Hegel, Kierkegaard developed another conception in his *Sickness unto Death*. Three statements comprise the definition in which he embraces the two aspects of the self. Man is spirit; spirit is the self; the self is the act of relating self to self. "The self is a relation which relates itself to its own self"; it is not a "synthesis" of its two factors, infinite and finite, or eternal and temporal, or freedom and necessity. In a sense the self is here both subject and object because it is the agent of relating as well as the object to which relation is made and the object which is related. How seriously we are to take Kierkegaard's definition may be a question left aside for the present since it does not affect a delineation of his position. The rest of *Sickness unto Death* makes clear that Kierkegaard is concerned with the untranscendable self-relatedness, the un-

5. Quoted, along with other references, by Carl G. Schweitzer, "Geist bei Hegel und Heiliger Geist," *Neue Zeitschrift für systematische Theologie und Religionsphilosophie* (Berlin), 6 (1964), 325f.

6. Ibid.

conditional solitariness, of every man. The human self is not the
theater of the action of the divine Spirit. It is man as over against
and then "grounded transparently" in the divine. To put it differently, the subjectival agent which relates the self to the self is pure
and unconditional subjectivity, even though it is temporal. It is the
temporal unconditional that stands over against the eternal unconditional; it is pure subjectival subjectivity that is over against the pure
objectival subjectivity of God. Thus Kierkegaard's definition of faith
is "that the self in being itself and in willing to be itself is grounded
transparently in God," and his definition of sin as the opposite of
faith is "before God in despair not to will to be oneself, or before
God in despair to will to be oneself."[7] The self is the necessity of freedom; it is the fact that in every act and passion *I* am always the agent.
This self as such can never become the object of thought since it is
unconditionally subjectival. Its freedom, or unconditionally subjectival character, is its necessity. It cannot use its freedom to escape
from its freedom. This realization erupts radically in the situation
of despair, the hopeless conflict of trying to accomplish what can
never be accomplished and of *having* to try it.

For Kierkegaard the unconditional subjectivity of the self is
evaluated by the object in view of which it exists. "The measure of
the self is always that in the face of which it is a self." Thus, the self
in view of God—the "theological self," as Kierkegaard calls it, with
some misgiving—not only is unconditional in its freedom, or its
subjectival subjectivity, but is evaluated in the face of the eternal
unconditional. "Only when the self as this definite individual is
conscious of existing before God, only then is it the infinite self."[8]
The self in the sight of God is not only subjectivally unconditional;
it is so over against the objectival unconditional. If the self accepts
its unconditional freedom as its "necessity"—that it must be subjectival—then it is "grounded transparently in God." Unlike Hegel,
therefore, Kierkegaard does not conceive of the human spirit as the
bearer of the divine Spirit. Rather it is temporal but unconditional
freedom which becomes conscious of itself over against the eternal
unconditional—the subjectival unconditional over against the ob-

7. *The Sickness unto Death* (New York, Doubleday Anchor, 1954), pp.
146, 213, 212. See also Louis Dupré, *Kierkegaard as Theologian* (New York,
Sheed and Ward, 1963), pp. 130f.

8. Ibid., pp. 210, 211.

jectival unconditional—and which, in the act of accepting its unconditional freedom, unconditionally transcends the opposition by being "grounded" in the objectival unconditional. One might conclude that here Kierkegaard does approach Hegel's position after all. If I am grounded transparently in God, is not God the depth of my subjectivity? In some sense this is certainly the case, but Kierkegaard's emphasis is on the opposition between the subjectival and objectival unconditionals. For him God is beyond the subject–object polarity insofar as he is the unconditionally *objectival Subject* over against whom I, or any man, is always a subjectival subject. For Hegel God is beyond the subject–object polarity insofar as he is the depth of both the subjectival and the objectival, expressing himself in and through my subjectivity and my objectifying.[9]

Tillich's "self" is a combination of these two conceptions. God is the depth of the subjectival and objectival (as in Hegel), but there is an infinite gap between the depth and the subject–object structure (as in Kierkegaard). The exact nature of Tillich's combination of these two notions is something we shall see in the course of this chapter.

If the designation "self–world polarity" can mean either the polarity of man-in-the-world or that of self-relatedness and relatedness to the objective world, the discussion of the being of God can be taken up in two different ways corresponding to this difference. I shall look first at Tillich's definition of God in relation to man-in-the-world, in which one side of the polarity is any man as a self-reflective being, and the other side is the whole over against him. In this case I am deliberately excluding from consideration the self now engaged in thinking these things and am taking up the position, as it were, of a metaphysical spectator, who sees before him a basic division of finite being into two kinds, self and world. It should be emphasized, however, that this bracketing

9. Thus, for Kierkegaard both subjectivity and objectivity have an unconditional element in them; for Hegel neither subjectivity nor objectivity is unconditional. For Kierkegaard faith is a decision which is also a gift, and the language of faith is a being-spoken-to as well as a speaking; for Hegel faith is a knowing which is also a being-known, and its language is a being-spoken-through as well as a speaking.

of the *I* is deliberate and provisional, to be supplemented by a second step in which the bracket is removed. Otherwise, one would only beg the question that historically conscious thought raises for the possibility of taking a metaphysical spectator's position at all.

On the assumption that the *I* has been excluded from direct consideration and that we provisionally occupy the position of metaphysical spectators, we ask how we see the relations of self, world, and God. Tillich's view can be defined in the following statements. First, God is not derivable either from the self or from the world or from both of them together. There is no idea in the mind, nor is there anything in the world, from which the existence of God might be inferred. The polarity of self and world is an ultimate datum. This is all we see, without being able to derive one pole from the other or to derive a third thing from them. This brings us to the second statement: God is manifested not as a third kind of being in addition to these two, but as the "ground" and "abyss" which appears in them and to which they are "transparent." The polarity is underivable from anything else, because anything else would be still on one or the other side of the polarity. The being of God is made known as that which suffuses both man and the world, as their ground and their abyss.

One should note two emphases in this definition. One of them is an opposition to supernaturalistic thinking which makes God a third kind of reality outside of man and the world. In Tillich's view he is not a third kind of being but the ground of the two irreducible kinds of being. The second emphasis is an opposition to an idealistic identification of God with the man-in-the-world totality. God is not a supernatural being, but he is not the unity of self and world in a larger whole either. The conception of ground and abyss opposes these specific tendencies of supernaturalism and idealism. The basic mistake of idealism on this point is that it overlooks or understates the infinite gap between God and the self–world structure of finite being, a gap which can be bridged only from the side of God and not from the side of the self in its world. Thus Tillich's early essays on religion, "Die Überwindung des Religionsbegriffes in der Religionsphilosophie" (1922) and

"Religionsphilosophie" (1925),[10] argue against a supernaturalistic view by insisting that God is not an object and against an idealistic view by denying that he is the unity or totality of man-in-the-world. He is neither an object (*gegenständlich*) nor the whole; he is the depth of the whole (*urständlich*) manifested as its ground and abyss (*GW, 1,* 379).

The depth of self and world appears when both poles become transparent to what is beyond their polarity. If what is beyond appears as destructive power, it is the abyss; if it appears as sustaining power, it is the ground. God as the ground and abyss of man and world can be known, accordingly, only as that which appears in their polarity, not as a third reality nor as a synthesis of the polarity into a higher unity.

But what is the difference between the depth and the whole? How can one understand the depth in any way that makes it different from either the parts or the whole of the self–world polarity? This is certainly one of the crucial questions in Tillich's thought. The answer can be briefly formulated if one says that the depth differs from the whole as something *directly meant* differs from something *symbolically meant*. Actually the position of a metaphysical spectator cannot be maintained if one explicates this difference, because it is connected with the temporality of the *I think*. Nonetheless, it can be described provisionally without taking direct account of the *I*.

If God is the ground of self and world, then anything can be as transparent to that ground as anything else. Anything can be a symbol which presents the depth to us. Thus, if the thing used as a symbol were taken from the world's side of the polarity, rather than from the self's, it would differ from other objects in the world because it would present the depth of subjects as well as objects. Its activity would consist of annulling and restoring its objective character. To be understood as a symbol, not as an object, the thing must be seen as having subjective characteristics as well as

10. The first is reprinted in *GW, 1,* 365–88; the second in *GW, 1,* 295–364. Also see his *Rechtfertigung und Zweifel* (Giessen, Alfred Töpelmann Verlag, 1924), p. 28.

objective ones, so that it represents the whole polarity, and its activity must be one of canceling and restoring its own objective standing, so that it represents the depth rather than the whole.

This difference perhaps can be best seen with regard to the self–world polarity itself, which can be taken nonsymbolically as a totality or symbolically as an expression of God. Anything can symbolize God, but only the full "synthesis of syntheses," the "synthesis of being and meaning in unity with the synthesis of the personal and its fullness," is, according to Tillich's statement, the "highest" and "always intended" symbol of God (*GW, 1, 334*). The difference between God and the totality is the difference between this full "synthesis" as directly meant and the same synthesis as symbolically meant. Tillich observes that even Hegel's "absolute spirit" could be interpreted in either way. If it is a totality, it is not a definition of God but a definition of the self–world whole. But if it is taken symbolically, it is a definition of God because it expresses the depth manifest in the totality.

Here then is the critical point for understanding the being of God. Described from the standpoint of a metaphysical spectator, the difference between a totality as a totality and a totality as a symbol is tantamount to the difference between a "finished" whole and a "living" whole—although this is not Tillich's way of putting it. In the first case the totality is completed; in the second case it is constantly being canceled and renewed. This canceling and renewing activity is the expression of the depth, as abyss and ground, which is present in the totality. When the depth is invisible, no such activity is seen in the whole. A nonsymbolic totality is a finished, standing whole, even if its constituent parts are in movement. A symbolic totality is one which can be seen constantly canceling and renewing itself, for this activity is the manifestation of what is beyond the whole. Only this activity, not the agent of it, is directly visible to the spectator, so that the God who is ground and abyss of self and world is known as the subject of that action, though he himself never becomes visible as a viewable reality.

If God is the depth of the basic self–world polarity, it follows that he is also the depth of any fundamental polarity, such as that of positive and negative. He cannot be equated with the positive alone or the negative alone; in moral terms, he cannot be identified with the good in contrast to the evil.[11] Thus, unlike Hegel's dialectical system where the positive and negative are steps in the development of an absolute totality which is an ultimate synthesis, in Tillich's symbolical whole the opposition of position and negation continues in the self-negation and self-positing of the whole. This continuing action expresses the depth which can never become part of the totality and presents us with the God who is not a self in contrast to the world, nor the good in contrast to the evil, but the depth manifest in both sides of the self–world or positive–negative polarity.

In other words, the "life" (canceling, renewing) of the whole, which gives it its symbolic character, is the action of God, and God is present in that living action. The whole is the be-ing of God, but it is not God himself. God himself appears only in his action of be-ing; and his action of be-ing, described in its totality, is the structure of man-in-the-world, in which man relates as agent to the world as patient or as responder to the world as power. This conception is behind a statement of Tillich's in the *Systematic Theology,* a statement which is remarkable because it occurs in only one place (though twice there) in all of his writings. He distinguishes God from the structure of being by saying that God is not subject to the structure: "He *is* this structure" (*ST, 1,* 238f.). "God *is* the structure of being"—this is tantamount to saying that what is elaborated as the structure of being becomes symbolic when it is interpreted as the be-ing of God, and this is a translation into metaphysical terms (I am still speaking from the standpoint of a metaphysical spectator) of the biblical understanding of the creation as the continuous creating of God. The self–world whole is, as a whole, the concrete aspect of the divine life. The self-canceling and self-renewing activity of the whole is transparent to its ground when it is seen as the action of God.

This of itself would not eliminate the "infinite gap" between

11. Hence the idea of a "transmoral conscience." Cf. Paul Tillich, *Morality and Beyond* (New York, Harper & Row, 1963), pp. 65–81.

God and finite being which Tillich insists upon against Romantic idealism. To guard against that misunderstanding, however, it is necessary to add that the difference between saying "The structure of man-in-the-world is the concrete action of *'God'*" and "The structure of man-in-the-world is the concrete action of *God*" (in the former case one is defining the word; in the latter case one is apprehending the meaning conveyed) is, like every difference between form as empty form and form as formal content, a qualitative one; there is a gap between the empty and the filled form. In one case the depth is absent from the form; in the other case the depth is present in the form; but the "filling" occurs at the initiative of the depth, not of the form. As Tillich puts it, "God is not only his own ground, but also his own abyss" (*GW*, *2*, 334). By adding this qualification, one can see the connection between Tillich's and idealism's doctrine of God. Like the idealist conception Tillich's is nonobjective, but unlike the idealist it maintains a distinction between God and the whole.

God is the ground and abyss of the self–world totality; the self–world structure is the be-ing of God—he *is*, as that structure. These are two ways of describing the relations of self, world, and God for a metaphysical view. A third way, which brings out a different emphasis, though it is the same conception, is drawn from the definitions of man as a microcosm and the world as a macrocosm. Any man is a microcosm, a gestalt, because he is a living entity centered in the self. The universe as a "world," as a structural whole with some sort of organizing center (such as the perspective of the man for whom it is "world"), is the macrocosm. This similarity between the being of a man and the being of the whole universe accounts for the similarity in the definitions Tillich gives of "self" and "world." The self, he says, is a "centered structure," and the world is a "structured whole" (*ST*, *1*, 172). Both of these definitions contain implicit references to an organizing center and the organized whole. On one hand, any centered structure is also a whole,[12] because its centeredness

12. Cf. *ST*, *1*, 169: "One can speak of self-centeredness . . . wherever the reaction . . . is dependent on a structural whole"; similarly, *ST*, *3*, 33.

is what distinguishes it from a mere collection of parts; on the other hand, any structured whole is also a centered structure, for the same reason. If the self is a centered structure, it is a whole organized around a center; and if the world is a structured whole, it has a center around which the whole is organized. The first is a microcosm; the second, a macrocosm.

For the microcosm, the center and the whole are easily specified. The center is the "self" of self-relatedness, and the whole is the individual man through which that self is active. The whole is the definite gestalt, whereas the center is the *I* expressing itself through the whole. In the case of the macrocosm, the situation is not so clear. Tillich seems to have three different ways of defining the whole and the center. One way is to say that the center of the whole world is the self for whom it is the world. The self viewing the world from its perspective is the center of the whole. In this case the center of the microcosm and the macrocosm are one and the same, or the distinction, if there is any at all, lies in the difference between the *I* as the center of the individual and the individual man himself, who is in turn the center of his universe. But this is scarcely more than a verbal distinction. Put in simplest terms, the self is the structuring center and the universe is the structured whole of the macrocosm.

A second way of defining the center and whole of the world is christological. Jesus as the Christ is the concrete logos, the single man in whom the structure of the cosmos is embodied.[13] As such he is a permanent center of the world, distinct from the selves of all other individual beings in such a way that the *I* of any man has its external counterpart in the figure of Jesus.

The third way—and Tillich never fully defined its relation to the second—is found in Tillich's ethical thought,[14] where the moral imperative places a limit upon any man's ability and right to structure the material of his world into a whole. The one thing that can never be objectified into the world without threatening

---

13. Tillich calls him the center of history, and history is the culmination of being universally. *ST*, *3, 366.*

14. *Morality and Beyond*, p. 22. Cf. below, Chap. 8, pp. 193–95.

the whole self–world relation is another person, who unconditionally demands recognition as a person, another structuring
center. Following this line of thought, one has to say that the
objectival center of the world for any man is any other man insofar as he is acknowledged as a person. So the center of the macrocosm is not the subjectival self alone, but the self externalized
objectivally in any other person. He too embodies in his person
the logos of the universe. He is another one for whom the whole
is a structured cosmos. Of these three ways of describing the relation between the microcosm and the macrocosm the second one is
no doubt fundamental for Tillich, as will be seen by an examina-
tion of his whole theological thought and the role played by the
christological paradox.

Even a metaphysical spectator's view of things, as I have been
describing it, makes clear how Tillich departs from Aristotelian
and idealistic conceptions of God. He emphasizes not only the
otherness of God, as the depth of man and world, but also that
the material for thinking God's being is given by the self–world
polarity—there is no third thing. God cannot be thought without
the self–world polarity, but he cannot be identified with it either.
The polarity cannot be synthesized into something higher; it remains an underivable polarity (*ST, 1,* 174). At the same time,
however, it is not a fixed whole, but a living process of cancella-
tion and reestablishment. Yet we must now turn to the fact that
Tillich's intention is not to present a view for metaphysical observation. It is necessary to remove the bracket placed around the *I*
engaged in reflective or responsive thinking here and now.

In the act of thinking, the self who thinks (the subjectival) is
unconditional, and what the self thinks (the objectival) is conditional. To think the depth of this relation would require thinking
something that is objectival and unconditional, for something that
is both unconditional and objectival would bridge the polarity
without synthesizing it into a more embracing whole. As objectival
it would represent the object, and as unconditional it would represent the agent of thought. Using the terminology of Tillich's early
writings, one can say that in the act of thinking the self is *uncondi-*

tional form, the world is *conditioned content,* and God, as the depth of that act, is *unconditional content and presence* (*unbedingter Gehalt*).[15]

But how can one think unconditional content if, in the very act of thinking, the content is always conditioned at least by the perspective of the thinking self? Indeed, the polarity of the self and world seems to make it impossible to do so. Either one allows an unconditional form (the unreflectible *I* in act) but no unconditional content; or one allows unconditional content which violates the unconditional form. The first presents the prospect of an ultimately empty autonomy, for there is nothing that cannot be reflected; and the second presents the prospects of a destructive heteronomy, a positing of an objectival unconditional which denies the unconditional form of the self. If God is to be defined as unconditional content and presence (*unbedingter Gehalt*), the question of the conception of God is how the unconditioned can appear objectivally without destroying the self's unconditional self-relatedness. This, Tillich says, is the question over which philosophy of religion, in its attempt to form a conception of God, repeatedly stumbles. Tillich's own answer can be stated briefly: "To view [*anschauen*] this infinite paradox [the objectival unconditional] is to think God; and when it is methodical, it is philosophy of religion or theology" (*GW, 1,* 386).[16]

---

15. *"Gehalt"* cannot be translated with a single English word. I have translated it in three different ways, depending on the context. Sometimes (particularly in the early writings) "Gehalt" is equivalent to "Inhalt" (content) and is contrasted with form. In such cases I use "content" as an English equivalent. In other cases "Gehalt" is contrasted with content as well as form, and then I translate it as "depth" or as "substance." (Tillich himself uses "substance" in English, and James Luther Adams, *Paul Tillich's Philosophy of Culture, Science, and Religion* [New York, Harper and Row, 1965], uses "import" for this meaning.) In still other cases it refers to that aspect of the objectival which cannot be grasped, which resists grasping; then I translate it as "power" or "presence." On the derivation of this last meaning, see my "Scope of Systematics," pp. 143, 146f.

16. "Religionsphilosophie ist Lehre von der religiösen Funktion und ihren Kategorien. Theologie ist normative und systematische Darstellung der konkreten Erfüllung des religionsbegriffs." *GW, 1,* 301.

After thought has become historically conscious, to think the reality of God requires thinking—or "viewing," as Tillich also says—a paradoxical reality or presence. In this case the thinking self, in all of its temporality, is included in the conception and no longer occupies the position of a metaphysical spectator. What is there whose objectivity cannot be removed by reflection—and which is therefore as unconditional as the reflecting self in its act —and whose presence is not dissolved by a doubting response? A paradoxical reality or presence, for this is objectival and yet unconditional. From this standpoint Tillich formulated the title of an early essay, "Die Überwindung des Religionsbegriffs in der Religionsphilosophie" (1922), which expresses the fact that paradox is the necessary form of every statement about the unconditional.

Tillich distinguishes three meanings of paradox (*GW, 1,* 367).[17] There is an esthetic paradox, which consists of the use of words in a contradictory and ambiguously suggestive way in order to communicate richness of personal content (*"'geistreich'"*). There is a dialectical paradox, which consists of the collision of two lines of thought, each of which is necessary in itself but contradicts the other when they are brought together. In both of these cases, Tillich says, the paradoxicality lies in the thinking self—in one case in the whims of its artistic construction, and in the second case in the limitations of its logical construction. There is a third paradox, however, which is rooted in the objectival rather than the subjectival and which appears at the point "where the unconditional becomes an object." In this case paradoxicality is as necessary as the lack of contradiction in scientific assertions. Unlike an esthetic or dialectical paradox, this one cannot be resolved; "it poses a [permanent] task for our viewing" (*GW, 1,* 367).

Moreover, the concept of religion in Tillich's treatment is

17. Schröer's discussion of paradox in Tillich restricts itself to *ST, 1,* and does not include references to *ST, 2,* 90–92, or to "Die Überwindung des Religionsbegriffs in der Religionsphilosophie." Henning Schröer, *Die Denkform der Paradoxalität als theologisches Problem* (Göttingen, Vandenhoeck & Ruprecht, 1960), pp. 157–63.

equally paradoxical. It conceptualizes something which is destroyed as soon as it is conceptualized, and yet the concept cannot be avoided. The task, therefore, is to use the concept of religion in such a way as to avoid its destructive power by recognizing its paradoxical character. This can be done by subordinating it to the concept of the unconditional (*GW, 1,* 368), that is, by conceiving the unconditional precisely in its unconditionality. Basically the problem of a philosophy of religion is the same as that of God's relation to the self–world structure. It can be approached from two different sides: How does the unconditional become manifest with reference to the thinking self in its act of thinking? How does it become manifest in relation to the world, or the object of thought?

Since the unconditional breaks through the ontological structure, the question of the concept of God or of religion can be raised from the side of the self or the side of the world. In the act of thinking I experience my subjectivity as unconditional. How do I come to know the unconditional which is God? This is to approach the question from the self-side of the polarity. Approached from the world-side the question is different. No object of my thought is unconditional, because it is conditioned at least by the fact that it is an object for me as a subject. How then can I think of God as the unconditional? The alternative seems to be that if anything is unconditional it is subjectival and immediately experienced, and if it is objectival it is not unconditional. Yet the conception of God as the unconditional tries to unite what is objectival and what is unconditional.

Accordingly, the conception of God can be developed along two different lines, corresponding to the two poles of the ontological structure. In the first case it is set forth as the relation between "self-certainty" and "certainty of God," which are two ways of experiencing the unconditional. In the second case it is set forth as the paradoxical statement, "God exists," which logically makes him part of the world even when ontologically he transcends the self–world polarity. We shall look at these two lines of thought separately.

Tillich opposes the idea that one can derive a certainty of God from the certainty of one's self. On the contrary, the certainty of the self rests upon the certainty of God. "The self participates in unconditional certainty only when it is meant as the locus of the self-grasping of the unconditional" (*GW, 1,* 369). The self is unconditionally subject in its grasping of the world, but it is not the ground of the world. The reality of the world is given to it, and that element of givenness withdraws it from conditioning by the perspective of the self. Thus, although the self is unconditionally subjectival in apprehending the world, it is not an unconditional being. To use Tillich's terms, the "form" of consciousness is unconditional, but the "content" is not. The unconditional self can grasp everything that is given to it and make it objective, but it cannot create the objectival content it grasps. It cannot be the basis of an objectival and unconditional content. The certainty of the self, therefore, is empty without a relation to the unconditional which is more than formal. Self-relatedness is unconditionally the form of consciousness, but it cannot guarantee its own actual being or the being of its world. Still less can it guarantee the reality of God.

Self-certainty cannot be used as a foundation for the certainty of God because objectival content cannot be derived from subjectival form. Nonetheless, every self-understanding, intentionally or unintentionally, contains a reference to the unconditional as the ground of its being at all. If there is no way from the unconditional form of self-consciousness to the unconditional ground of real being, there is a way from the latter to the former. There is no way from *I* to God, but there is one from God to *I*. This is what Tillich calls the event in which "the ground contained in consciousness of self breaks through the autonomous form of consciousness" (*GW, 1,* 379).

Even though it is always implied, the reference to the unconditional ground may not be intended and may not be conscious. Whether it is intentional and conscious or unintentional and not conscious distinguishes the religious from the nonreligious self-consciousness. The self can experience its certainty in such a way that "the unconditional relation to reality" contained in it is in the foreground, or in such a way that it is in the background while the being of the self is in the foreground. In the former case it is a "religious" self-understanding; in the latter it is non-religious (*GW, 1,* 378). But this is a difference in intention and not in the real state of affairs, since self-grasping implicitly includes a reference to the ground of the self's being at all. This, however, means that the subjectival unconditional is not the ground but the *medium* of unconditional being. Its form is unconditional, but what it mediates is a depth that breaks into the form and embraces both the self and its object, the form and the content. The acting subject is a medium "in which and through which" the unconditional is grasped; it is the place (*Stätte*) at which the unconditional grasps itself through the self's grasping of its object.

Thus, with respect to the self-side of the ontological polarity, to think God as the unconditional involves the awareness of the depth of the unconditional form. The paradox here is that the form of the unconditional—the *I* in the act of thinking or being— is broken through by a content which is really unconditional, and the self which is unconditionally subjective becomes known as well as knowing, grasped as well as grasping, acted upon as well as acting. It experiences its activity upon the world as a medium for the power that is the ground of the world as well as of the self. When the paradox is reached, it bridges the gap between self and world. From the side of the subjectival it is experienced as the depth of subjectivity; from the side of the objectival it is the depth of objectivity; and it is both of them at once.[18] When the self becomes aware of the real ground of its unconditional form, it knows itself as the "locus of the self-grasping of the unconditional." It is the paradoxical awareness in which the acting subject is also acted upon, not by another subject, but by the depth of subjectivity acting in and through it. In the self's thinking God, God is thinking himself.

If it is true that the paradox is unavoidable when approached

18. Thus the "constellation" of ecstasy and miracle (*ST, 1,* 117).

from the side of the self, it is also true when approached from the side of the world. The subjectival paradox has an objectival counterpart. Indeed, Tillich devotes more attention to the objectival question, namely, the relation of God and the world. Against Romantic idealism he maintains that God can no more be derived from the world than from the self. Consequently, the statement "God is" can be interpreted only in the light of the distinction between the world and God. It assigns God a place in the world—he is one of the many beings that are—even though, as the unconditional, he cannot be an object or the whole of objectivity.

To understand the paradox objectivally, therefore, we must be clear on the relation between God and the world, religion and culture, faith and unfaith. To say "God is" is to place him among the things of the world, yet he is not an object in the world. The symbol "God"—that word or object in and through which the unconditional is manifest—is a reality which transcends its objectivity, whether it is a single object in the world with symbolic power or the whole world-synthesis with symbolic power. The paradoxical character of the statement that God exists derives from this fact. On one hand this object or this whole world-synthesis is objectival; on the other hand it is unconditional. By combining the objectival and the unconditional, it bridges the duality of self and world from the side of the world, since it speaks of an unconditional which, even though unconditional, is not the form of self-relatedness. "God exists," or "There is a God," is a paradoxical assertion in which the content of the statement (the manifestation of the unconditional) contradicts the form of the statement (which conditions God by making him objectival) and, by so doing, bridges the gap between subjectival and objectival.

This objectival unconditional is not derived from the self or the world, but it is the implicit basis of both, for consciousness of the world is destroyed if the consciousness of its unconditional depth is lost.[19] The unconditional in self-certainty is purely formal,

19. This is the fault of idealism. It "hebt den Abgrund in Gott auf, das Göttlich-Schöpferische, in dem auch das Dämonische enthalten ist, und sieht nicht die Negativitäten des Unbedingten gegen die Formsynthesis, die Welt" (ibid., p. 334).

and without a corresponding content it is nothing. The totality of the world synthesis is conditional, and without an unconditional form it is chaos. What self-certainty needs is content for its unconditional form; what world-consciousness needs is unconditional form for its content. The self, though unconditional, cannot produce its contents; it must receive them. The world, though having content, is not unconditional. The subjectival unconditional cannot stand without an objectival unconditional. Therefore, to the extent that an unconditional content intrudes upon self-consciousness, it is the awareness of God; and to the extent that an unconditional form intrudes upon the world content, it is the presence of God.[20]

Tillich's methodological development of these ideas is found chiefly in *Das System der Wissenschaften nach Gegenständen und Methoden* (1923) and *Religionsphilosophie* (1925), which serve as the background for the *Systematic Theology*. I shall follow Tillich's thought in these early writings first and then indicate how they are worked out in the *Systematic Theology*.

The methodological problem for philosophy of religion and systematic theology is like that of the concept of God. Philosophy objectifies all things; religion insists that God cannot be objectified. Philosophy maintains that whatever cannot be objectively known is not real; religion insists that God cannot be objectively known. Yet each of them makes a kind of total claim. How can one bring them together as a philosophy of religion or as a theology that is a specific exemplification of that philosophy of religion? Tillich's most concise statement of this problem is given in the opening paragraphs of *Religionsphilosophie,* and the solution which he expounds in this treatise is the one which he advances in the notion of a "self-transcending" idea of God in the introduction to the second volume of *Systematic Theology*.

"In religion philosophy comes upon an object that resists being

20. The "unconditional form" of the *System der Wissenschaften* becomes "the question of God" in the *Systematic Theology*. Cf. *GW, 1,* 125, 227, with *ST, 1,* 207.

made an object of philosophy" (*GW, 1,* 297). This simple fact imperils religion as well as philosophy. Religion feels attacked at its very center by a "concept" of religion, which seems to oppose the "revelation" upon which it is based. Revelation speaks of the divine activity, religion of the human; revelation is singular and absolute, religion is always repeatable; revelation speaks of the entrance of a new reality into life and spirit, religion speaks of a life-reality that is always there and a spiritual function that is necessary; revelation speaks of what is beyond culture, a concept of religion speaks of an aspect of culture. Thus, the concept of religion threatens the life of religion at its very heart, and the philosophy of religion seems to occupy a strangely self-defeating position. Either it dissolves the object it is trying to understand, or it forsakes its philosophical method in the face of religion. Either it misses religion by maintaining its philosophical method, or it ceases to be philosophy by sacrificing its method.

If its essential aim is to understand everything as it really is, philosophy cannot be content with failing to understand religion religiously or with sacrificing its objectifying method. If it dissolves the religious element in religion it ceases to be philosophy simply because, as philosophy, it must seek to understand its objects for what they essentially are, and religion will not let itself be dissolved. But if, on the other hand, it tries to halt before religion and to say to itself, This far and no farther, it imperils not only philosophy of religion but all philosophy. "If there is any object that is in principle not accessible to philosophy, its right to every object is brought into question." Why? Tillich answers that philosophy would then not be in a position to draw a line between the forbidden object of religion and other spheres. "If it gives in at one point, it gives in altogether" (*GW, 1,* 298). Revelation could claim all domains, and philosophy would have no weapon with which to resist the claim. Indeed, in the nature of the case revelation, as the intrusion of the unconditional into the conditional, does not let a limit be set to its claim. Revelation and philosophy make total claims, each in its own name.

Furthermore, the fact that this is not only a "dialectical" but a real problem is shown, Tillich notes, by the history of philosophy and theology. In some periods, as the early Middle Ages, the whole view is theological; in others, such as the Enlightenment, it is philosophical. In still others a synthesis is aimed at, either from the side of theology (as in the high Middle Ages) or from the side of philosophy (as in idealism and Romanticism); or they simply coexist, as in English empiricism and theological Kantianism. All such syntheses, however, founder upon the question, Who determines the boundary line? Indeed, no solution to the problem of philosophy and religion (revelation) is possible at all unless there is a point in philosophy as well as in revelation where the two are identical.

Philosophy and religion, however, do reach a point at which they meet, and hence the problem is soluble. The point of juncture is that of the paradox. Philosophically expressed it is the point where an *unconditional* object is reached, for this is the point at which objectivity (and the method for establishing objectivity) transcends itself; religiously expressed it is the point where an unconditional *object* manifests itself, for here the unconditional— or, in our present terms, objectival subjectivity—(and the method for responding to it) transcends itself.

After settling in the United States Tillich discovered the flexibility of the English word "concern" and began calling God man's "ultimate concern,"[21] for which the German counterparts are such phrases as *das, was uns unbedingt angeht.* The utility of this phrase lies in the fact that "concern" contains both subjective and objective references. It is my being-concerned-about as well as that-which-concerns-me—the state of concern as well as the object eliciting concern. The relation between the subjective and objective meanings is, accordingly, reciprocal. The object about which I am concerned is the object which concerns me. "Ultimate" or "unconditional" qualifies both sides of the concern. Whatever object can concern me unconditionally is no longer

21. See Tillich's comments on this in D. Mackenzie Brown, ed., *Ultimate Concern: Tillich in Dialogue* (New York, Harper & Row, 1965), pp. 11, 26.

simply objectival, and whenever I am unconditionally concerned my state of concern is no longer simply a subjective state. In the phrase "ultimate concern" Tillich thus found a formulation for the conception of God as the paradoxical unconditional. The question of method can then be stated as the question of how to approach an "ultimate concern" philosophically and religiously. The peculiarity and strength of Tillich's conception and the method appropriate to it lie in its connection of the philosophical and the religious in such a way as to avoid the emptiness of a philosophical autonomy and the destructiveness of a religious heteronomy.

Because the point of juncture can be found philosophically and religiously, it can be approached from either direction. In the method of correlation of the *Systematic Theology* the point of juncture is given a dual character which embodies the two approaches to it. Reached from the side of philosophy it is the *question* of the unconditional; reached from the side of religion it is the unconditional as a *concrete answer*. This is to say that the point at which objectivity first transcends itself is expressed as a question;[22] the point at which unconditionality transcends itself is expressed as a concrete answer. Ultimate concern philosophically expressed is a question; it is that for which one is always asking. This question is unconditional in philosophy because what it seeks is not any particular object but objectivity as such, and because it is the untranscendable ground of philosophy as philosophy. Ultimate concern religiously expressed is a concrete answer. As religious it is, of course, unconditional; but as concrete it transcends the unconditionality to become objectival—it is unconditional objectivity as an answer rather than a question. The question of the unconditional is reached through ontological analysis; the answer is methodologically reached through "critical phenomenology" (*ST*, *1*, 107); and the two together comprise the "method of correlation."

---

22. "There is an unconditional element in the very act of asking any question" (*ST*, *1*, 208).

The background of the method of correlation, however, lies in Tillich's early writings from the 1920s. Accordingly, as noted previously, I shall first direct attention to that earlier material, discussing it under the four topics of the "metalogical" method, the method of "coincidence," the theonomous and autonomous elements, and the hermeneutical question. All of these contribute to the final formulation of the method of correlation which unites an ontological analysis with a critical phenomenology of religion.

Tillich's work on the conception of God was always attended by work on a method appropriate to it. First it was the quest for a method in the philosophy of religion[23] and later, as a concrete expression of the same, the quest for a method in systematic theology. Methodologically, the first problem one must take account of is the fact that the act and content of religious understanding cannot be separated—what religion is and whether it is true are one question, not two. A frequent and fundamental mistake on the part of many philosophies of religion is that they separate the object intended in the religious act from the act itself (*GW, 1,* 274). The nature and the truth of religion are then treated as two separate questions. This separation invalidates the religious character of religion in advance, for it presupposes that a religious act is equally possible whether its object exists or does not exist, and it tries to find a religious object that could be treated apart from the religious act. But one cannot empirically describe the religious act and speculatively evaluate the truth of its object without sacrificing the religious nature of both. Whatever can be empirically described or speculatively evaluated is not religious. The only method appropriate to religion is one in which the act and the object of the act are not separated. This, however, means that the assertions made in such a philosophy are paradoxical, and the method appropriate to them is one which Tillich calls the metalogical method.

The metalogical method, a forerunner of the *Systematic Theol-*

---

23. Cf. *GW, 1,* 274: "Religionsphilosophie hat nur ein Recht als theonome Sinnprinzipienlehre."

ogy's ontological analysis and critical phenomenology, combines a critical with an "intuitional" and "dynamic" (individual–creative) element. It is logical because it directs itself to the pure forms and metalogical because it transcends the forms. Insofar as it is logical, it is like the critical–dialectical method, which understands its objects by abstracting the functions and categories of meaning (*Sinnfunktionen* and *Sinnkategorien*) from the actualities in which the meaning is embodied (*Sinnwirklichkeit*) and by bringing them together dialectically as the conditions for a meaningful construction of reality. Functions and categories are known when they have been given their place in the construction of reality. The logical aspect of the metalogical method consists of an analysis of religion as a function and category implied in the structure of meaningful reality. Yet the method goes beyond the logical task in two ways. It seeks to grasp not just the form but the living content in the forms; it distinguishes between the essence and the norm of anything. Thus, to the formal element three others are added—the dynamic, the intuitional, and the individual–creative.

The living dialectic that suffuses all reality is that of form and content. These are the elements of meaning found in all reality. In understanding the essence of a phenomenon, the metalogical method takes account of the living dialectic by directing its attention not to individual objects but to the tensions and polarities which are the principles constituting both form and content of the object under study. These principles express the inner dynamics of the reality. Because of the infinite tension between form and content, the particular objects (*Sinngegenstände*) are left to empirical study; they cannot be grasped metalogically. The metalogical method sharply distinguishes, therefore, between the forms and the objects of meaning. It studies the forms not of individual things but of the polarities which are essential to their being at all, and it leaves the objects themselves to empirical study. It keeps the "dynamic dialectics of the elements of meaning" distinct from "empirical experience" (*GW, 1,* 314).

These two characteristics also distinguish the metalogical from the phenomenological method, insofar as phenomenology is not concerned with the dynamic dialectic of the constitutive elements but with the individual forms, and insofar as it does not leave the objects themselves to empirical study. Thus, this metalogical method can provide a basis for the critical evaluation that is lacking in phenomenology, and it can elevate empirical study to a "living understanding of essences" without introducing a kind of second-order, mystical empiricism above objective empiricism.

The intuitive element, which is also part of the metalogical method, is related to the basic principle of mysticism—that the principles of the macrocosm are found in the microcosm.[24] Epistemologically this is expressed as the statement that the world is filled with meaning by spirit—man fills the world with meaning. That is to say, in man the elements which constitute reality reach their fullest expression; he is a mirror of the universe. But this implies that the elements of all meaning—namely, form and content—are universally (*schlechthin*) the elements of being (*Wesenselemente*). Meaning and essence are constituted by these same basic elements. Hence the development, particularly in Western mysticism, of psychological terminology to grasp the content of reality signifies a new method and a new way of thinking. Germinally it is the metalogical method, for this mysticism employs psychological terminology in order to grasp the living content in the forms of meaning—"die Schau der mit lebendigem Gehalt erfüllten Sinnformen" (*GW, 1*, 315). It is not a way of viewing some metaphysical and independent beings. The opposition between form and content is one which applies only to the viewing itself, not to reality, since in reality there is no form without content and no content without form.

Finally, the individual–creative element, which methodologically is related to pragmatism, also comes from the inner dynamics of the polarity of forms. This dynamic polarity makes possible a

---

24. This principle is applied in Tillich's ontological analysis (cf. *ST, 1*, 168) and is reflected in the use of "inside" and "outside" terms for ontological concepts. Anxiety and courage, for example, are inside terms for being and nonbeing.

constructive understanding of the historical ways in which the forms have been filled by spirit. It leads to a normative position by way of the history of spirit, driving toward a balance of the tensions in creative solutions to problems that have arisen from the historical process. This concrete concept of norm distinguishes the metalogical method from the critical method. Criticism is concerned only with the pure forms and finds no significance in the concrete forms. The metalogical method looks at the concrete forms also.

If the metalogical method is followed, it should, in Tillich's understanding, avoid the disjunction between the nature and the truth of religion (*GW, 1,* 327). If the religious act is the act of being directed toward the unconditional, it is pointless to ask whether there is or is not an unconditional, or whether the act is directed toward something real or not. If religion is essentially the unconditional aspect of every human act, such a question is pointless because the question itself—"Is there an unconditional?" —presupposes "the unconditional meaningfulness of the cognitive sphere."

Moreover, this method is applicable not only by philosophy but by all the humanities, or "self-interpretive sciences" (*Geisteswissenschaften*) (*GW, 1,* 235).[25] It is designed to correct the deficiencies of formalist criticism and uncritical phenomenology or pragmatism. Tillich developed it in view of both the strengths and weaknesses of criticism, phenomenology, and pragmatism. In other words, this method grew out of a consideration of how to grasp the phenomenon of religion appropriately, and it was then applied universally as an answer to the problem of understanding both the form and the content of the objects of study.

The metalogical method thus provides the main characteristics of Tillich's method in the *Systematic Theology*. The intuitive element is represented in the principle, used in the ontological analysis, that man is a microcosm—a being in whom all the elements

25. Tillich notes that he used the method in his philosophy of religion, his *Masse und Geist,* and his *Die Idee einer Theologie der Kultur* before he had a name for it or knew of its methodological significance. *GW, 1,* 235, n. 2.

of the structure of being are present. The dynamic element is represented in the typology of religion as well as in the interpretation of the movement of history (*ST, 1*, 218ff.; *3*, 364ff.). The fact that a metalogical understanding includes structural forms as well as historical content is represented by the double approach to ultimate concern through analysis and through description. The individual–creative element is represented in Tillich's view of every theological system as a point of crystallization, individual and temporary in its formulation, a beginning as well as an end (*ST, 3, 4; GW, 1*, 111).

The method of the *Systematic Theology* differs from the metalogical method chiefly in its emphasis upon the double and correlative approach to understanding ultimate concern (and implicitly all things human). This difference is reflected *in nuce* by the translation of *Sinn* (meaning) and its combinatory forms of *Sinnfunktion, Sinnkategorie,* and *Sinnwirklichkeit,* which are used in the *System der Wissenschaften,* into the two terms of the *Systematic Theology,* "being-itself" and "the meaning of being," the first of which is philosophical and the second theological.[26]

The metalogical method grew out of the general question of understanding human reality and grasping the unconditional in it. A second line of thought, also contributing to the methodological background of the *Systematic Theology,* is developed specifically with respect to metaphysics, a term which Tillich later discards.[27] In the *System der Wissenschaften* he describes this discipline as the "will to grasp the unconditional" (*GW, 1*, 253). The unconditional includes the unconditional meaning (*Sinn*) that is the prius of every meaning (*Sinnerfassung*), the unconditional form that is the prius of every form (*Sinnform*), and the unconditional content that is the prius of every content (*Sinngehalt*). The methodological problem in metaphysics is raised by the fact that it must use concepts, which express the formal element of reality, in order to grasp and convey the content of reality. Like science, meta-

26. Cf. *ST, 1,* 22, with *GW, 1,* 255f.
27. *Love, Power, and Justice* (New York, Oxford University Press, 1954), pp. 23f.; *ST, 1,* 163.

physics uses conceptual forms; like art, its intention is to express the content rather than the form of reality. This fact makes for the presence of a scientific element and an artistic element in metaphysical thought. Nonetheless, metaphysics is not a synthesis of the scientific and artistic; it is, rather, an expression of the original unity out of which the two have proceeded (*GW, 1,* 254).

The original unity is unconditional because it is the presupposition or prius of any subjectival–objectival distinction. This gives rise to the paradoxical character of metaphysics. It must use forms of the conditional in order to grasp the unconditional. But which forms? Here its dependence on the sciences is evident. It must use the concepts which have been fashioned by the sciences, but it must use them symbolically in order to convey the unconditional. It cannot fashion its own concepts without working heteronomously on the sciences in their understanding of reality. The central symbol for the unconditional is the unity of the real itself. The way that unity is seen—the categories out of which it is constructed and the values that are expressed through the construction—produces the "system of metaphysical symbols" (*GW, 1,* 254). Such a system cannot be an arbitrary construction; it must use intelligible forms that convey the unconditional.

Metaphysics must begin with being (*Sinn*) rather than beings (*Sein*) because the unconditional is not an object among objects.[28]

28. *Sinn,* of course, means "meaning," and *Sein* means "being"; but since *Sinn* of the early writings is *Sein* (being-itself) in the later, and *Sein* of the early writings is "world" in the later, I have fused the two usages here. The change is to be traced no doubt to Heidegger's distinction between *Sein* and *Seiendes.* In "The Religious Symbol," a translation of a 1928 German article, published in the *Journal of Liberal Religion, 2* (Summer 1940), 13–33, Tillich uses the term "being-in-itself" to refer to objectivity, "being-for-us" to refer to subjectivity, and the "unconditioned transcendent" to refer to their depth as expressed in religious symbols. One should perhaps note that "being-in-itself" is not equivalent to "being-itself," since the latter, in Tillich's terminology, refers not to the objectivity of the subject–object structure but to its depth as conceptually grasped. The usage can be confusing, as is evidenced by the discussion elicited by the article in the *Journal of Liberal Religion,* but Tillich retained it in the revision of that article in *Daedalus, 87* (Summer 1958), 3–21.

Its first task is to work out the elements that constitute being and meaning at all, for seeing these elements is the only way of grasping the unconditional meaning (*Sinn*) that founds all meaning. In particular such a view answers three questions: What is the relation of the unconditional to the things that are? What is the relation of the unconditional to the creative process of spirit? What is the unity (*Sinneinheit*) of the process of being and the process of spirit? These are all questions about the meaning of being (*Sinnfragen*) rather than questions about what there is (*Seinsfragen*). The first one is answered by ontology or the metaphysics of being; the second one is answered by the metaphysics of history; the third is answered by the metaphysics of the absolute idea. Thus, the task of ontology is to show "in what way being as a whole, as a universal structure, is a symbol for the unconditional" (*GW, 1*, 255)—to show how the whole of being is a symbol for the ground and abyss of being. The task of a metaphysics of history is to interpret the meaning of the spiritual–historical process (*Geistesprozess*) in the light of the unconditional meaning which is its ground. The task of the metaphysics of the absolute idea unites the other two. It is a view (*Betrachtung*) of the universal process in which the opposition between intention and fulfillment in meaning is overcome. The unity of intention and fulfillment is the highest symbol for the unconditional; the task of a metaphysics of the absolute idea is to exhibit that symbol. Its method is the method of coincidence (*GW, 1*, 256), in which the unconditional is seen in the conditional forms.

Like the metalogical method, the method of coincidence used in a metaphysics of the absolute idea is an important part of the background of the method of correlation. Uniting the unconditional of being (*Sein*) and the unconditional in spirit (*Geist*)[29] into the unconditional of the "absolute idea" is a way of relating the objectival and the subjectival expressions of the unconditional. But here again the chief difference between the earlier formulation and that of the *Systematic Theology* lies in the fact that the

---

29. "Geist ist Selbstbestimmung des Denkens im Sein" (*GW, 1*, 210).

latter "correlates" rather than "unites." The phrase "the absolute idea" is, of course, eliminated altogether in Tillich's later writings, but what is more significant than this elimination is the fact that the "unity" envisaged in a metaphysics of the absolute idea is achieved not as a synthesis but as a correlation.

A third development in the background of the method of correlation can be seen in Tillich's discussion of autonomous and theonomous elements in the self-interpretive sciences (*Geisteswissenschaften*). In the *System der Wissenschaften* Tillich discusses the autonomous and theonomous intentions in these three sciences—philosophy, self-interpretive history, and systematics. Philosophy, in this arrangement, is the study of the functions and categories by which the various realms of meaning are marked and constituted. It is the study of the principles of being and meaning. Self-interpretive history (*Geistesgeschichte*) is a study of the material of being and meaning. Since the study of principles becomes concrete in the study of history, which is the arena of the "individual and creative fulfillments of meaning" (*GW, 1,* 238), self-interpretive history studies the material produced by the historical process in the light of the principles of meaning. It is a "receptive understanding" (*GW, 1,* 239) in that it takes up the material and interprets it from the point of view of the principles. It stands between philosophy, from which the principles come, and systematics. Systematics, in this arrangement, is the study of norms of being and meaning. A norm, in contrast to a principle, is concrete. A principle is general, a norm concrete but universal. It aims at being the "right and valid solution . . . for the problems that self-interpretive history produces on the basis of the tension of the elements of being and meaning [viz., thinking and being or form and content]" or the "concrete fulfillment of the abstract universal principle of being and meaning [*Sinnprinzip*]" (*GW, 1,* 241).[30]

---

30. Tillich defines "Sinnerfüllung" thus: "Der Begriff besagt, dass die Dinge in der Richtung auf die unbedingte Form stehen und dass diese Richtung ihre Erfüllung findet in den geistigen Schöpfungen. Nicht ideale Normen, die jenseits des Seins stehen, aber auch nicht eine dem Geist

Each of the three self-interpretive sciences moves, like everything else, in the polarity of form and content. But whether the form or the unconditional content is primarily intended determines whether the scientist's approach is autonomous or theonomous. That is to say, attention can be directed primarily to the autonomous forms in which the science is expressed or to the unconditional as manifest in the forms. In one of Tillich's definitions, the difference is stated thus: "Theonomy is direction toward being as pure content, as the abyss of every form of thinking [*Denkform*]. Autonomy is direction toward thinking as bearer of the forms and their validity" (*GW, I,* 272). Both elements are always present, but the emphasis can fall on one or the other. Thus, if it is theonomous, philosophy has the task of determining the relation of theonomy and autonomy in general and in particular functions and their categories (*GW, I,* 273). Theonomous philosophy is not simply philosophy of religion as opposed to philosophy of culture; rather it is philosophy as concerned with the theonomous elements in all culture. Indeed, Tillich can justify a philosophy of religion only if it means a "theonomous study of the principles of being and meaning [*Sinnprinzipienlehre*]" which does not oppose or supplement the autonomous study but works with it. The highest goal of philosophy of religion as a special study is to cancel itself in favor of a theonomous philosophy which is also autonomous, one which is directed toward forms as well as unconditional content. Similarly, self-interpretive history seeks the theonomous content in every cultural creation; it is not only history of religion.

Theonomous philosophy and theonomous history—that is, the study of theonomy in relation to autonomy in the principles and the material of meaning—culminate in theonomous systematics, which is the same as theology. Theology is "theonomous study of

---

gegenüberstehende sinngeformte Wirklichkeit ist Trägerin des Sinnes. Der Sinn ist überhaupt nicht gegeben, weder real noch ideal, sondern er ist intendiert, und er kommt im Geiste zur Erfüllung. Jedes Wirkliche trägt die Intention auf Sinnerfüllung; denn jedes Wirkliche ist auf die unbedingte Form gerichtet" (*GW, I,* 233).

norms (*Sinnormenlehre*)," or "theonomous systematics" (*GW*, *1*, 276).[31]

In his discussion of theonomous metaphysics Tillich clarifies the relation between the theonomous and autonomous elements in the theoretical sphere.[32] Depending upon its relation to the autonomous element, the theonomous intention appears in the theoretical sphere as myth, dogma, or metaphysics. Myth and metaphysics denote the extremes, the dogma the synthesis. In myth the theonomous intention is most direct; in metaphysics, least direct. Myth is an immediate from of theonomous metaphysics which lies before the rise of autonomous sciences (*GW*, *1*, 279). Metaphysics, on the other hand, uses the concepts or symbols with which autonomous science has provided it and is the most rational form of grasping the unconditional. But if the theonomous element predominates in myth, the autonomous element is nonetheless present insofar as every myth also contains "a will to understand the world"; and if the autonomous element predominates in metaphysics, the theonomous element is nonetheless present insofar as metaphysics also contains "a mythical will to know the unconditional."

Thus myth and metaphysics move in the same polar dialectic as objectivity (*Sein*) and subjectivity (*Denken*) or content and form. They are synthesized in dogma, in which scientific concepts are used as theonomous symbols. The conceptual character of the concepts represents the autonomous element; the symbolic character gives them a theonomous direction. Dogmatic formation is different from mythical formation because it lacks the immediate freedom of myth; it is different from scientific conceptualization because it lacks rational open-endedness. Like metaphysics it is a deliberate rather than spontaneous production; like myth it aims

31. There is no theonomous science or art because they are of a different order, but there is a theonomous or autonomous attitude (*Haltung*) in them. *GW*, *1*, 279.

32. The theoretical list includes science, art, metaphysics; the practical list, law, community, ethos.

at theonomous content. If it loses this mediating position, it becomes heteronomous—as when it attributes to its rational symbols unconditionality and infinity. But if it avoids that danger and succeeds in retaining the theonomous intention as well as the autonomous conceptual material in a creative way, it performs its synthesizing task and becomes "theonomous metaphysics."

As we shall see, the idea of a theonomous metaphysics is worked out in the *Systematic Theology* in two ways. One way is to bring out the theonomous intention of ontological concepts by correlating them with their mythical counterparts. This is exemplified in the typology of religions compared with the corresponding philosophical systems.[33] The second way is to convert the ontological concept into a predication made of God. This is exemplified in the statement, "God is freedom and destiny," where the ontological concepts of freedom and destiny are predicated of God.

A fourth root of theological correlation lies in the task suggested by the term, "historical theology" (*GW, 1,* 276f.).[34] In one sense historical theology is theonomous history of man and does not restrict itself to any one religion or even to religion as contrasted to the whole history of spirit. In a second sense historical theology is "normative exegesis." It makes reference to given classical documents. Theology is carried on within a concrete history and is thus bound to the classical expressions of theonomy—"the classical symbols in which the theonomous conviction found its expression." In this respect it is like legal theory. Normative exegesis aims at individual–creative interpretations of classical expressions of theonomous conviction. Though it is individual–creative, or "confessional," it nonetheless has a universal intention which prevents the "confessional" element from cutting off the historical process.

An exegesis of this sort involves two tasks. The first is to portray the original spirit of the religious documents, and the second is to transpose them into contemporary consciousness. There is

33. See below, Chap. 3, pp. 85ff.
34. Cf. Hans Georg Gadamer, *Wahrheit und Methode* (2d ed. Tübingen: J. C. B. Mohr, 1965), pp. 311ff.

always a degree of tension between the two. Where the tension is not great, no special problem is created by the transposition. Where the tension is great, the transposition may fail in two different ways. Either the original normative document is adjusted to the present historical consciousness—as happened in "the grand but contradictory attempt of the allegorical method"—or one's contemporary consciousness is heteronomously subjected to a legalistically understood (*exakt erfasst*) document of revelation. The former loses the theonomous conviction; the latter inevitably turns one away from the original document. Neither of them can be finally successful. Normative exegesis is based upon a living connection with the religious intention of the classical documents; therefore, it can neither adjust nor heteronomously subject. If such a living connection does not exist and cannot be found, normative exegesis is not possible; it is replaced by a completely reportive analysis of documents.

This consideration raises a question which Tillich does not take up here. Can the documents of Christian revelation ever cease to be possible objects of normative exegesis? Can it happen that a living connection with the religious intention of the Old and New Testaments is lost? Tillich's answer, as far as he ever gives one, seems to be that as long as man is "historical" this cannot happen because the religious intention of the Hebrew–Christian documents is related to the meaning of man's historical situation itself. They express the paradoxical answer to man's historical being. A living connection with this intention is possible as long as man still experiences his historical character, as long as he is existentially man. But then a second question arises. Are there other religious documents, not from the Hebrew or Christian tradition, of which the same could be said—that they can never cease to be possible religious documents as long as man is man?[35] Tillich's answer to this is not definite. Sometimes he seems to say, "No," but perhaps it would be more accurate to say that he regards this

35. As would be suggested by Hajime Tanabe, "Todesdialektik," in *Martin Heidegger zum 70. Geburtstag,* ed. Neske, pp. 93–133.

as a question that cannot really be answered by a Christian,[36] since every adherent of a religion would consider the documents of that religion to be as irreplaceable as the biblical documents are for Christians, and there is no neutral position from which to view all of them. Yet this remains one of the major unanswered questions in Tillich's writings.[37]

We have seen in this chapter how Tillich develops the conception of the unconditional in opposition to supernaturalism and idealism and in connection with the basic self–world polarity of being. Immediate experience knows only the unconditional of self-relatedness and is therefore threatened with an ultimate emptiness, the emptiness of formal autonomy. Objective experience knows content but no unconditional, and when it tries to resist dissolution into the form of self-relatedness it is threatened by a destructive heteronomy. Tillich resolves the problem of the self in its world, immediate experience and objective experience, self-relatedness and relatedness to the world, in the paradoxical conception of the unconditional, or God. This solution is presented in the development of that concept itself and then in the development of a method related to it. Particularly in the *Systematic Theology,* as compared with earlier descriptions of method, we can see that the problem of self and world is an ontological form of the problem of critical reflection and doubting response. It is soluble from neither side alone, but only from a correlation in which one side opens to the other. The self of immediate experience, which is unconditional but ultimately empty, is met by a content that is unconditional; and the world of objective experience, which has content but no unconditional, is met by an unconditional that is its form. God, who is the unconditional, breaks in as unconditional content in the self and unconditional form in the world—content,

36. *Christianity and the Encounter of the World Religions* (New York, Columbia University Press, 1963), pp. 33, 89, 96f., 57. Cf. *ST, 3,* 369.

37. Cf. Huston Smith's review of Tillich's *The Future of Religions* (ed. Jerald C. Brauer [New York, Harper & Row, 1966]) in *The Journal of Religion,* 47 (April 1967), 184–85.

in a correlation of "ecstasy" and "miracle." The problem of the self in its world is not resolved by fusing the two into a third and higher reality, or by reducing one to the other, but by the emergence of the ground–abyss in each of them and in both of them simultaneously. This is what happens when the self comes into view of a paradoxical reality and presence.

CHAPTER 3

Subjectivity and Objectivity in the Objectival

The basis for Tillich's distinction between a metaphysics of being and a metaphysics of history (*GW*, *1*, 255), which was mentioned in the preceding chapter, and for his two approaches to the referent of religious symbols,[1] is the recognition that the unconditional is known in objectival subjectivity as well as in objectival objectivity. The terms designating the two disclosures are "God" and "being." The unconditional is disclosed in objectival subjectivity in the experience of the holy—the experience of objectival subjectivity as such. It is disclosed in objectival objectivity in the ontological analysis which, based on the shock of possible non-being, opens the self-transcending aspect of being. The unconditional sought in such an analysis is being as such, or the quality of objectivity as such, in objectival beings. Since the referent of a religious symbol is the unconditional, it can be known by experience of the holy (objectival subjectivity) as well as by ontological analysis (objectival objectivity). Like subjectivity and objectivity, however, the two approaches are correlative.

Phenomenologically one can describe the experience of the holy, but one cannot critically evaluate the phenomena described. Ontologically one can analyze the being of man in his world, but one cannot find an object that is being as such. Moreover, phenomenology is concerned with a particular symbolic object and the experience connected with it; ontology is concerned with anything that is at all and the experience connected with it. The two fulfill each other in correlation, when it is shown that an ontological analysis and a description of the holy have the same referent

1. "The Meaning and Justification of Religious Symbols," in *Religious Experience and Truth*, ed. Sidney Hook (New York, New York University Press, 1961), pp. 3–11. See esp. p. 7.

and that the character of being, which I am always seeking to grasp in every being, and the content of the symbol, by which I am always grasped, are one. Symbols that express the holy and ontological concepts that express being represent objectival subjectivity and objectival objectivity, God and being.

These considerations on correlative ways of naming and knowing the unconditional object and presence take us further into the discussion of themes treated in the previous chapter. Though it is true, as it will be with the other steps of this discussion, that here we are dealing more with the radiation of a single pattern into a new context than with a new section in the territory of a whole problem, Tillich's discussions of the relation between "God" and "being," between the experience of the holy and ontological analysis, between the outer and inner relations to the content of a tradition, and between religious symbols and philosophical concepts disclose new aspects of the pattern by which he addressed the problem of certainty for historically conscious thought. The question posed by the disclosure of two ultimates is how it is possible to recognize two ultimates and understand their relation to each other without destroying the ultimacy of either one. Tillich's three-step pattern requires that one see first the totality of each of the two opposites, then how the two converge in such a way that one opens to the other for its completion, and finally where and how the paradox, the object and presence which cannot be removed, appears in these contexts.

The pattern here is the following. God and being are both ultimate, but they converge in the statement that God is being-itself. This convergence is made possible by the fact that there is an ontological element in the symbols which embody a response to God, and there is a symbolical element in the concepts which grasp being. The ontological element in the symbols lies in the fact that they objectify God. The symbolical element in the concepts is the fact that they can never grasp being-itself—their underlying theme is an open question. The objectifying element in all symbols can be justified by the recognition that God is being-itself; that is to say, ontological concepts do grasp the reality of the symbols. In this way ontology fulfills symbolical theology. On the other hand, the inadequacy of all concepts for grasping being-itself is answered by the recognition that the religious symbols make present the very being which ontological concepts seek to grasp. The present chapter is not concerned with the third step of the pattern—the paradoxical reality which embodies an indissoluble certainty for historically conscious thought—since that aspect is discussed in the next chapter.

In his autobiographical introduction to *The Protestant Era* (1948) Tillich recalls that from the beginning his study of theology moved between an "outside" and an "inside" view of Protestantism. To the outside view Protestantism is one factor in the whole world–historical process; to the inside view it is the form of Christianity to which one is bound by tradition and faith —that is, by an "existential experience of its meaning and power."[2] In the first case the observer tries to see Protestantism for what it objectively is. In the other case, the observer responds to it as the meaning which gives everything else its meaning. To relate these two views one must know how to bring together objectival objectivity and objectival subjectivity.

Seeing things objectively requires a method for ascertaining or securing objectivity. Generally this is the method of critical reflection, but there are many specific variations of it. In Tillich's work too, the methodological emphasis to which the objective point of view is related changes from time to time. At first it was the study of philosophy, later it was the historical-critical study of religious documents, and finally it was the "experienced and interpreted general history of our period."[3] Tillich became acquainted with classical Greek philosophy when he attended the humanistic *Gymnasium* in Königsberg-Neumark and Berlin, a kind of educational institution where "the religious and humanistic traditions . . . have been, ever since the Renaissance, in continuous tension."[4] Philosophy represented the outside, objectifying point of view here. Later, at the university, the representative of objectivity and of the universally human was historical criticism of religious traditions and documents. Tillich especially credits Ernst Troeltsch with having helped him overcome all apologetic remnants in the use of historical criticism.[5] In his use of this historical method Tillich parts company with the supranaturalism he found in Barthian rejections of the right to radical historical criticism. He first expressed this position in a series of theses presented to a group of theologians on Pentecost in 1911. In retrospect he refers to these theses as a determinative document of his own development.[6] They are addressed to the question of how Christian teaching would be understood should it happen that the nonexistence of the historical Jesus became probable.[7] Finally, the outside view was represented by the endeavor to understand Protestant theology within the framework of an interpretation of the great events of this century, starting with the First World War, which opened "the abyss" that could henceforth never be closed.[8]

With respect to these two ways of viewing, the task was to correlate the criterion of the biblical picture of Christ (as the concrete objectival subject) with the changing circumstances and general features of human being and history (as the objectival object). Tillich himself attests autobiographically that he sensed the polarity of the two. He experienced the tension between the classical humanist tradition at the *Gymnasium* and the Christian tradition at home, between the rightness of the claim of historical criticism to autonomy and the power of the Christian biblical tradition,

4. "Autobiographical Reflections," in *The Theology of Paul Tillich,* ed. Kegley and Bretall, p. 9.

5. Cf. Ernst Troeltsch, *Die Absolutheit des Christentums und die Religionsgeschichte* (1901).

6. *Auf der Grenze* (Stuttgart, Ev. Verlagswerk, 1962), p. 37. (English translation: *On the Boundary* [New York: Charles Scribner's Sons, 1966], p. 50).

7. His answer is contained in the distinction between Jesus as an object of historical research and the biblical picture of Jesus as the Christ. See below, Chap. 4, pp. 107ff.

8. *Auf der Grenze,* p. 39. (*Boundary,* p. 52.)

between the vocational claim of philosophy and that of theology. Of each of these tensions it can be said, as Tillich said of his divided vocational interests, that it would have been easier to leave the boundary in favor of one or the other but for the fact that it was an inner impossibility.[9] The solution could be found only in the difficult stance of maintaining the independence and reciprocity of both, in being a theologian as a philosopher and a philosopher as a theologian. From the tension between the humanist and the religious traditions in Tillich's early years there resulted "either a decision against the one or the other side, or a general skepticism or a split-consciousness which drove one to attempt to overcome the conflict constructively." The latter choice, "the way of synthesis," was Tillich's.[10] The *Systematic Theology* formulates that experience and that choice in universal terms.

There is more involved here than a biographical datum about Tillich. The universality of the tension he recounts resides in the fact that it has to do with the fundamental relation of objectivity and subjectivity. Philosophy and humanism on one side and theology and religion on the other can neither replace nor ignore each other. To have seen this is to have seen, at least implicitly, that a religious tradition is most objectively approached when it is apprehended precisely in its objectival subjectivity, its power of eliciting response; and the philosophical tradition is most subjectively approached when it is apprehended in its objectivity. Similarly, if historical criticism is the method by which objectivity is established[11]—as it was in the nineteenth century—then it stands in polar opposition to objectival subjectivity, the concrete picture of Jesus as the Christ. And if the structure of finite being is polar, then subjectivity and objectivity require each other. Life goes on through their interaction. However the question is, How is the connection made between them?

9. Ibid., p. 43. (*Ibid.,* p. 58.)

10. *The Theology of Paul Tillich,* p. 10.

11. On historical criticism and objectivity see Tillich's reply in Thomas A. O'Meara, O. P., and Celestin D. Weisser, O.P., eds., *Paul Tillich in Catholic Thought* (Dubuque, Iowa: Priory Press, 1964), p. 302.

Tillich makes the connection first by means of a limiting experience and a limiting concept, formulated in his philosophy of religion. In his autobiographical remarks Tillich describes this philosophy as an endeavor to express the experience of the abyss and the idea of "justification" as the philosophical limits of philosophy.[12] The abyss is the infinite inaccessibility of substantial content, dramatically experienced by European intellectuals at the outbreak of the First World War.[13] The idea of justification, applied to thinking and knowing, expresses the fact that knowledge of God is possible in spite of one's distorting perspective. The experience of the abyss and the idea of the justification of the doubter, by expressing the limit of objectivity, make connection with objectival subjectivity. The abyss removes the foundation of everything that is, and critical reflection removes the foundation of any truth. Yet a man does exist, in spite of the threat of the abyss; and he does know, in spite of his inability to provide an ultimate foundation of truth. The thinker is "justified" in spite of his doubt, truth is expressed in spite of untruth, and a man does exist in spite of his anxiety.

How does this provide the connection between object and subject—between that upon which I act and that which acts upon me? The answer is that at the point where the negative appears in the objective—as the abyss—objectivity is in transit to the subjective. The negation of an object is the nonobject, and in terms of the polarity of finite being a nonobject is implicitly a subject. Hence, the negation of all objectivity, which is experienced as "abyss," opens objectivity to objectival subjectivity. Conversely, the negation of objectival subjectivity, which is expressed in religious doubt, opens it to objectivity. When I doubt the objectival subject, my relation to it changes from one in which I respond to action upon me to one in which I grasp something through my

12. *Auf der Grenze,* p. 39. (*Boundary,* p. 52.)

13. Emil Brunner, for example, says of this war: "For me, as well as for most of my educated comrades, the catastrophe of war in our time was at first something inconceivable." Charles W. Kegley, ed., *The Theology of Emil Brunner* (New York, Macmillan Co., 1962), p. 7.

action upon it. My failure to respond, as an *act* of doubt, passes over to the action of critically reflecting. An object that loses its objectivity is opened to subjectivity, and an objectival subject that ceases to elicit response is opened to objective grasping. Thus, the limit of the ontological, ontologically expressed, is the concept of nonbeing, through which the nonobjectivity of being first grasps me; and the limit of the theological, theologically expressed, is the concept of doubt, through which I first grasp the objectivity of the objectival subject.

That the connection between these two can be made is a fact of paramount importance for Western man, who is heir to both of them and lives in the tension between them. In an essay on two types of philosophy of religion,[14] Tillich attributes the ever-increasing loss of religious consciousness in the West, with its attendant emptiness, to the failure to make this connection. It has resulted in a division between the traditions representing both poles or in the self-defeating attempt to subsume one under the other—as when God is conceived of as a supreme being. The solution lies in correlating objectivity and subjectivity, in finding the point at which each connects with the other and then interpreting them reciprocally. This reconciliation can be achieved only through transcending the split between the subject and the object, whether the split is between the subjectival and the objectival or between objectival subjectivity and objectival objectivity, both of which are involved in Tillich's essay now under discussion. Attention in this chapter is on the latter of the two—the correlation of objectival subjectivity and objectival objectivity, or God and being.

Tillich begins by recalling the fact that Western man won his spiritual freedom from mythological powers in two developments, one of which is religious and the other philosophical. The beings which mythological figures represent are those powers that subject man to them without regard for his freedom. Religiously they were conquered by their subjection to the god of the prophets of

14. "The Two Types of Philosophy of Religion," in *Theology of Culture* ed. Robert C. Kimball (New York, Oxford University Press, 1959), pp. 10–29.

Israel, who as the god of justice could become the universal God without destroying man's autonomy. Philosophically they were conquered by their subjection "to a principle more real than all of them," the principle of being, which was able to become universal because it embraced all ontological qualities. When Western man subjected the gods to the God of justice and the ontological powers to being-itself, he became free of them. "The gods disappeared and became servants of the absolute God, or appearances of the absolute principle."[15] The distinction between beings and being or gods and God was achieved; it is the distinction between objects and objectivity as such, and between subjects and subjectivity as such.

Against the background of this development Tillich interprets *Deus est esse*—God is being—as a correlation, not as a definition or equation. The fact that there were two developments and two manifestations of the absolute makes the question of their relation unavoidable since the absolute seems to exclude such duality by its very nature. How they are related is an abiding question, to which correlation is Tillich's answer. "God is being" expresses the ultimate unity of the God of justice and the principle of being, an identity which can be expressed only by a method that preserves the character of both within their relation to each other. This is to say, however, that God is ontologically understood and being is theologically understood.[16]

Here Tillich sees the basic alternative, which yields the two types of philosophy of religion, the ontological and the cosmological. One type recognizes the ultimate identity of the two principles, the other makes God only objective. The ontological type recognizes the identity of God and being, both of them pointing to what is prior to the split between subjectivity and objectivity. The cosmological type interprets God as an object in the realm of the objectival. This type, however, is ultimately self-defeating because a God who is an object of argumentation or thought cannot be truly God; atheism is the natural consequence.

15. Ibid., p. 11.
16. Ibid., p. 12.

Argumentation, which objectifies, necessarily misses God, who is objectival subjectivity. Hence Tillich can ascribe the ever-increasing loss of religious consciousness in the Western world to the cosmological conception of God represented in the thought of Thomas Aquinas, Duns Scotus, and William of Occam. He is concerned with reversing that direction by setting forth the conception of God as "the prius of subject and object,"[17] the unconditional of which man is unconditionally aware. At this point in the essay, however, Tillich moves from the correlation of objectival subject and object to that of the subject–object structure with the depth of that structure, a phase of correlation which belongs to a later discussion here.

In *Biblical Religion and the Search for Ultimate Reality,* Tillich takes up the question of Western man's dual heritage at greater length, calling it "an especially urgent question of my own theological thought."[18] Biblical religion and the philosophical search for ultimate reality seem, Tillich grants, to embody fundamentally opposing traditions which cannot be intermixed. This can be seen if one compares the primary terms in each of them, the biblical conception of God and the philosophical conception of being. In biblical religion, as in all religion, God is a person who meets and is met by man. In encountering God, man meets an objectival subject. On this point the difference between the biblical and the nonbiblical God has to do not with their personality but with the degree of their exclusiveness. In all religions God is met as a thou, but in biblical religion the relation is exclusive. God is not only a thou but also unconditional. If religion is the "name for the reception of revelation,"[19] then the difference between the biblical and nonbiblical religions is not in their character as religion but in the revelation which has been received in them. Biblical religion is founded upon the revelation of objectival subjectivity as such, not simply upon the revelation of an objectival subject.

17. Ibid., p. 21.

18. *Biblical Religion,* p. vii. This book is an expanded version of the James W. Richard lectures at the University of Virginia in 1951.

19. Ibid., p. 3.

In contrast to the religious conception of God, the philosophical conception of being is objective. Philosophy deals with the "encounter of subject and object in the cognitive experience" rather than with the "personal encounter in the religious experience."[20] It is related to the objectivity, not the subjectivity, of the objectival. It strives for a view of reality as a whole or a grasp of the being in all beings. But since we *participate* in being (because we are beings) and *encounter* a personal God, the subjectivity which we meet and the objectivity in which we find ourselves seem to be at irreconcilable odds. Can there be a connection then between biblical religion, which radically expresses man's response to objectival subjectivity, and the search for ultimate reality, which expresses man's endeavor to grasp the objectivity in which he stands?

Tillich analyzes the many ways in which the conflict is illustrated. Two important examples are the questions of attitude and ethics, of how we are related to the objectival and how we understand the meaning of our actions. The philosopher, in his attitude, is at a distance from his object, viewing it in theoretic detachment. He seeks to grasp the objectively real, the reality that is embodied in every objectival being. He questions, criticizes, objectifies— activities which express a cognitive distance between him and the material he works on. The believer, on the other hand, is grasped by the objectival subject. He is not neutral toward it but responds to it. He does not question or criticize but listens and receives what is given to him. These two attitudes sharply express the difference between biblical religion and the philosophical quest.

A similar conflict is visible in ethics. For biblical religion ethics is a matter of decision, made for or against the God whom man encounters; for philosophy ethics is a matter of finding universal principles of action that can be applied to specific cases. (I am departing somewhat from Tillich's statement of the conflict—as the conflict between the ethical character of biblical religion and the nonethical character of ontological thought—in order to emphasize the difference within ethics itself. But the point being

20. Ibid., p. 25; cf. p. 20.

made is the same.) In biblical religion man's decision is what counts; he must "decide for or against Yahweh, for or against the Christ, for or against the Kingdom of God."[21] This seems to be quite different from the nonpersonal character of the ontological principle. The ethical command of the Bible presupposes a free response of man to God; the ontological principle presupposes man's participation in the principles he seeks. That is to say, since man participates in being, he can ask the question of being objectively, without needing to decide for or against it; but since he confronts the personal God as a subject outside of himself, he cannot treat him with objectivity but must react with existential involvement. He must decide, and in deciding he also determines his own destiny. Ontology has to do with man's universal destiny as man; the biblical demand has to do with a man's free decision which determines his own destiny.

Yet, in spite of how sharply they seem to contradict each other, biblical religion and the philosophical quest do imply and require each other.[22] Biblical religion involves the question of ultimate reality, and the question of being involves an encounter with the unconditional power of being. The problem is only how that mutual implication is to be interpreted, and Tillich's answer is that they are correlative. They arise and can initially stand independently of each other, but intrinsically they connect at a point to which each one leads in its own way and by its inner dynamics.

> In both biblical religion and ontology an ultimate concern is the driving force; in both of them the "No" of doubt is taken into the "Yes" of courage; in both of them a participation in concrete experiences and symbols gives content to question and answer; in both cases an ultimate trust in the power of being makes human surrender and search possible. This analogy of structure keeps one side open for the other.[23]

21. Ibid., p. 45.

22. "There is an element in the biblical and ecclesiastical idea of God which makes the ontological question necessary. It is the assertion that God *is*" (ibid., p. 82).

23. Ibid., p. 63.

In our present terminology, this says first that the relations of re-flective understanding (search) and free response (surrender) are implied in one's relation to the objectival itself, as being and as God. Secondly, both of them move through the negative and posi-tive moments of questioning and receiving and of doubting and affirming. Thirdly, each of them opens upon the other. Each is incomplete alone, as objectivity or subjectivity is incomplete with-out the other. At least implicitly the philosopher is also respond-ing to objectival subjectivity and the believer is grasping objectival objectivity. This can be shown, moreover, in biblical and philo-sophical literature itself.

If it is true that a philosopher is theoretically objectifying and a believer existentially responding toward the objectival, it is also true that there is an element of involvement in a philosopher and an element of detachment in a believer. Thus the biblical account of conversion experiences has parallels in philosophical literature. For biblical faith reason is, like all other human functions, under the destiny of sin; it is "blinded" and unable to recognize God if its eyes are not opened by a revelatory experience. But philoso-phers also attest a kind of conversion or revelatory experience which contrasts with the ordinary state of mind. "The sudden awareness of the light of the ontological question, the breaking-through the surface on which one lived and moved before—these events are described like a religious conversion." So ontology pre-supposes something that is not a matter of detached observation or of objectification. It presupposes an encounter with ultimate reality, and in this sense one can speak of a philosophical faith as "faith in ultimate reality."[24]

To be sure, Tillich notes a difference in philosophical and bibli-cal conversion related to the fact that religion is a matter of one's whole being while philosophy is a cognitive endeavor. Yet when the cognitive function is involved in the encounter with ultimate reality—when "it is existentially moved"—it cannot really be separated from the other functions, and so the two conversions

24. Ibid., pp. 65, 66.

are not at all dissimilar. What is in the background of one is in the foreground of the other. The cognitive function is in the background for the believer and in the foreground for the philosopher; a man's whole being is in the foreground for the believer and in the background for the philosopher. This contrast would be even less than Tillich allows it to be if the comparison were made, as it should be, between philosophy and theology rather than between philosophy and religion. Such a comparison would relate the cognitive function in responding to objectival subjectivity with the cognitive function in grasping objectival objectivity.

Similarly the believer who responds to God implicitly also seeks ultimate reality. He could not be concerned ultimately with a god who were less than ultimate reality. "Only if God is ultimate reality, can he be our unconditional concern; only then can he be the object of surrender, obedience, and assent."[25] As a believer man responds unconditionally to God; as a philosopher he asks whether his God is indeed ultimate reality.

Again, the difference between biblical and philosophical ethics is not as exclusive as it initially appears to be. The ethical thrust of the biblical writings, where man is placed over against God and decides for or against him, contrasts with the ontological conception of man as participating in being; one represents man's freedom and obedience, the other his destiny and participation. Nevertheless, they do approach each other, as several biblical conceptions show.[26] The biblical conception of grace refers to a decision which is also participation. When a man looks back upon his decision for God, he sees that it was not only his decision but God's decision in him. "After the decision we realize that it was not our own power but a power which decided through us." In this conception freedom and destiny, the biblical and the ontological, are brought together. Both destiny and freedom are ontological as well as ethical, and both "are transcended and united in

25. Ibid., p. 58. This single sentence and its converse would describe the motive force of Tillich's whole systematic thought.
26. Ibid., pp. 67–69. Subsequent quotations are from these pages.

the religious symbol of sin and grace." Similarly the contrast between obedience and participation is transcended in the conception
of the "law of love" and of the presence of the divine Spirit in us.
Here obedience proceeds from participation. "He who is united
with the will of God voluntarily acts and does more than any law
commands."

There would be no search for ultimate reality if one had not
already encountered it, and there would be no religious worship of
a being who was less than ultimate reality. This, in short, is why
philosophy and religion are open to each other. Not only does the
ontological search raise the question of God, but the religious encounter raises the question of being. Thus, in the biblical and ecclesiastical idea of God the ontological question is raised as soon
as we say that God, the one we encounter in religion, *is*. If the "is"
were taken to mean that God "can be found in the whole of potential experience," then the concept of the whole of reality, within which he can be found, would be more basic than the concept
of God; God would be "subject to the structure of reality."[27] But
such an interpretation of God's being does not adequately express
the object of religious encounter. The only interpretation that expresses its holy character is the one that says he is being-itself—the
ground and abyss of every being and every person; he is ultimate
reality.

In such statements as "God is being-itself" or "God is the personal itself," Tillich says, religion and ontology meet. The predicate in each of them is an ontological concept, whereas the
subject is a religious symbol. In the sentence "God is" the being
which is attributed to God is that of the ground of everything
and everyone. In this way the objectivity of being that we seek in
everything and the subjectivity that we encounter are related to
each other. They can be connected because the ultimate reality
for which we search is also a power that has confronted us—as a
question; and the God whom we encounter is also the ultimate
reality for which we search, else the encounter with him would

27. Ibid., p. 82.

not be ultimate. "Two ultimates cannot exist alongside each other," and what is really ultimate must comprise both the objective and the subjective expressions of the ultimate. Similarly the ultimate concern of a believer comprises both, for it is "concern about that which is really ultimate and therefore the ground of his being and meaning."[28] From the objective meaning of "ultimate" as well as from faith's concern, the objectival subject and objectival object must be related. The method of correlation defines that relation in such a way as to preserve both the polarity and the ultimacy of the two.

The correlative connection of these two ultimates is also Tillich's answer to the question of the referent of a religious symbol. One of the criticisms of his interpretation of religious symbols[29] is that he provides no way of stating the referent of symbolical assertions nonsymbolically. If the referent cannot be stated nonsymbolically, the symbol does not seem to have any definite meaning; if it can be stated nonsymbolically, it seems to contradict Tillich's assertion that religious symbols are primary religious language. William Alston finds the mirror of this dilemma in the *Systematic Theology,* where "it looks very much as if [Tillich] is trying to translate [the religious symbols] into ontological terms" in spite of his claim that " 'every symbol opens up a level of reality for which nonsymbolic speaking is inadequate.' " This is to say that "Tillich is unable to carry out his own principles when he comes to try to explain particular religious symbols."[30] And for a good reason—in the "traditional conception," according to Alston, the symbolizandum can be given also in nonsymbolic language. Thus, in the figure of a shepherd used to represent divine providence, the

28. Ibid., pp. 58f.

29. William P. Alston, "Tillich's Conception of a Religious Symbol," in *Religious Experience and Truth,* ed. Hook, pp. 12–26. Cf. William L. Rowe, *Religious Symbols,* pp. 186f., 220. Alston's essay represents a kind of criticism which is widespread but unproductive. On this point see Lewis S. Ford's review of J. Heywood Thomas, *Paul Tillich: An Appraisal,* and Kenneth Hamilton, *The System and the Gospel: A Critique of Paul Tillich,* in *The Journal of Bible and Religion,* 32 (July 1964), 279–81.

30. Alston, p. 25.

shepherd is the symbol and God's providential care for his creatures is what is symbolized. Since we can know God's providential
care in a nonsymbolic way, we can say that this is what the symbol
symbolizes.

Alston's criticism misses the point, however, because the issue is
not whether the referent of a religious symbol can be given nonsymbolically but whether it can be given *noncorrelatively*. That it
can be given nonsymbolically Tillich does not deny; that it can
be given noncorrelatively he does deny. This is to say that our
contact with the ultimate by way of ontological concepts and our
contact by way of religious symbols cannot be reduced to each
other. A religious symbol cannot be transformed into an ontological concept, nor can an ontological concept be transformed into a
religious symbol, without losing the characteristic which is essential to each. Our responding to objectival subjectivity cannot be
reduced to our grasping of objectival objectivity. They can be related to each other only correlatively; the ultimate by which we
are grasped and the ultimate which we grasp—God and being—
are united in the depth of objectivity and subjectivity. A living
knowledge of that depth involves both the subjective and the objective terms, neither of which can replace the other, and each of
which interprets the other. What Alston overlooks is the fact that
"God's providential care" is no less symbolic than the figure of a
shepherd. We may know what providential care is nonsymbolically, but the difference between somebody's providential care and
God's providential care is as great as the difference between the
figure of a shepherd and God. Thus this phrase cannot serve as a
nonsymbolic designation of what is meant by the comparison of
God with a shepherd, since it can be understood only by correlation with a nonsymbolic counterpart, such as the idea or conviction that our being is ultimately meaningful.

In other words, the referent of a philosophical concept and that
of a corresponding religious symbol are the same. But my relation to the referent is different. Through a philosophical concept
I grasp it, but through a religious symbol I am grasped by it. Such
philosophical and religious terms could be called first-order con-

cepts and symbols. On the other hand, a *theological* concept of the *second order* is one which defines the nature of religious symbols (not their referents) and correlates them with philosophical concepts.[31]

Tillich's conception of systematic theology rests, accordingly, upon a distinction between religion and philosophy and also upon a distinction between first-order and second-order terms. This can be seen most clearly if we examine the standing of Tillich's highly controverted statement, "God is being-itself."[32] This he calls the one literal statement theology makes. It is the statement with which theology, in making explicit what is implicit in primary religious expression, must begin, because it is "the most abstract and completely unsymbolic statement" that can be made of God. Nothing can be said about him before this statement is made, for it places all theological statements into their proper domain.[33] It serves to relate "God" and religious symbols to "being" and concepts which elaborate the ontological structure. It prevents confusing religious language with nonreligious language, but it also states how the two can be related. All theological interpretation of religious expression, therefore, depends upon this basic identification of the reference of religious terms.

The question arises whether this statement itself is symbolic or literal. At first Tillich treated it as symbolic. Later, according to his own report, a criticism by Professor Urban of Yale[34] brought

31. George F. McClean, "Symbol and Analogy: Tillich and Thomas," in *Tillich in Catholic Thought,* ed. O'Meara and Weisser, p. 160, is surely incorrect when he says that, for Tillich, a symbol results from an encounter but cannot contribute to it. Cf. Tillich's reply, ibid., pp. 307f., and also *Dynamics of Faith* (New York, Harper & Brothers, 1957), p. 96: "'Adequacy' of expression [of the truth of faith] means the power of expressing an ultimate concern in such a way that it creates reply, action, communication."

32. Or, "God is the power of being in all being," or, "God is the ground of being." *ST, 1,* 239; *3,* 294. For a discussion of the first-order and second-order terminology in Tillich, see my "The Scope of Systematics," pp. 136–49.

33. It also reduces (Tillich notes in connection with his discussion of the reconstruction of the trinitarian dogma) the predominance of the male element in the symbolization of God, a predominance which is characteristic especially of Protestant theology. *ST, 3,* 294.

34. *The Theology of Paul Tillich,* p. 334.

to his attention the fact that to be intelligible the statement which delimits the symbolic area must itself be nonsymbolic. If it were symbolic it could not perform the function of delimiting exactly the symbolic realm, for it would be a part of that realm. Under the impact of this criticism, Tillich says, he became "suspicious of any attempts to make the concept of symbol all-embracing and therefore meaningless." The one unsymbolic statement in theology, which protects the whole theological domain from becoming meaningless, is the correlative identification of God with being-itself; it is the statement "which implies the necessity of religious symbolism . . . and as such [is] beyond the subject–object structure of everything that is."[35] Other theological statements follow from this and are explicit assertions of what is implicitly contained in religious thought and expression. If one considers only the formulations of the first volume of *Systematic Theology* and of *The Theology of Paul Tillich,* Tillich's position on this question seems to be clear—"God is being-itself" is the one literal theological statement.

As an unsymbolic statement defining what is the domain of theology, "God is being-itself" would seem to be philosophical in character.[36] Yet it cannot be only philosophical, for it would contradict the principle that philosophy and religion must each reach the point of juncture from its own side since neither can delimit the other. Hence, in the introduction to the second volume of

35. Ibid.

36. So John B. Cobb, Jr., *Living Options in Protestant Theology* (Philadelphia, Westminster Press, 1962), p. 281, can conclude that Tillich subordinates the distinctively Christian elements in understanding ultimate reality to philosophical ones. Cobb's conclusion is rather widely shared by theologians, but I think this is due less to Tillich's characterization of the statement "God is being-itself" than to the general lack of acquaintance with the way Tillich in his early writings carefully delineated his position on two points: the distinction between the totality of living and the depth of being, and the distinction between theology and a philosophy of religion. Walter Hartmann, *Die Methode der Korrelation von philosophischen Fragen und theologischen Antworten bei Paul Tillich* (Göttingen, 1954), pp. 47–49 has, by contrast, noticed the importance particularly of the first distinction and has concluded that this is the very thing which Tillich uses to prevent deriving a concept of God from a concept of being.

Systematic Theology Tillich expresses himself somewhat differently. That there must be one nonsymbolic statement to found theology was an unchanging part of his position since the discussion with Urban. What that one statement is, however, he seems to give differently in *Systematic Theology* II as compared with other places. The question has arisen, he writes here, whether "there is a point at which a non-symbolic assertion about God must be made" (*ST*, 2, 9). There is such a point, he answers, and it is "the statement that everything we say about God is symbolic." In some ways this seems to be a better identification of the nonsymbolic statement than the other. It so delimits the symbolic realm that it can be exactly located in relation to other realms, and it also preserves the symbolic character of every statement occurring within that realm. But if it is theology's one literal statement, then, contrary to *Systematic Theology* I, the other statement, "God is being-itself," would not have to be literal at all.

At least one interpreter, therefore, has taken the position of Tillich in the second volume of the systematics to be an alteration of his earlier one.[37] Yet it is doubtful that Tillich intended it to be a change in position.[38] For one thing, immediately after defining the one nonsymbolic assertion as the statement, "Everything we say about God is symbolic," he goes on to call it "an assertion about God." Strictly taken, of course, it is an assertion not about God but about our assertions concerning God. Only indirectly is it an assertion about God. But taken as such, it would have to be identical in content with the statement "God is being-itself." Secondly, in the same paragraph Tillich clarifies the dialectical

37. William L. Rowe, "The Meaning of 'God' in Tillich's Theology," *Journal of Religion*, 42 (October 1962), 274–86; *Religious Symbols*, pp. 28ff.

38. Langdon Gilkey, *Maker of Heaven and Earth: The Christian Doctrine of Creation in the Light of Modern Knowledge* (Garden City, N.Y., Doubleday Anchor, 1965), p. 357, n. 17, refers only to the formulation from *ST*, 2, 9, but he equates the content of the statement "Everything we say about God is symbolic" with that of "God is being itself"; thus, "If all language about God is symbolic, this implies directly the transcendence of God, and so His status as being itself."

character of the primary assertion about God by using formulations like those in *Systematic Theology* I. "If we say that *God is* the infinite, or the unconditional, or *being-itself,* we speak rationally and ecstatically at the same time. These terms precisely designate the boundary line at which both the symbolic and the non-symbolic coincide"(*ST, 2,* 10; italics added). It is the boundary line because an awareness of being-itself or the unconditional is nonsymbolic—"the state of being ultimately concerned . . . is universally human" (*ST, 2,* 9)—but any statement of the content of that awareness is more than literal; it is "a combination of symbolic with non-symbolic elements."

Tillich expresses this same idea somewhat differently in another essay, "The Nature of Religious Language."[39] He distinguishes the nonsymbolic and symbolic elements always present in the term "God," which is not simply a symbol because "our image of God" has nonsymbolic elements as well.[40] The nonsymbolic element is that "he is ultimate reality, being itself, ground of being, power of being"; the symbolic element is "that he is the highest being in which everything that we have does exist in the most perfect way." Taking the two together means that "we have a symbol [i.e. an image of a perfect being] for that which is not symbolic in the idea of God—namely, 'being-itself.' "

It is important, however, Tillich continues, to distinguish these

39. "The Nature of Religious Language," *The Christian Scholar, 38* (September 1955), reprinted in *Theology of Culture,* pp. 53–67. I cite from the latter. See also *Religious Experience and Truth,* p. 315: "In the word 'God' is contained at the same time that which actually functions as a representation and also the idea that it is *only* a representation. It has the peculiarity of transcending its own conceptual content." Cf. Ernst Cassirer, *Philosophie der symbolischen Formen* (Darmstadt, Wissenschaftliche Buchgesellschaft, 1964), p. 286: "Die Religion vollzieht den Schnitt, der dem Mythos als solchem fremd ist: indem sie sich der sinnlichen Bilder und Zeichen bedient, *weiss* sie sie zugleich als solche,—als Ausdrucksmittel, die, wenn sie einen bestimmten Sinn offenbaren, notwendig zugleich hinter ihm zurückbleiben, die auf diesen Sinn 'hinweisen', ohne ihn jemals vollständig zu erfassen und auszuschöpfen." Tillich's criticism of this is in *Religious Experience and Truth,* p. 309.
40. *Theology of Culture,* p. 61. Subsequent quotations are from this same page.

two elements in order to avoid false interpretations of religious experience. These false interpretations can be overcome if two
things are said. First, the awareness of something unconditional
"is in itself what it is, is not symbolic," and can be called " 'being-
itself,' *esse qua esse, esse ipsum.*" Second, in our relation to this
ultimate "we symbolize and must symbolize" because "we encounter him with the highest of what we ourselves are, *person.*"
In other words, Tillich maintains that we are literally—that is,
nonecstatically—aware of something unconditional, which we call
being-itself; and being-itself means literally that of which we are
aware. But as soon as we characterize it, we speak symbolically,
because our experience of what being-itself is is ecstatic—we experience it, and therefore it is objectival, but we experience it also
as our own depth, and therefore it is subjectival. This is more
than an awareness that we "are," in spite of the threat to our being; it is an experience of the meaning of our being at all. Literally we are aware *that* we are; symbolically we experience *what*
our being means. The literal element is our awareness of the unconditional; as soon as we say what that unconditional is we have
passed beyond the literal.

Thus, Tillich's exposition in "The Nature of Religious Language" corroborates the suggestion that whether we say, "The
one literal statement is the assertion that all we say about God
is symbolic," or say, "The one literal statement is that God is
being-itself," we are stating the same thing. If this is the case, then
the modification of the wording in the introduction to *Systematic
Theology* II does not represent a change in Tillich's position but
an alternate formulation demanded by a specific context.[41]

This, however, raises another question. If the statement "God is
being-itself" is nonsymbolic and if it refers to the boundary be-

41. Thus, his statement in *The Theology of Paul Tillich*, p. 339, describes
a position that did not change: "Being as the negation of possible non-being
is the basic cognitive position, which precedes in logical dignity every characterization of being." Cf. his "Rejoinder," *The Journal of Religion*, 46 (January 1966), Pt. 2, 186: "One point in which one who has experienced the
shock of non-being cannot make any concession [is] the ultimacy of being."

tween the unsymbolic and the symbolic, can it be "completely unsymbolic," as Tillich calls it in *Systematic Theology* I? It cannot if the expositions in *Systematic Theology* II and "The Nature of Religious Language" are to be clarifications of the connection between symbolic and nonsymbolic expressions. The point where the two meet, Tillich says in *Systematic Theology* II (*ST, 2,* 10), "is itself both nonsymbolic and symbolic." If "God is being-itself" designates that point of meeting, it must reflect the same double character; it must be symbolic and nonsymbolic. Moreover, if, according to "The Nature of Religious Language," God has a literal meaning (the unconditional of which we are aware) and a symbolic meaning (the image or language about God which conveys the answer to our quest), the presence of the term "God" in "God is being-itself" would keep it from being completely unsymbolic. "God" is literal as a question and symbolic as an answer. Finally, in Tillich's usage a question itself is quasi-symbolic in that it pushes beyond the ordinarily given. Thus, if "being" can refer to what is experienced as the power to be at all as well as to what is conceptualized in an elaborated ontological structure,[42] it too has something of a double character; it is quasi-symbolic as well as conceptual and nonsymbolic. For what is experienced as the power of being cannot be fully conceptualized; it is that toward which the ontological concepts point as always beyond them.

In view of the double character of "God" and of "being" we can say that "God is being-itself" asserts that the question (which is identical with the abstract, nonsymbolic element in "God") is answered by the concrete element in God (the definite sound or imagery conveyed by the term "God"). It says that our awareness of the unconditional is completed by the imagery which embodies the unconditional. The juncture, then, between the concept of being and the symbol of God is made at the point where the concept of being becomes quasi-symbolic as the question of being-

42. Cf. *ST, 1,* 236: "The concept of being as being, or being-itself, points to the power inherent in everything, the power of resisting nonbeing," and *ST, 1,* 164: "Is not the term 'structure of being' a contradiction in terms, saying that which is beyond every structure itself has a structure?"

itself and the symbol of God becomes the awareness of the unconditional. Insofar as the statement "God is being-itself" is an expression of the fact that the nonsymbolic and the symbolic elements are correlative, it is completely unsymbolic and is interchangeable with the statement, "Everything we say about God is symbolic." But insofar as it is a statement about God and is not interchangeable with the second statement, it is both literal and symbolic.

The difference here corresponds to what I have called first-order and second-order terms. As a first-order assertion, "God is being-itself" is both symbolic and nonsymbolic; it expresses a response to, as well as a grasping of, the objectival. As a second-order assertion, it is a nonsymbolic statement of the fact that the religious is interpreted by the philosophical, and conversely, at the points where they open upon each other; but it is nonsymbolic in the way that a meta-language is and not in the way that ontological concepts are.

This discussion of "God is being-itself" thus far has assumed, but not yet questioned, the fact that in Tillich's formulation the statement moves in one direction only. It is never converted into "Being-itself is God." This reflects his conviction that being-itself is not a symbol, even if, as already noted, it may be a question and serve a quasi-symbolic (this is not Tillich's term) function.[43] Yet there is a line of thought in Tillich which suggests that "God is being-itself" is convertible. Indeed, it would perhaps be more consistent with the basic pattern in Tillich's thought to acknowledge its convertibility than to deny it. If it is convertible, then being-itself, like God, must be usable symbolically as well as literally (and quasi-symbolically).

In his express utterances on the subject Tillich denies its symbolic character. He does not necessarily deny that it *could* be symbolic but that it is *in fact* symbolic. "Is 'being-itself' symbolic,

43. Klaus-Dieter Nörenberg, *Analogia Imaginis: Der Symbolbegriff in der Theologie Paul Tillichs* (Gütersloh, Gerd Mohn, 1966), p. 120, concludes from Tillich's avoidance of the converse formulation that for Tillich being is God in a "theopanistic" and not a "pantheistic" sense.

and therefore theological and not philosophical?" he asks in reply to a critic.[44] He answers, "I do not think so." Being-itself is not symbolic "because . . . every philosophy has an implicit or explicit answer to the question: What does the word 'is' mean?" In other words, all philosophers "say something about the character of being which logically precedes all statements about that which participates in being." If besides making statements about the character of being a philosopher is ultimately concerned about being-itself, then "words like 'ground' or 'power' of being appear which express both the theoretical and the existential relation of the mind to being-itself," and every element in the structure of being "has . . . the same dual character"—it not only characterizes being as being but can express ultimate concern.

For Tillich, then, being-itself is not symbolic, because being is restricted to a characterization of the universal structure. However, since every characterization of the structure, or of its elements, *can* also refer to ultimate concern, a symbolic element can indeed be present. Yet the symbolic expression of such a concern is not the term "being-itself" but terms like "ground of being," or, in a more openly religious way, "God." Being-itself is that of which the whole structure is a structure and that to which the structure points only in the form of a question. It does not answer the question; it does not concretely embody an ultimate concern.

On the other hand, there is a line of thought in Tillich's writing which somewhat counteracts this disclaimer. It is exemplified in his history or typology of religion (*ST, 1,* 218ff.), which is drawn from the tension in the idea of God. If God is an "ultimate concern," the idea of God implies both absoluteness and concreteness, and a typology can be based upon the various possibilities of relating the absolute and the concrete elements. We cannot be concerned about the nonconcrete, and we cannot be ultimately concerned about the relative. But "the concreteness of man's ultimate concern drives him toward polytheistic structures; the reac-

44. *The Theology of Paul Tillich*, p. 335.

tion of the absolute element against these drives him toward monotheistic structures; and the need for a balance between the concrete and the absolute drives him toward trinitarian structures" (*ST, 1,* 221). Moreover, since there are two ways of being related to the ultimate, as the "holy" and as "secular," the typology includes the directly religious as well as its philosophical "transformations." Secular objects can become divine powers, and divine powers can be "reduced" to secular objects. "This means that the secular ultimates (the ontological concepts) and the sacred ultimates (the conceptions of God) are interdependent." Ontological concepts have religious substance in their background, and ideas of God have secular implications. Grasping the ultimate presupposes a manifestation of it, and responding to the ultimate implies a way of grasping it.

Tillich then provides a typological analysis which includes the religious and philosophical expressions. Polytheistic structures are characterized by "the lack of a uniting and transcending ultimate" (*ST, 1,* 222) since each of the gods claims ultimacy in its own sphere. A reaction from the ultimate element begins when the claims of the various gods conflict with each other, and it leads toward a monotheism, in which the ultimate predominates over the concrete. However, since it is not possible to maintain a living relation to an abstract ultimate, an absolute monotheism is no more possible than an absolute polytheism. It invites a polytheistic reaction and then either reverts to polytheism or becomes "exclusive monotheism," in which one god is ultimate and universal "without the loss of his concreteness and without the assertion of a demonic claim" (*ST, 1,* 227). Historically this happened with the God of Israel, Yahweh, who as the God of justice is independent of his nation and of "his own individual nature" and can assert a universal claim without being "imperialistic." He is universal not because he *disregards* but because he *regards* the claims of everything that is. His radical transcendence, however, makes it difficult to retain concrete elements in a conception of him. If they are lost, exclusive monotheism merges with mystical monotheism or with a philosophical absolute, or it combines the concrete and absolute in a trinitarian monotheism. "Trinitarian monotheism is concrete monotheism, the affirmation of the living God" (*ST, 1,* 228). In philosophical terms the tension of the absolute and concrete elements results in the interaction of the principle of pure identity with the pluralistic principles, being-itself with "the relativities of reality" (*ST, 1,* 231). Each of the religious types, therefore, has a philosophical counterpart. The counterpart to trinitarian monotheism, which is the culminating type, is "dialectical realism" (*ST, 1,* 234).

Schematically, the religious types and their transformations can be represented thus:

ULTIMATE CONCERN
(Concrete–Absolute)

I. Concreteness Predominating

Religiously	*Philosophically*
Universalistic Polytheism (Special divine beings are embodiments of universal, all-pervading power.)	Monistic Naturalism (An all-pervading but secular, presence is in natural beings.)
Mythological Polytheism (Deities are relatively fixed powers and represent "broad realms of being and value.")	Pluralistic Naturalism (There is a plurality of ultimate, and secular, principles.)
Dualistic Polytheism (There are two powers, representing the divine realm and the demonic realm.)	Metaphysical Dualism (There are two ultimates—such as the Greek matter and form.)

II. Absoluteness Predominating

Religiously	*Philosophically*
Monarchic Monotheism (One power rules over and represents a hierarchy of powers.)	Gradualistic Metaphysics (There is a hierarchy of powers of being with an absolute or highest being.)
Mystical Monotheism (The One is transcendent, beyond all realms of being and value.)	Idealistic Monism (The unity of being is in a ground, or identity, in which manifoldness disappears.)

(*cont.*)

| Exclusive Monotheism
(One concrete god is ultimate and
universal.) | Metaphysical Realism
(Essences, or ideals, are but tools
for dealing with the given reals.) |

III. Absoluteness and Concreteness United

Religiously	*Philosophically*
Trinitarian Monotheism (A concrete being is paradoxically ultimate.)	Dialectical Realism (Reality itself is dialectical; the concrete is present in the ultimate.)

Three aspects of this typology are notable. First, the transformation of types is given in only one direction. The religious types are transformed into the philosophical ones. Second, the philosophical types interact among themselves, as do the religious types, but they also react to the religious types. Pluralistic naturalism, for example, is a reaction not only to monistic naturalism but also to universalistic polytheism.[45] Third, the religious types interact among themselves but do not react to the philosophical. All of these facts would be consistent with the view that "God is being" is not convertible. But they do not seem to be consistent with the parallelism and correlative standing of ontological elements and mythological gods. If the gods are expressions of ontological elements, their conflict gives rise to the question, Who is the true God? The first answer to this question is the God of justice (in exclusive monotheism). Then a second question arises: Who is the God of justice? If the answer to this question were only Yahweh of Israel, it would not be capable of universalization—and indeed would not express the justice of his divinity. The only way of answering this question satisfactorily seems to be to say, Being-itself is that true God.

If this is the case, the relation between the philosophical and religious terms would be such that the conflicts of the gods give rise to a question which is answerable by the ontological ultimate, and the conflicts of the ontological polarities give rise to a question that is answered by the theological ultimate. The parallel typology, accordingly, would be an exemplification of the fact

45. Cf. *ST, I,* 232.

that the question with which critical understanding (philosophy) ends is answered by a religious ultimate, and the question with which doubting response ends is answered by a philosophical ultimate.

This line of thought in Tillich would naturally lead to the conclusion that being-itself is, in certain contexts, a symbol.[46] For, according to a parallel typology of religions and philosophies, both "God" and "being" can refer to the ultimate as a question and also convey it as an answer; and where one is a question, the other is an answer. Out of the mythological expressions of objectival subjectivity (gods) there arises the question, Who is God-himself? Out of the ontological expressions of objective objectivity (ontological concepts) there arises the question, What is being-itself? The answer to the first is the symbol of objectival objectivity (being), and the answer to the second is the symbol of objectival subjectivity (God).

Tillich's *usage* of the terms does not allow this full reciprocity. But this can be accounted for by the fact that he writes primarily as a theologian. The fundamental direction of his thought, on the other hand, both allows and suggests that the "first (but not the last) statement" about God and being is indeed convertible.[47]

William Rowe has also reached the conclusion that Tillich's "being-itself" is symbolic.[48] This is what he sees as "the fundamental problem in Tillich's theory of religious symbols" which has given rise to most of the major objections critics have advanced against this theory. The problem, as Rowe analyzes it, lies in the fact that being-itself and ontological statements describing being-itself are incapable of clarifying symbolical statements of theology. If it is true that being-itself is a symbol, and if it is true that statements which describe being-itself (ontological statements) are symbolic too, it is impossible for ontological

46. Heidegger and Jaspers could be cited as examples to support this conclusion.

47. One might also note that in *ST*, 1, 279, the argument at the bottom of the page (God is love; God is being-itself; being-itself is love) is valid only if "God is being-itself" means the same as "being-itself is God."

48. *Religious Symbols*, pp. 182–93.

statements to clarify the symbolical statements about God that appear in theology. The ontological statements in this case need as much clarification as do the theological ones. Contrary to Tillich's claim, then, ontological statements cannot be used as literal statements to clarify theology's symbolical statements. Having seen that Tillich's being-itself is somehow symbolic, Rowe is able to fault the superficiality of the critiques of Tillich's theory made by William Alston and Paul Edwards, though he concludes that Tillich's theory is inconsistent with the principle that a symbolic statement is meaningful only if its cognitive content is expressible by some literal statement. He chooses not to try to settle the question of the validity of that principle itself, only suggesting[49] that it may not be tenable.

However, most of the difficulties which Rowe still sees here can be resolved, I think, by relating them to a different framework, which better states Tillich's intentions. Instead of dealing with the meaning of symbolic statements in terms of whether "being-itself" and "God" are both symbolic and whether there are ways of "reducing" these symbolic terms to literal ones, it accords more with Tillich's intentions and with the implied structure of his thought to deal with it in terms of the correlative standing of the depth expressed as being-itself and the depth expressed as God. The principle Tillich uses is not that just any literal statements can be used to clarify just any symbolic statements, but more specifically that conceptual statements (in the sense of statements that grasp and articulate the structure of being) can be used to interpret mythological statements (in the sense of statements that symbolize that same structure), and that the concept of being-itself, which is the concept by which we endeavor to grasp what the articulated ontological structure is a structure of, can be used to interpret the religious symbol of God, which expresses the power always working through the mythological gods.[50] If Tillich is understood along these lines, as I have

49. Ibid., p. 192.
50. Consequently it would not be correct to say, as Rowe (p. 188) does, that "being-itself is the ground of life" would be an ontological statement

been setting them forth in this analysis, then I do not see that any of the problems Rowe still finds in Tillich's theory of symbols remain. One could hardly deny that much of this theory needs further clarification and elaboration, but none of the critics[51] seems yet to have uncovered any fundamental problem that cannot be avoided *if* one takes the theory to mean what I have stated in these chapters.

I think this applies also to the difficulties Lewis Ford finds in the metaphysical, though not the religious, use of symbols.[52] Instead of seeing "personal commitment" as the factor which gives content to religious symbols,[53] and instead of seeing the ontological dimension as something additional to the religious use, as Ford does, we should perhaps understand Tillich's view to be that the ontological concept gives objective content to the religious symbol[54] and the religious symbol gives power to the ontological concept. Such a reciprocal fulfillment is possible because of the quasi-symbolic character of the concept of being-itself and the partially conceptual character of God, and because of the parallel between the mythological structure arising from the man–god encounter and the ontological structure arising from an analysis of the self–world relation. Ford rightly sees that there is a polar structure in religious symbols as well as in ontological concepts.[55]

---

which correctly interprets the symbolic, religious statement "God is living." On the contrary, the two statements which interpret each other would have to be "God is living" and "Being-itself is the creator," for only thus do we have a strict correlation between the symbolic and the conceptual. "God is living" assigns an ontological predicate to a religious subject; "Being-itself is the creator" assigns a religious, symbolical predicate to a conceptual subject. Correlative interpretation requires that the statement which interprets Cs must be the statement Sc, where c or C refers to an ontological concept and s or S refers to a religious symbol.

51. Rowe's study is the best that has come from the logical analysts, and it takes much more care to be attentive to Tillich's language and intentions than other studies of this kind.

52. "The Three Strands of Tillich's Theory of Religious Symbols," *Journal of Religion, 46* (January 1966), Pt. 2, 104–30.

53. Ibid., p. 126.

54. See below, Chap. 8, pp. 186f.

55. "Strands," pp. 107f.

But because he has not identified the reason for this similarity exactly, he has overlooked the correlative element involved in the issue.

To conclude this discussion of the relation between subjective and objective aspects of the objectival sphere are two observations about unclarified points. First, Tillich makes no use of the fact that in the assertion "God is" the concept of being is expressed as action. He lets "God" and "being" stand as representatives of two ways of relating to reality, correlated with each other by their common relation to the man who uses them and by their ultimate identity in the ground of both of them. However, Tillich does not deal explicitly with the fact that being is here expressed as a verb, or as action.[56]

A second observation has to do with some examples from biblical and ecclesiastic material which Tillich cites to show that ontological elements are implied in religious expressions. If Jesus said, he writes, that even the hairs on our heads are numbered and that no sparrow falls to the ground without the knowledge of the Heavenly Father, these statements are indirectly ontological because they imply that God is not only a person but also a participant in everything that happens. Again, when Luther, transcending his "sometimes unreflective biblical personalism," said that God is nearer to creatures than they are to themselves and that he gives the power "to the arm of the murderer to drive home the murderous knife,"[57] these statements imply that God is not only a person but a participant in all beings. "God as the power of being in everything is ontologically affirmed." The murderer commits the murder, but the hidden subject of the act is God, who acts through the finite subjectivity of the murdering man. A sparrow falls to the ground, but the hidden subject of the happening is God. In these examples we can see more than illustrations of the point Tillich is immediately making. They also show that, in Tillich's usage, objectival subjectivity in the sense of "he" rather

56. R. Scharlemann, "Concepts, Symbols, and Sentences," *Theology Today,* 22 (January 1966), 513–27.

57. *Biblical Religion,* p. 84.

than "thou" is called ontological. The conception of God as the hidden subject of all actions is an ontological conception.

From this it follows that "God" and "being" are correlated in another way, which Tillich never elaborated fully. God as a thou-subject, which is religious, is correlated with being, which is onto-logical, by means of the conception of God as a he-subject, which is, at least implicitly, ontological.[58] There is a parallel to this in objectival objectivity (although there are no illustrations for it in Tillich's writings). The objectival objectivity of being as the "it" which I grasp is connected with objectival subjectivity (thou) by means of an "it" which is the subject of its own action—the "it" of such sentences as " 'it' is." Such an "it" is a subject even though it is objectival and thus is intermediary between subjec-tivity and objectivity. From both directions, therefore, this third-person objectival subjectivity ("he" or "it") provides a connec-tion between the thou-subject of religious encounter and the it-object of ontological grasping.

58. A point which is worth noting in adjudicating the debate between Til-lich and Reinhold Niebuhr concerning whether ontology can include historical dynamics. See below, Chap. 8, pp. 189ff.

CHAPTER 4

Subject and Subject

In correlating "God" and "being" and the methods appropriate to them, Tillich provides a connection between the qualities of objectivity and subjectivity as they are located in the objectival sphere. From here we are naturally led to the question of how the subjectival and objectival subjects are related. Are there expressions of the subjectival which need to be interpreted by means of an objectival subject, and conversely? Or can we give direct expression to the meaning of the subjectival without reference to an objectival counterpart? The areas which these questions circumscribe are ethics, in which a subject encounters another subject, and christology, in which a subject encounters another subject who is both concrete and universal. In reference to "God" and "being" the correlation is needed because we are dealing with two ultimate terms and we must ask how they are related. Simultaneously we are also dealing with two activities of the self, both of which are fundamental. Is the responding activity shut out by the grasping activity? Here again correlation is the only answer which preserves both activities in their completeness. In moving from any "self" to my concretely existing I-myself we come to a different aspect of the question. God and *I* are two unconditionals; God and being are two ultimates; I-myself and a concrete paradoxical object are correlative to each other in another way. Here correlation is necessary because I cannot know what my act of existing means without an externalization of it, with reference to which my act takes place. This is the case for two reasons: first, my acting *I* is unconditionally subjectival—I can never get a look at it; and second, the character of existence is such that I am split from my true self, and I cannot, therefore, see my actual self in my objective self. The first point has been discussed already.

The second point will be taken up in the present chapter. The relation of subjectival subject and objectival subject, in Christian theology, is that of our relation to the picture of Jesus as the Christ. This picture is characterized by the fact that it is a concrete ultimate—which is to say, it is indistinguishable in its function from "God," and it is the picture of a concretely existing man.

Tillich distinguishes existence from essence as well as from life (*ST, 1,* 66f.). Both essence and existence are abstractions from the actual life-situation. The place where we find ourselves is life, which is a mixture of essential and existential elements. To speak of essence or of existence is to speak of one of the elements in life but not of life itself. The difference between the two abstractions is that essence refers to the structure of being and existence refers to the distortions in that structure. Thus, whereas the mark of the essential structure is finitude, the mark of existence is estrangement; whereas the polarities in the structure are essentially in balanced and dynamic tension, in existence they contradict each other. Instead of a structure of finitude, existence is a structure of destruction, a structure that works against itself because it is severed from its ground. Instead of supporting each other, self and world contradict each other. Similarly, freedom works against destiny and destiny against freedom. Existence reaches its final point when the poles are completely in conflict and isolation.

In both the subjectival and the objectival spheres the polarity is broken. The self is divorced from its center; the whole is divorced from the center of the world. Expressed in other terms, existentially "I" and my "self" are in conflict. The act of existing is the act in which I work against my concrete actuality.

We saw in a previous chapter that the self–world polarity is really a dual polarity. On the side of the self, there is the "center" (the *I*) and the concrete whole being (the this-ness); on the side of the world, there is the "whole" structure and the being which serves as its center. In existence, the split involves both sides. There is a division between the *I* and its concrete being and between the whole of the world and that which serves as its center. But this division results from the separation between the *I*, which is unconditional in its acts of being, and the unconditional, which is unconditional for being at all—between the ego-self and the ground of all being. The subjectival and objectival unconditionals are separated from each other. Essentially there should be an external subject that is related to the whole world in the way that the *I* is related to bodily being. Existentially that subject is lost sight of, and there is nothing that can make a connection between the *I* and the this-ness of concrete being or between the self and the world.

Thus, it is under the conditions of existence that the distinction between the *I* of *I am* and my being in this body, between my act and my objective presence in the world, becomes acute. The split between the polar elements of the ontological structure is manifested as a split between the self and its concrete being. It is a condition in which the exercise of freedom, for example, fails to achieve true destiny, and destiny seems to be unrelated to the fulfillment of freedom.

Because of this self-contradiction stamped upon it, existence culminates in a state of hopeless self-contradiction, the state of "despair." Despair, in this context, does not mean simply a feeling of futility. It means a situation in which the *I* is engaged in a continuous activity which it can neither complete successfully nor withdraw from. Again, it does not mean a situation in which I destroy myself, for the polar character of the ontological structure implies that no element can be destroyed without a simultaneous destruction of its polar opposite. If destiny were lost, freedom would be lost also. But existence is not the actual loss of either freedom or destiny, for that would mean that at least negatively existence could succeed or find a way out of its despair. On the contrary, the despair of existence lies in the fact that I continuously endeavor to destroy my individual being—and with it my freedom—but the endeavor can never succeed; on the other hand, I cannot desist from the endeavor. The ego-self cannot escape the state of self-contradiction in any way; it can neither cease its activity against itself nor accomplish that end. Sheer despair is the state in which my whole activity is that of trying to accomplish what cannot possibly be accomplished—the undoing of myself. This is formulated in Tillich's description of existence as a "structure of destruction" (*ST*, 2, 60). This "seemingly paradoxical term" refers to "the fact that destruction has no independent standing in the whole of reality but that it is dependent on the structure of that in and upon which it acts destructively."

The culmination of existence is formulated in a question different from that which expresses the limit of essential finitude. The question of finitude has to do with what is beyond the polarity of self and world or, mythologically expressed, of man and god. The question of existence is the quest for a way out of the state of despair. It arises at the point where the ego-self recognizes the insoluble contradiction between what it aims to do and what it can do. It cannot provide its own way out, since every activity is but an expression of the fact that it neither can nor will escape from its division within itself. Again, existence overcomes its limit differently than essential finitude. For finitude the symbol "God" provides the effective source of its courage. It sustains the tension of the polarities in the ontological structure. For existence this symbol is, however, the objectival presence of the New Being. The New Being is encountered in a man in my world who, though under the conditions of existence, transcends them. He represents both the state of existence and that of essential being. Expressed in other terms, he is *a* subject who is nonetheless subjectivity as such and *an* object (in the sense that his presence is external to me) who is also objectivity as such. He is an objectival subject who is also the depth of subjectival subjectivity. He is a man who is also the embodiment of mankind, the center of the world. The world is to his concrete being what my bodily self is to my self-center.

It is important to note, however, that in Tillich's conception this figure of Jesus as the Christ is not a being who exists *in my place*. Tillich enunciates, as one of the principles to be used in developing the doctrine of atonement further (*ST*, 2, 176), an alternative to "substitutional suffering." This term does not correctly express the relation between the divine and the human in suffering. God "participates" in existence but does not substitute for it. Nor is the existence of Christ a substitute for the existence of the creature. "The suffering of the Christ [is not] a substitute for the suffering of man." "Free participation," not substitution, defines the relationship. God's participation in creaturely suffering and the creature's "participation in the divine participation, accepting it and being transformed by it," define the relationship more adequately. In other words, the New Being in Jesus as the Christ does not take the place of my own act of existing, but it makes it possible for me to get beyond the impasse of despair at which existence ends, not as someone else's act in my place, but by something which empowers my own act, even though in the first place I meet it outside of myself.

The peculiarity of our relation to the picture of Jesus as the Christ is connected with this fact. He is what makes it possible to "succeed" in existence. This is to say, he is not objective to us only in the sense that we can critically understand his objective being or critically respond to his power upon us. The way he is objectival to us can perhaps best be expressed by saying he is a being *in view of whom* we are able to actualize our own being beyond despair. He is an object which, as it were, "triggers" an act of ours that takes us beyond the state of hopeless self-contradiction. In view of him, we can do something that we are not able to do when we have nothing outside of us in view. If God is the source of our courage to be, the picture of Jesus as the Christ is the objectival being in view of which we are able to be ourselves. In the present chapter we will see how Tillich develops this basic idea as another context for the basic pattern of correlation and a paradoxical reality.

Historical research has shown, Tillich believes, four stages of development in the christological symbols (*ST, 2,* 109). Since the christological symbols are correlated with the problems of existence, the stages of that development are important for interpreting existence. Moreover, this is a point at which historical research can make a direct contribution to theological interpretation.

Such research into the origin and life of symbols has shown, first, that the symbols arise and grow "in their own religious culture and language." Then, second, they come to be used as "expressions of [the] self-interpretation [of the men for whom they have become alive] and as answers to the questions implied in their existential predicament." Third, they are transformed as they are used to "interpret the event on which Christianity is based." Fourth, their meaning is distorted by the endeavor to restore them to the meaning of the first stage by people who live in an age beyond it. They are distorted "by popular superstition, supported by theological literalism and supernaturalism." The importance of recognizing these stages lies in the fact that, as in all spiritual developments, there is a correlative progression between the interpreter and the material he is interpreting. There are transformations in man's self-understanding correlative to the transformations in the meaning and use of the symbols. The three basic stages of this transformation should be explained, therefore, with reference to both the subjectival and the objectival side of the relation.

The symbols which arise and grow "in their own religious culture and language" are used by men who are not yet aware of their existential situation. They are at one with their world and with their own humanity, not yet aware of a real severance between man and nature or between what an existing self is and what an essential human being is. Since they are not conscious of that difference, it is possible for them to speak of themselves in objective terms, as one part of their world. Every man among them is conscious of himself only as part of a whole world. He speaks of himself in the same terms as he speaks of the world. When christological symbols—of which Tillich expressly discusses the following seven: Son of David, Son of Man, Heavenly Man, Messiah, Son of God, Kyrios, Logos—are used in this pre-existential or precritical stage, they are not specifically existential expressions. They are concrete portrayals of universal aspects of being.

At the second stage the same symbols are used by men who have become conscious of a "fall" into existence. They are conscious of a gap between what they actually are in their act of existing and what they could and should be as real men. They therefore use the symbols expressing universal aspects of being, not in order to objectify what they are, but in order to express the difference between their essential and their existential being.[1] Thus, the symbol "Son of Man," as used at the first stage, refers to the unity of God and man which, in ontological terms, is the unity of man with the ground of his being. The negative aspect has not yet been experienced, neither as the threat of nonbeing nor as the consciousness of a split between a self's true being and his actual being. But at the second stage "Son of Man" is used to contrast the actual situation of men with the man from above, and to express anticipated or received answers to the problem of that gap. "The Man from Above is contrasted with man's situation of existential estrangement from God, his world, and himself. This contrast includes the expectation that the Son of Man will conquer the forces of estrangement and re-establish the unity between God and man" (*ST*, 2, 109).

At the third stage the symbols are ascribed to Jesus. This one man receives the title "Son of Man" and the other christological symbols. That is to say, one man is given the predicates of man prior to the fall into existence even though, as a man, he too exists. Tillich's way of formulating this point is to say that essential Godmanhood appears under the conditions of existence. "In Jesus as the Christ the eternal unity of God and man has become historical reality" is his reformulation of the assertion, "Jesus as

1. "Existentialism as a universal element in all thinking is the attempt of man to describe his existence and its conflicts, and the anticipations of overcoming them." "Existential Aspects of Modern Art," in *Christianity and the Existentialists*, ed. Carl Michalson (New York, Charles Scribner's Sons, 1956), p. 129.

the Christ is the personal unity of a divine and a human nature"
(*ST*, 2, 148). The symbols applied to this one man Jesus express
the fact that he, as it were, existed "successfully." His existence
differs from that of others insofar as they do not successfully
exist, but at the same time it makes the conquest of existence
universally possible.

It is at the fourth stage, however, that Tillich's own systematic
construction is operative. At this stage the symbols are no longer
working in any of the other three ways, but they still have power.
So they survive either as superstitions or as theological literalism
and supernaturalism. Instead of this kind of survival Tillich's
systematic interpretation is intended to restore them to their original power.

These stages, as Tillich sets them forth, are reflected in the
systematics insofar as the section on christology moves at the
level of existential interpretation. In order to see what the role
of the christological symbols is it is necessary to discuss the dialectic of existence at greater length than previously.

The term Tillich uses to characterize existence is "estrangement." This word suggests both of the marks of existence. Existence
is separated from essential being in such a way that it can neither
regain it nor execute a divorce from it. It cannot "succeed" in
either direction. This continuing failure provides the dialectic of
existence. In the state of essential finitude, the self can accept its
finitude because it does not lose sight of the power of being
which encompasses the self's act as well as its objective presence.
Under the conditions of existence the self opposes its finitude.
Thus the dialectic of finitude is related to transcending the ontological polarity, but the dialectic of existence is related to resisting
it from within it. There is a similar difference in the relation of
positive and negative elements for finitude and for existence. In
finitude the threat of nonbeing is taken into the power of being in
a continuing act of courage; this is possible because finite being
has not lost its rooting in its eternal ground. In existence the threat
of nonbeing cannot be taken into courage because the finite
polarity is opaque to its ground. The threat of nonbeing appears

—to put it mythologically—as the demonic power of a God who destroys what he creates by plunging it into a hopeless self-contradiction.

This inability to see beyond the destroying power provokes the self's resistance. The self resists the power which threatens to negate it, to assert its own being in opposition to it. However, it cannot do so by the power of something that embraces its world and itself, but only by the power of its own unconditional freedom or responsibility. It resists the threat—which is to say, it resists its own finitude—but it cannot succeed in its resistance. Whatever it does, the finitude of its being finally overcomes the infinite element of its freedom.

Thus, what produces despair (*ST*, 2, 69) is not the experience of finitude itself, for that can be taken into the experience of the courage to be. Rather, it is the experience of failure in the self's attempt to resist finitude. The self *must* resist because it cannot see anything beyond the opposition between its unconditional freedom and its limited finite being. The only unconditional outside its own free act is the negative. If the self resists that threat, it loses itself by being defeated, finitude overcomes it. If it does not resist the threat, it loses itself by giving up its unconditional freedom. Tillich attributes this resisting action on the part of the self (*ST*, 2, 69) to the fact that man essentially belongs to the eternal, but because he is excluded from it under the conditions of existence, he tries to transform finitude itself into the eternal. His resistance against the negative elements in finitude springs from a truth, but the resistance itself works against the truth from which it springs. The structure of finitude is "good in itself, but under the conditions of estrangement it becomes a structure of destruction" (*ST*, 2, 71). In other words, the self's unwillingness or inability to accept that structure turns it into a structure of destruction. The structure of destruction, we should remember, refers to the fact that the self neither can escape from having to resist its finitude nor can succeed in its resistance; it can neither gain itself nor lose itself. "One is shut up in one's self [in despair] and in the conflict with one's self. One cannot escape, because one cannot escape from one's self" (*ST*, 2, 75).

In the nature of the case, self-salvation is impossible under the conditions of existence. Whatever the self does is part of its act of hitting wide of its true being. Tillich points to this in his analysis of false ways of salvation, which are the various types of self-salvation. One type is religion of the law. A man can be saved if he is obedient to the law of love. But the very fact that love has to be commanded makes its fulfillment impossible. Thus, even the law which formulates the nature of essential being expresses existential distortion by the very fact that it is a law. Similarly, ascetic self-salvation, in which everything finite is denied by the self, fails because the denial of the finite expresses, not the eternal, but the distortion of essential being. The wish to deny finitude itself expresses existential estrangement, and whether it succeeds or fails it would not provide an escape from existence. This inherent defeat is true of all ways of trying to save one's self from existential estrangement. The self is confirmed in its despair by the only activity it thought could provide an escape.

In sum, the dialectic of finitude is such that the threat of non-being is posed and continually answered by a courage rooted in a power beyond the polar ontological structure itself. The dialectic of existence is such that the self must oppose the negative implied in the structure of finitude; but because it cannot successfully resist it, even though it must try to do so, it is continuously in despair. Even the self's attempts to save itself by religious means end in magnifying the despair instead of providing a way out. There is an insoluble conflict between the act of the self and the finite being of man. Finitude resists the negative by accepting it; existence resists the negative by trying to deny it.

What then is the way out of despair? Here is where the christological element comes into consideration, for the picture of Jesus as the Christ provides a way out. That is to say, this picture is not another object for the self's activity, otherwise it would simply become part of the existential distortion. Rather, it is an object in view of which the self finds it possible to "be" under the conditions of existence. It is an object which, in a unique way, corroborates and eliminates the state of despair. It is objectival, but it is neither an objectival object nor simply an objectival subject; it is the subjectival in objectival form. This point will now be explored at more length.

The objectival reality in view of which existence becomes possible is, in Tillich's thinking, the picture of Jesus as the Christ. The picture both confirms and transcends the existential situation, and this is its power of new being. It is a peculiar combination of corroboration and reversal of the self's situation of self-contradiction.

In one way it is a reversal of what I experience my own self to be. The self is aware of being existentially estranged from what it essentially is because it is estranged from its own ground. The self is alone, unable to see beyond the polarities of its being to its own depth. The picture of Jesus as the Christ is the picture of another man, an objectival subject, who, in a way directly opposed to what I actually am, does indeed actually exist as what he essentially is. He does not become separated from the ground of his being even though he is engaged in the act of existing.

Again, in existence the self resists the finitude of its being because finitude appears as demonic. The self must resist it in order to retain its freedom, but it must inevitably fail in its resistance. The picture of Jesus as the Christ is that of one who accepts his finitude, even when, under the conditions of existence, he cannot see beyond the polarities of his being. The self sees him as existing, but also as succeeding in that act of existence. That is to say, he is an externalization of my act of existing as well as of my human being, but he is a reversal of it because he succeeds where I fail.

On the other hand, the picture is of one who corroborates rather than reverses my experience of my self. He experiences the situation that I experience as despair, as being alone with myself without seeing a way out. He experiences defeat at the hands of the powers representing finitude—death and guilt. "If Jesus as the Christ were seen as a God walking on earth, he would be neither finite nor involved in tragedy" (*ST, 2,* 133).

This is the point, however, at which the picture takes on power. The way in which this happens Tillich seems to see as follows.

Everything that the man in the picture does every existential self is also doing, with one exception. He *accepts his defeat* by finitude *as a victory*. In view of his accepting his defeat as a victory the existential self sees a possible way out of despair. The very self-contradiction into which it has been brought is not defeat but a hidden victory. The fact that the self cannot recover its essential being, though it must try to do so, and that it cannot successfully resist finitude, though it must try to do so, now becomes a fact of quite different significance. The defeat is transcended as soon as it is accepted, and it becomes a victory. New being is thus a possibility even for the existential self, because the only activity required of it is the activity in which it is already continuously engaged. In Tillich's reformulation of the Reformation principle of justification through faith and its understanding of the bondage of the will, the existential self at this point becomes aware that it is accepted in spite of its unacceptability. Its state of despair is confirmed and corrected at one and the same time.

The significance of this new possibility for the existing self can perhaps be seen best if we compare its parallel in the situation of temptation before the fall (*ST, 2,* 31–44). The possibility of the fall is rooted in man's finite freedom. Man can turn against the ground of his finitude and against his own freedom (though he cannot succeed at it). The temptation which appears in the state of "dreaming innocence" arises from anxiety over losing oneself either by failing to actualize one's freedom or by failing to achieve one's destiny. Under the conditions of existence this temptation appears demonic, for it seems to bespeak a situation in which man cannot win. If he decides to exercise his freedom, he loses his unity with God; if he decides not to exercise it, he loses his free self. In either way, however, he loses himself because he cannot retain both his freedom and his destiny. In terms of the story of the fall in Genesis, one can put it thus: If Adam obeys the prohibition against eating the fruit of the one tree, he loses his freedom; if he disobeys it, he loses his destiny or his unity with God. Since he must do one or the other, his choice is not whether he will lose himself but only which path he will take to that end.

As a matter of fact, man always chooses—according to Tillich's interpretation of this story (*ST*, *2*, 36, 44)—to actualize his freedom; but from the perspective of existence, his refusal to actualize his freedom would lead to the same consequence—estrangement from himself.

This situation, which inevitably leads to defeat, is not reversed, as far as its external appearance is concerned, in the presence of the New Being. Jesus is faced with defeat in a similar way. If he refuses to fulfill his mission, he gains his freedom but loses his destiny; if he fulfills it, he loses his freedom but retains his destiny. His actual choice is the opposite of Adam's; instead of sacrificing his unity with God in order to actualize his freedom, he sacrifices his freedom in order to retain his unity with God. Yet the consequence at first seems to be the same since he does lose that unity also. This, in any case, would be suggested by the cry of dereliction.

All of the features of self-defeat which characterize Adam's decision characterize this one too. Yet the picture of the New Being is more because, as completed by the story of the resurrection, it puts existential defeat into a new light. What appears in Adam to be but a choice between two ways of losing himself turns out, in the strength of the picture of Jesus as the Christ, to be a choice between two ways of gaining himself. It should be noted, however, that this picture of a New Being is not just a new interpretation of man's existential situation but a new happening, a new "manifestation" of God.[2]

The existential situation is put into a new light by the cross, because what the picture of Jesus as the Christ shows there is the fact that self-defeat is the existential way of achieving the self's victory. There is nothing the self need do in order to regain its

2. *ST*, *2*, 175: "Manifestations are effective expressions, not only communications. Something happens through a manifestation which has effects and consequences. The Cross of the Christ is a manifestation in this sense. It is a manifestation by being actualization. It is not the only actualization, but it is the central one, the criterion of all other manifestations of God's participation in the suffering of the world."

essential being, except to let itself be defeated; and it cannot help letting itself be defeated because, in one way or another, that is what it continually is doing. For this reason, the picture is capable of providing the way out of despair without doing violence either to the self's freedom or to its destiny.

A specific illustration of what this means can be seen in Tillich's discussion of the involvement of Judas and the Jewish leaders in the crucifixion of Jesus (*ST, 2,* 132–34). With regard to all of them Tillich notes that Jesus shares "the tragic [rather than ethical] element" of their guilt. He made his enemies guilty by his conflict with them, and Judas could not have become a traitor if he had not belonged to the intimate group of disciples; the betrayal could not have happened "without the will of Jesus." In regard to Judas, therefore, Jesus becomes "tragically guilty." The guilt did not disrupt his "personal relation to God," but it was nonetheless a guilt resulting from involvement in the conditions of existence.

If we look at the happening from the side of the leaders of the Jews, who represented faithfulness to the divine law, or from that of Judas, who, let us conjecture, represents willful freedom, then the crucifixion has reversed the situation of aboriginal temptation. That is to say, at this point in history two opposed decisions converge in a common result. Among the people involved in the deed, those who would consciously have chosen to act against the will of God and those who would consciously have chosen to act in accordance with it would have converged in carrying out the execution. Thus each of them was a unique combination of obedience and disobedience to the will of God.[3] Judas was too. Even if his betrayal was an act of faithlessness, he was nonetheless faithful to Jesus' mission. As part of the picture of Jesus as the Christ, he was a unique combination of faithfulness and unfaithfulness.

If we compare this unique situation with the universal situation

3. To speak in terms of "obedience" and "disobedience" is to give a somewhat more Barthian cast to the exposition since Tillich does not use such phraseology here.

of the fall, we can see how it manifests new being under the conditions of existence. In the temptation leading to the fall, man is placed before a decision to obey or disobey God. If he disobeys, he loses himself because he does not actualize his freedom; if he obeys, he loses himself because his freedom cuts him off from his destiny. Whether he obeys or disobeys, he loses himself. In the crucifixion of Jesus, man is again faced with a decision to obey or disobey the will of God. But in this case, if he disobeys it, he gains himself because his disobedience is an obedience of another order; if he obeys it, he gains himself because his obedience involves him in a disobedience of another order. By this crucifixion existence is salvaged because human freedom and destiny are restored. Freedom is preserved because man can act in either of two radically opposed ways. Destiny is preserved because, regardless of which of the two radically opposing decisions he makes, man affirms his unity with the divine ground of his being.

If the analysis I have given here is a substantially true account of Tillich's understanding, then it is easy to see why, for him, Jesus as the Christ embodies the New Being which is the final revelation of God. It is final in the sense that whatever comes after it chronologically has already been anticipated in it. All subsequent decisions made within human existence as now constituted are included in or between the two extremes anticipated in Jesus —a decision for the will of God, and a decision against the will of God. His appearance is a happening of such a kind that it focuses the problem of historical being itself and introduces a decision about its ultimate meaning. If we circumscribe the term "historical being" by saying it is the situation expressed in the fact that all of our knowing and doing occurs within a perspective or a shaping on the part of the *I,* and that we cannot say for certain whether the ultimate consequences of that shaping are for or against our true being, then the worst possible act is one in which the historical self makes a decision that contradicts its eternal being. This exactly is the decision which determines "existence" in contrast to "being" or "life." Therefore, a happening that discloses such a decision in a central and finally interpretive way will express the meaning of existence itself. What *is* the meaning of a human decision against the eternal ground? The answer provided by the picture of the crucified is that even a decision against God is implicitly a decision for him. This meaning is expressed in one way in the myth of the fall and in another way in the picture of Jesus as the Christ. In both cases man is drawn into a situation where each of two opposite decisions eventuates in the same consequence. In the myth of the fall the consequence is the lostness of existence; in the story of the crucifixion it is the salvation of existence. What appears as inevitable defeat in the fall emerges as a hidden victory in the crucifixion and resurrection of Jesus. It is the appearance of the paradox which even historically conscious thought cannot dislodge by reflection or doubt.

The picture of Jesus as the Christ, however, is not a portrayal of something that happened to him alone. It also communicates the power of his victory to those who are transformed by it. That is to say, an existing person is related to the picture through faith rather than historical research. It is not an object to be studied but a transforming power. (What such transforming power means we have seen above—the picture can occasion a free act which, though it is made by the existing self, takes the self beyond the despair of existence.) This brings us to the question of the relation between the historical Jesus and the biblical picture of Jesus as the Christ, one an object of research, the other an objectival pole of a faith relation. Here is where Tillich's definition of the paradoxical certainty becomes more problematic.

Tillich distinguishes two meanings in the term "historical" (*ST*, 2, 107). It can refer to "the results of historical research into the character and life of the person who stands behind the Gospel reports," and it can be used to say that "the event 'Jesus as the Christ' has a factual element." In the first case it does not affect the object of faith at all. In the second case it does. "If the factual element in the Christian event were denied, the foundation of Christianity would be denied" (*ST*, 2, 107). In this sense the reality of the historical Jesus is "guaranteed" by faith itself. Faith guarantees, according to Tillich's distinction, "a personal life in which the New Being has conquered the old being," but it does not guarantee that his name was Jesus of Nazareth (*ST*, 2, 114).[4]

Yet Tillich also introduces a kind of circularity into his statements of what faith guarantees. No special trait of the picture can be verified beyond the usual limits of historical probability. What can be stated with certainty is the fact that "through this picture the New Being has power to transform those who are transformed by it," because no historical criticism can "question the immediate awareness of those who find themselves transformed" by the picture (*ST*, 2, 114). Nor, for that matter, can historical research ever provide the foundation for faith. The reason for this is suggested by Tillich's wording—the picture has power to transform those who are transformed by it. If such a statement stood in isolation, it would be too self-evident to need stating. Of course it is true that if I am transformed by something, that something has power to transform me—how else could I have been transformed by it! But Tillich is saying more than such a triviality. He is saying, first, that there is an indissoluble connection between the act and the object of faith and, second, that faith and historical research imply two distinct relations of the self to its object.

The starting point is the fact that the self, upon coming into view of the picture, finds that it is transformed; it can see its existence as victory rather than defeat and can live a different form of life from before. The fact that this happens with reference to a definite picture is conceptualized in the idea of the power of that picture to transform. As long as the self continues to find itself transformed by that object, it stands in a relation of faith-response, and no research it undertakes can undercut that immediate relation. For those, however, who do not find themselves transformed when they come into view of this picture, it is not an object of faith.

If, then, the historical Jesus refers to this man as accessible to investigation, he cannot be the foundation of faith, since the very relation implied on the part of the self to that object is not a re-

4. Cf. *Dynamics of Faith*, pp. 87–89 and "Rejoinder" pp. 191–94.

lation of faith. There is no way of moving from an act by which I establish the credibility of what is said about this man to an act in which the same object is a power to which I freely respond. Of course, it may happen that a man who is engaged in historical research at some point confronts the figure of Jesus as a power transforming his existence. But when that happens, his relation to the object is changed from that of a researcher to that of a responder. The movement from historical research to faith-response is a transition from one sphere to a quite different sphere. For this reason, no result of historical research can remove the picture's power, and no act of responding faith can provide a guarantee for the reliability of the results of historical research. What establishes the relation of faith is simply the fact that the picture of Jesus as the Christ has the power of eliciting the self's response to it. If it does not have that power, it is not an object of faith.

This difference is illustrated by the examples Tillich cites of what faith can and cannot guarantee.[5] Faith cannot answer such questions as whether present editions of sacred books are identical with the original text, when various books were written, whether the Book of Genesis has more myths and legends than actual history, whether apocalyptic expectations of a final catastrophe as found in the Old and New Testaments originated in the Persian religion, how much legendary, mythological, and historical material there is in the stories of the birth and resurrection of Christ, which reports of the early church are most accurate, whether the Mosaic Law comes from Moses, whether words ascribed to Jesus in the New Testament were actually spoken by him, whether the man pictured as Jesus the Christ in the New Testament did have the name Jesus. What faith can answer are such questions as whether the Old Testament law has unconditional validity for those who are grasped by it, whether the reality "which is manifest" in the New Testament picture of the Christ has saving power "for those who are grasped by it, no matter how much or how little can be traced to the historical

<hr/>

5. *Dynamics of Faith;* pp. 87–89; *ST*, 2, 107, 114.

figure who is called Jesus of Nazareth."[6] We could add another point that Tillich does not state directly. Faith cannot guarantee in any given case that the objectival reality (the picture) which thus far has had transforming power will in future continue to have it. No one who responds to the liberating power of the picture of Jesus can know for certain whether ten years hence it will have the same power for him. What faith can guaranee on this matter will be discussed in Chapter 7; it is connected with Tillich's assertion that the symbol of the cross contains a criterion against its own "idolatrous abuse."[7]

What establishes the object of faith is, in other words, simply the fact that it has the power to elicit a response. In the case of the New Testament picture of Jesus, what the self confronts is both an objectival subject and an externalization of the subjectival awareness of the self. It is not another man or the description of a man now dead, but rather a living picture, a figure, portrayed in story, imagination, and so on, which has the power of providing a way out of the existential impasse. Faith can guarantee the reality of what is expressed in that picture for the simple reason that faith is the response to its power. There would be no faith in the first place if the picture did not elicit the response it does.

It is not difficult to see how Tillich distinguishes the object of faith and the object of historical research, and why he can say that one of the things faith guarantees is that there was a real man —whatever his name or traits may be—behind the picture expressed in the New Testament. Nevertheless there is one aspect of this question which he leaves largely unanswered. It can be made clear by a comparison with Shakespeare's Hamlet. Here too we can say the picture portrays a real man, one who is caught in the paralysis of existence.[8] Yet even though it portrays a real man, we do not conclude that there must have been an actual man behind Shakespeare's dramatic portrait. The two cases seem to be

6. *Dynamics of Faith*, p. 88.
7. Ibid., p. 104.
8. For the impression this drama made on Tillich, see Adams, *Paul Tillich's Philosophy of Culture, Science and Religion*, p. 66.

of the same sort. Hamlet is the product of Shakespeare's response to the situation of existence as well as to the particular man he is portraying. The picture of Jesus as the Christ arises from the way in which certain people saw in this man the presence of New Being. In both cases a single man is portrayed in such a way that he expresses the meaning of existence and New Being—in one case (Hamlet) the meaning of existence itself, in the other case the presence of New Being in existence.

Should we therefore conclude that there has to have been one actual person behind Shakespeare's portrayal? Or should we conclude that the picture of Jesus the Christ, though it is the picture of a real man, need not have arisen in response to any single person in the world? It could have come from someone's, or some group's, recognition and creative expression of the truth that new being is present even in existence. In this latter case, the question whether there was one actual person upon whom the New Testament picture is based must be settled by historical research, whose conclusions would move within the usual range of probability and improbability. It would be possible, depending upon the nature of the evidence, to conclude that, like Hamlet, the picture of Jesus as the Christ is a composite.

A possible rejoinder to this line of thought would be to say that there is a difference between the picture of Hamlet and the picture of Jesus in that the former expresses existence and the latter the conquest of existence. An expressive portrait of existence, as in Hamlet, does not necessarily imply one real man behind it because the condition of existence is universal. A portrayal of the New Being would imply its special appearance in one man because, unlike existence, it is not universal. Therefore there could not be a picture of Jesus as the Christ if there were not an actual person upon whom the picture was based. In this regard the New Testament picture would differ from other real pictures.

Such an answer seems to reflect some of the things Tillich says about the New Being, but it contradicts his assertion that the power of the New Being *is* universally present. Its presence in the picture of Jesus differs from its presence elsewhere as a "final" manifestation—that is, the one which contains a criterion by which all are judged, including the one in which the criterion appears—differs from others. But revelation itself is universally present. Moreover, the existential situation does not normally appear in radical form either, even though it is universal. Normally it is mixed with essential elements. Consequently, the distinction between final and universal revelation has an exact counterpart in the universal and radical (or aboriginal) forms of existence. If one argued that the finality of the revelation in Jesus necessarily implies an actual person behind the picture, one also would have to argue that the radical character of Adam's decision guarantees an actual person behind the portrayal in Genesis.

It does seem, then, that the question whether the biblical picture is based upon an actual person or upon something else—say, a creative insight into the meaning of existence—is answerable only by historical research and not by faith. This is not to say that faith is based upon this research, for faith, in line with Tillich's view, would continue to rest upon the power of the picture to elicit it. But faith would not be able to guarantee that the reality behind the picture was an actual person rather than a composite or an artistic creation.

In other words, if this comparison between the Hamlet of Shakespeare and the Jesus of the New Testament is valid, then, contrary to what Tillich says, faith cannot guarantee that the reality behind the picture was an actual person. In one of his last writings Tillich seems to incline toward this view. In reply to an article by D. Moody Smith,[9] he says: "Suppose . . . the New Testament picture of Jesus is essentially a creation of Mark . . . then 'Mark' was the bearer of the Spirit through whom God has created the church and transformed . . . many in all generations, including myself. Then this 'Mark' has expressed the inner events he has experienced in the symbolic image of the Christ story." But even here Tillich seems to be referring to the factual details of the actual person behind the picture, not to the question whether there was such a person or not.

9. "Rejoinder," p. 192.

CHAPTER 5

Structure and Depth

In Tillich's conception myth and cult cannot be reduced to any of the other functions of reason (*ST, 1,* 80f.). They are not primitive forms of science or morality, nor are they esthetic counterparts of cognitive expressions. On the contrary, they embody what Tillich calls the dimension of "depth," which "precedes" the structure. They are "expressions of the depth of reason in symbolic form" and "lie in a dimension where no interference with the proper functions of reason is possible" (*ST, 1,* 81). Since the basic ontological and rational structure is the self–world or subject–object polarity, "depth" refers to what is beyond this polarity. But since every expression, even myth and cult, must occur within the polarity—every myth, for example, has to be told *by someone*—the difference between expressions of depth and those of structure is that the structural material is used differently. In one case the structure itself is directly meant; in the other case the structure is used to point to something beyond it. Myth and ritual are, as it were, structures of the depth of structure. One way of stating the difference between an expression of structure and an expression of depth—a way which Tillich himself never uses— is to say that direct expressions of structure present the elements for what they are, whereas expressions of depth present the same structural elements as being there *in spite of* the fact that they need not be. Thus, if I say of an object, "*x* is a being," I am calling attention to the fact that it is a thing within a world (however limited the world may be). This is a statement of its fundamental ontological structure. If I want to call attention to its being there in spite of the fact that it need not have been, or that there was a time when it was not there and there will be a time when it is no longer there, then I should give expression to the depth of its being. In such a case, if I were using the biblical symbols, I would say, "*x* is a creature," rather than "*x* is a being." The structure implied in the word "creature" is exactly the same as that implied in "being," but the former is used to express "depth" and the latter is used to express the structure itself. The distinction between the holy and the secular makes the same point. "Everything has the dimension of depth, and in the moment in which the third dimension is actualized, holiness appears" (*ST, 3,* 218).

From this difference three tasks follow, as three more versions of correlation. First, there is the task of relating philosophical expressions of structure with religious expressions of depth. Second, there is the task of relating cultural expressions of depth with its traditional religious expressions—the nonparadoxical with the paradoxical expressions of depth. Third, there is the task of relating religious expressions of structure (mythology, rather than myth) with philosophical expressions of depth. The first task brings together reason and revelation and being and God; the second involves culture and religion; the third relates mythology (or the typological history of religions) with the depth of being. This third task Tillich does not actually carry out, but one can discern outlines of it and project its construction. In each of these cases one side of the correlation completes the other by some intermediate steps, which will be described here.

In relating the structure of reason and being to the depth of reason (revelation) and being (God), we are dealing with philosophical expressions of structure and religious expressions of depth. Philosophy's primary role is to articulate the ontological-rational structure; religion's primary role is to express its depth. The problem in relating the two is to discern which mythical expressions correspond to which philosophical concepts. In doing this, theology mediates between "the mystery which is *theos* and the understanding which is *logos*."[1]

In working out this connection, we need to bear in mind two

---

1. *The Protestant Era,* p. xiii.

considerations. First, since the element of depth is what "precedes" the structure of reason or being, its manifestation occurs both subjectively and objectively. In Tillich's terminology, depth is apprehended only in a correlation of "ecstasy" and "miracle" (*ST*, *I*, 113, 117), for these two terms refer to its emergence subjectivally and objectivally. Indeed, the two terms can be defined reciprocally—ecstasy is the miracle of the mind, and miracle is the ecstasy of reality (*ST*, *I*, 117). For this reason every interpretation of myth or cult must take into account both sides of the structural relation. They represent the emergence of depth not only in the world of the people who used them but also in the people themselves as they used them. The recognition of this fact is what Tillich proposes to foster by his conception of the "ontological" type of philosophy of religion.[2] It is the type which interprets God as the depth of the subjectival as well as the objectival sides of a structure. Thus, when man meets God, he does not meet a stranger but "something that is identical with himself although it transcends him infinitely."[3] The historical schools or movements which represent this type are identified by their refusal to treat the symbol "God" as only subjectival or only objectival. Thus, German idealism would belong to the ontological type because it reestablished God as "the *prius* of subject and object" (even though Tillich believes it was mistaken in trying to derive all contingent contents from the Absolute). Pragmatism would also belong here "in so far as it . . . refuses to accept the cleavage between subject and object as final."[4] In short, the principle at work in the ontological type of philosophy of religion is this: "Man is immediately aware of something unconditional which is the prius of the separation and interaction of subject and object, theoretically as well as practically."[5]

Second, the term "structure" in Tillich's usage embraces both the *act* and the *object* of thought. This is especially clear if we

2. *Theology of Culture,* pp. 10–29.
3. Ibid., p. 10.
4. Ibid., pp. 21f.
5. Ibid., p. 22.

look at the original derivation of the polar structure as presented in his *System der Wissenschaften* of 1923. He begins there with the two terms "thinking" and "being." Thinking is the act in which consciousness directs itself toward something, with the aim of grasping it objectively. Being is that toward which the act of thinking is directed. These two terms are subsequently, and deliberately, replaced by two others, "form" and *"Gehalt,"* which not only designate the structural elements of reality but also take on the connotations of thinking and being. They do so because of the relation between thinking and being. For thought, being is not only that which is grasped but also that which resists grasping. To the extent that it is grasped it has form; to the extent that it eludes grasping it has Gehalt. Every reality is always more than what it can be thought to be. Therefore, when the term "form" is used to designate a structural element, it refers both to the act of thinking, insofar as it grasps reality, and to that in reality which it grasps. It is both "forming" and "the form." Similarly, Gehalt refers to being, insofar as it cannot be grasped in the form, and to that which resists the act of grasping. Thus it connotes both the ungraspable "substance" in the form of reality and also the power that resists the act of thinking; it is the act which, as it were, comes at the subject rather than goes out from the subject. Taking the several meanings together, we have "form" used for the act of thinking as well as for the static or fixed element in the objectival reality, and we have "Gehalt" used for the dynamic element in reality as well as for the power that resists the act of thinking. These meanings are carried over into the terminology of Tillich's later writings, so that what he means by the basic structure is not only the dynamic and static poles of a standing structure but also the acts of relating and being related (*GW, 1,* 118ff., 238).[6]

Thus, the self–world structure refers not only to that which shapes (self) and that which is shaped (world) but also to the

6. Ford, "Tillich and Thomas: The Analogy of Being," *Journal of Religion, 46* (April 1966), 229–45, shows how this conflation of act and object also characterizes Tillich's use of "being" (as *ens* and as *esse*).

acts of shaping and being shaped. Similarly, the subject–object structure of reason refers not only to the fact that in all knowledge there is someone who knows and something which is known but also to the act of knowing and of being known. Tillich expresses this fact by saying that the structure of being, with all of its details, is something in which man lives and through which he acts. Such structures "are immediately present to him"; indeed, "they are he himself" (*ST, 1,* 169). In speaking of the basic "ontological structure," therefore, we are referring not only to what is universally implied by the presence of anything in its world but also to the act through which man relates to the world. In speaking of "being," we are speaking not only of what is grasped as objectival but also of the act of being related to the objectival as such.

From this it follows that the depth of the structure is the depth not only of objectivity and subjectivity but also of the act through which a subject is related to its object. The difference between the two is reflected in Tillich's distinction between God and the unconditional. "God is unconditioned, that makes him God; but the 'unconditional' is not God," for the meaning of the term "God" is "filled with the concrete symbols in which mankind has expressed its ultimate concern—its being grasped by something unconditional."[7] The unconditional refers to the act in which the self is unconditionally aware. The term "unconditional" implies the "unconditional demand upon those who are aware of something unconditional."[8] In other words, the "unconditional" refers to the kind of awareness in which the act and the object are one—"awareness of the unconditional is itself unconditional."[9] It is the act which corresponds to the symbol "God," in which the object of the act is objectified. God is that to which the self is related in the religious act; the unconditional is the act of relating and being related.[10] One can express this difference by saying that

7. *Theology of Culture,* p. 24.
8. Ibid.
9. Ibid., p. 23.
10. Tillich stresses the fact that the religious act is an act of the whole

God is the depth of the standing structure, and the unconditional is the depth of the act of structuring and of being structured. But the two are never separable, and Tillich in any case does not systematically employ the two terms to mark the distinction.

In the following exposition I will not make a point of this distinction, but it is to be remembered that "structure" is used for that which is the structure and for the act of structuring and being structured. "Depth" similarly includes both meanings. Thus, God as the unconditional which "precedes" the structure is the depth not only of its subjectival and objectival poles but also of the act in which the subjectival is related to the objectival. In religious language "God" is speaking as well as being spoken.[11]

If God is the prius of the division into subjectival and objectival, then to interpret religious (symbolic) language theologically we must show how that language uses the elements of the structure in order to express depth, or, more exactly, how the structure of language expresses its own depth. Two areas are chiefly involved here. One is covered by the term "God," the other by "revelation." In both of these cases Tillich's procedure is to work out the structure and then to relate expressions of its depth (God, revelation) to parts or aspects of it. His intention is to make the structure "transparent" to its depth and to see what structure is present in expressions of depth. The means by which he does this can be described quite simply. The structure of being is opened to its depth *when the concepts expressing that structure are used as predications of "God."* The structure of reason is opened to its depth *when both sides of its form–Gehalt polarity are used in the expression of revelation* (truth-itself).

---

self, not of just one function. In *Theology of Culture,* he thinks Schleiermacher injured the understanding of religion when "he cut 'feeling' (as the religious function) off from will and intellect, thus excluding religion from the totality of personal existence and delivering it to emotional subjectivity." In *ST, 1,* 15, however, he ascribes the fault not to Schleiermacher as much as to his successors who misinterpreted "feeling" as emotion.

11. Cf. *ST, 3,* 120: "We can only pray to the God who prays to himself through us."

Tillich has four levels of ontological concepts, all of which come into consideration with regard to the meaning of God.

I. The basic ontological structure
"Self" and "world"

II. The elements which constitute that basic structure
"Individuality" and "universality" (individualization and participation)
"Dynamics" and "form"
"Freedom" and "destiny"

III. Characteristics of being which are the conditions for existence
The duality of essence and existence
Finitude and infinity
Finitude in relation to
freedom and destiny
being and nonbeing
essence and existence

IV. The categories of finite being and knowing[12]
Time, space, causality, and substance[13]

The task of theological interpretation is to let these concepts which express the ontological structure also express the depth of being, and to let the symbol for the depth of being ("God") be structured by reference to these same concepts. To do so, one applies polar concepts to God in such a way as to express the fact that he includes and transcends them both. This means that one must distinguish the literal meaning of the concepts from the symbolic ones and also balance the two sides of the polarities.[14] By ascribing both polar characteristics to God without implying a conflict between them, one so interprets the polarities that God participates in them at the same time as he is infinitely beyond them. His participation in them is communicated by our speaking of him as, for example, free *and* destined; his transcendence of them is communicated by speaking of his freedom and destiny in

12. Finitude at this level is determined by the positive and negative sides as present in the categories, e.g. that time is both creative and destructive—it brings the new as well as destroys the old.

13. There are an indefinite number of categories, but these four are theologically significant.

14. Cf. *ST, 1,* 244.

such a way that the opposition between the two poles never becomes a contradiction. "Within the divine life, every ontological element includes its polar element completely, without tension and without the threat of dissolution, for God is being-itself" (*ST, 1,* 243). He is "equally 'near' to each of them while transcending them both" (*ST, 1,* 245).

With the exception of "self" and "world," which to Tillich provide no symbolic material at all (*ST, 1,* 244), this procedure can be followed through the various levels of ontological concepts. *Individuality* and *universality* (or individualization and participation) are both ascribed to God. If he is called the absolute individual, he is also called the absolute participant; "the one term cannot be applied without the other" (*ST, 1,* 244). He is personal, but also a universal presence. *Dynamics* and *form* are similarly ascribed to him—in scholastic theology under the terms "intellect" and "will." Both of them belong to God, the power which breaks through form as well as the form which power is given. Again, *freedom* and *destiny* are both attributed to God. He is free, and he is also his own destiny. To call him free is to say that there is no power outside of him to which he is subject (since the depth of being is the power of being-itself); "that which is man's ultimate concern is in no way dependent on man or on any finite being or on any finite concern" (*ST, 1,* 248).[15] To say that he is destined—or, more exactly, that he "is his own destiny"—is to recognize his participation in the historical and developing aspects of objective being.

In connection with the categories—the fourth level of ontological concepts—the same principle is at work, even where there are special words to serve as symbols supplementing the ontological concepts. The symbol "eternal" is related to the category of time. In ascribing eternity to God, we are relating both the creative and the transitory character of time to its own depth (eternity). God includes temporality in himself in such a way, however, that he is sovereign over both of its aspects. Similarly,

15. Tillich makes no special point of the difference between the adjectival and the nominative forms—"God is free" and "God is freedom."

"omnipresence" serves as a symbolization of the category of space. When it is ascribed to God, it expresses his presence in every space as that which is infinitely transcendent to it. To put it in different terms, a man who says "God is omnipresent" is conceptualizing not only the positive and negative aspects of his relation to space but also his awareness of the depth to which these two aspects are opened. An adversative connotation always seems to be present in such statements. To say "God is omnipresent" implies having experienced the negative and positive aspects of space and having experienced also the power that transcends them. To say "(But) God is omnipresent" is to recall, in the category of space, the experience of ground or depth as over against the experience of structure alone. For the categories of causality and substance Tillich uses the symbolic expression, "the creative and abysmal ground of being" (*ST*, *1*, 238).

With the third level of concepts, Tillich's procedure is to say that God is beyond the dualities indicated there. He is beyond the split between essence and existence as well as that between infinite and finite. His essence and existence are one, and he includes finitude in his infinite being.

At first it is puzzling why Tillich does not allow the same to be done with "self" and "world." Why can this polarity not be opened to its depth by saying God is the self and God is the world? Tillich's reason is that self and world are "kinds of being" (*ST*, *1*, 244) rather than "qualities of being" which are applicable to all beings. For example, every being has both freedom and destiny, but no being is both a self and a world. At the same time, Tillich does not object to ascribing selfhood to God or to speaking of a whole structure (a logos) in him.[16] Nor, of course, does he deny that God is the depth of the self as well as the depth of the world. But if there is selfhood and something like "worldhood" in God himself, why could we not say "God is the self and the world" in the same way that we say "God is freedom and destiny"—he is his own self as well as his own world?

16. Cf. O'Meara and Weisser, eds., *Tillich in Catholic Thought*. Also cf. *ST*, *1*, 251, on the divine "logos" and "Spirit."

To understand why Tillich denies this possibility, we need to look beyond his stated reason and recall that he uses "self" to mean both the element of "self-relatedness" in beings and also "any man." In this latter sense, any man is a kind of being, distinct from all nonhuman beings. To call God a self in this sense would be to make of him another human being. A second unstated reason why Tillich does not use "self" and "world" symbolically is the fact that, since Kant's philosophical critiques, the terms "self" (as the totality of subjectival activity), "world" (as the totality of the objectival), and "God" (as the absolute totality) have occupied a special standing as ideas of the whole. However, Tillich's interest, from his earliest writings, has been to maintain that God is not the whole but the *depth* of the whole.[17] This fact undoubtedly excludes a feeling for symbolic possibilities in "self" and "world." Apart from these two special considerations there is no sufficient reason why one could not say "God is the self and the world" in order to do with the self–world structure what is done with the elements of that structure—to make self and world transparent to what is their depth, and to give structure to that depth.

In relating reason and revelation one follows the same procedure as in relating being and God. There is a basic structure of reason and elements constituting that structure, which correspond to the structure and elements of being. The structure and its elements are present in all four functions of reason—the cognitive and esthetic, and the legal and communal. The first two constitute the theoretical sphere, because cognition and art are the ways in which the subject grasps (receives) reality. The latter two are the practical sphere, because law and community are the ways in which the subject shapes reality. If revelation is the manifestation

17. In his "Religionsphilosophie," however, he does allow for a use of the absolute whole (i.e. the whole which includes subjectival and objectival wholes) as a symbol for the divine depth. *GW, 1,* 334: "Die absolute Synthesis ist . . . unmittelbar betrachtet Einheit des Bedingten; als Einheit des Bedingten aber ist sie *Welt.* Die gleiche Idee kann also unmittelbare und symbolische, religiöse und kulturelle Bedeutung haben; sie kann Gott und die Welt sein."

of the depth of reason in the cognitive function (*ST, 1,* 129), then the truth of revelation is related to cognition as God is related to being.

The basic structure of reason is subjectivity and objectivity. Truth within that structure always means truth objectively or truth subjectively or some mixture of the two. But the truth of revelation embraces both sides of the structure completely. It is knowledge in which the depth of the knowing subject and the depth of the known object emerge simultaneously. In such an act of cognition, the subject is aware of expressing the depth of himself simultaneously with his seeing into the depth of the world; and the depth of the world grasps him simultaneously with his grasping of it. This is the correlation of ecstasy and miracle in reason. "Something happens objectively as well as subjectively in every genuine manifestation of the mystery [i.e. the depth of reason]" (*ST, 1,* 113). Therefore, any interpretation of the truth of revelation must relate it to both sides.

The elements in this basic structure are three polarities—the autonomous and heteronomous, the relative and absolute, and the formal and emotional elements. These are three specifications of what Tillich, in his early writings, called the form and Gehalt (*GW, 1,* 118ff., 238). The first element refers to the subject's conditioning of the object, and the second to the object's conditioning of the subject. The truth of revelation transcends the polarities involved. It is theonomous and therefore includes the subject's action upon the object as well as the object's action upon the subject. It is concrete yet absolute and therefore transcends the alternative of relativism and absolutism. It is rational and yet mysterious and therefore transcends the alternative of formalism and emotionalism. Thus, if "Jesus was crucified" is to be taken as a statement of revelational truth, it must be understood differently than when it is taken as a statement of historical truth. As the latter it would imply that something happened to a man called Jesus, and what happened to him was that he was put to death on a cross. Whether or not he was actually crucified is a fact that can be established, with greater or lesser degrees of probability, in exactly the same way as other facts of historical reporting. But as a statement of revelational truth it would be taken as expressing someone's experience of the depth of his own being and the depth of his world, an experience related to the happening called the crucifixion of Jesus. It would therefore be characterized by both polar elements of reason. It would be absolute and relative, autonomous and responsive, formal and emotional. It would be absolute because it could never be undercut by any action of a subject or any happening in an object, but it would be relative because the concrete terms in which it is couched would not have relevatory power for all subjects. It would be autonomous because it resulted from an act of cognition on the part of the subject—it expresses the depth of his activity or freedom—but it would be responsive or destined because it resulted from a power of depth coming to the subject through an object. It would be formal because all of its objective contents could be objectively grasped, but it would be emotional because its objective contents would be of ultimate concern to the subject.

In the briefest description, then, expressions of depth are related to the rational structure when they are interpreted as expressions of ultimate concern. The truth of theological (or religious) statements can be brought out only when they are interpreted as expressions of our being concerned about that which concerns us, or as expressions of what concerns our being and not-being. "Only those propositions are theological which deal with their object in so far as it can become a matter of ultimate concern for us," and "only those statements are theological which deal with their object in so far as it can become a matter of being or not-being for us" (*ST, 1,* 12, 14). These two formulations state what Tillich calls the two formal criteria of theology.

The correlating procedure takes on additional weight if we emphasize the active side of the relation implied in such terms as "form" and "Gehalt." One relation (Gehalt) is that in which the subjectival is responding to the objectival, and the other (form) is that in which the subjectival is grasping the objectival. In correlating the two, we are bringing together the vocabularies by which we respond to something and grasp something. Thus, "God" and "being" are the two terms by which a relation of the subjectival to the depth of the objectival is actually accomplished. In speaking or thinking the word "God" in its original meaning, a subject is relating himself to the objectival in an action of response to its depth. In speaking or thinking the word "being-itself" in its original meaning, a subject is engaging in an action of grasping the depth of the objectival. The two words represent, as it were, the "routes" upon which the self travels to the objectival. They are not tools by which a subject can refer to realities that he knows apart from them, but the very means by which he is carried to reality. To correlate them means to engage in an action which is both a grasping and a responding—a doubting and a reflecting.

If, then, the first task for correlation is to connect philosophical expressions of structure with religious expressions of depth, the way in which the *Systematic Theology* interprets ontological concepts theonomously shows how Tillich carried out one of the programs announced in his *System der Wissenschaften*. There he had envisaged dogmatics as a synthesis of the mythical and metaphysical (*GW, I,* 279). By myth he meant an immediate form of theonomous expression, and by metaphysics an autonomous understanding. Dogmatics "synthesizes" the two by using metaphysical concepts, as do the sciences, but using them in order to express depth. In the *Systematic Theology* we see the pattern by which this theonomous interpretation of metaphysical concepts is made. Concepts are interpreted theonomously when they are *predicated of God.* Thus, the concept of freedom becomes theonomous when we say that God is free in unity with his destiny. The concept of destiny becomes theonomous when we say that God is his own destiny in unity with his freedom. Indeed, the most fundamental ontological concept, that of being-itself, becomes theonomous when we say that God is being-itself. Such a theonomous interpretation of ontological concepts is more than just a technical device. But if one were to reduce Tillich's procedure to a formula, the *Systematic Theology* provides it—ontological concepts are transformed into theonomous or "dogmatic" terms when they are made predicates of God.[18]

A second aspect of relating depth and structure correlatively is found in the difference between religious and cultural expressions of depth. Tillich's formulation of the relation states that religion is the substance and culture the form of a society. Yet there are cultural expressions of depth, and there are religious expressions of depth. This fact imposes upon theology the task of relating two different expressions of depth. In general terms this is the sphere of theology of culture.

Cultural forms are subjective as well as objective. Their religious substance is also expressed subjectively and objectively. A theology of culture hopes, by analyzing the character of the depth which is expressed through cultural forms, to provide a connection for those forms with direct religious expressions of depth. It provides an intermediate step, at which the indirect expression of depth in a culture is related to the direct expression of depth in religious symbols. The ontological approach to a philosophy of religion is the most embracing instance of this sort of correlation. Hence Tillich can say that it can overcome, as far as "is possible by mere thought,"[19] the "fateful gap" between religion and culture. For if a basic connection between religion and culture has been provided by an ontological interpretation of religion, in which the depth of culture and the form of religion are set forth, then "cosmological principle" can be interpreted to mean that the unconditioned can be recognized in the "cultural and natural universe."[20]

---

18. This feature is just as significant as the "dialectic of affirmation and negation" they exhibit, as Ford, "Strands," pp. 106–13, points out. It is not only the case that polar opposites are always involved in concepts used as symbols, as Ford clearly shows, nor is it strictly the case, contrary to what Ford says (p. 127), that such concepts symbolically "refer to being-itself" or are "applied" to being-itself, but also, and more correctly, that they are used according to the technique I have described: polar ontological concepts are turned into symbols, or symbolically deepened, by being predicated of "God."

19. *Theology of Culture,* p. 29.

20. Ibid., p. 26.

Tillich's theological analysis of culture may rightly be said to serve a religious purpose, but not in the sense that cultural forms are made subservient to religious expressions. It does not demand, for example, that painting be used for depicting the Christ and things connected with him or that philosophical thought be used for defending a statement of the Christian gospel. On the contrary, a theological analysis of cultural forms aims at uncovering the dimension of depth in all cultural forms in order to make religion intelligible to culture and culture expressive of religion.

Culture is, however, historically conditioned. Not only do its forms—such as its philosophical terms or its artistic techniques—change from age to age, but the way in which it gives expression to the dimension of depth also changes. Every identifiable historical era, therefore, has its distinctive expression of religious substance. The term which Tillich uses to designate such a historically distinctive expression is "style." Style is a concrete expression of depth which is characteristic of an age or a group. The concept of style lies midway between "structure" and "depth," for it is a definite structuring of the experience of depth.[21] Its most immediate application lies in the sphere of art, but its broader application is the whole of human culture, including the practical as well as the theoretical functions. It is, in brief, a cultural expression of the experience of depth. According to Tillich's analysis, every work of art (and by implication every product of cultural activity) contains three elements—subject matter, form, and style. The subject matter is what a work treats in one way or another; the form is what makes a work what it is—for example, a work of art or a work of philosophy; and the style is what expresses the common experience of the ultimate as found in a certain historical era or cultural group. Style is the "immediate expression" of ultimate concern, qualifying "the many creations

21. Artistic "style is the over-all form which, in the particular forms of every particular artist and of every particular school is still visible as the over-all form; and this over-all form is the expression of that which unconsciously is present in this period as its self-interpretation, as the answer to the question of the ultimate meaning of existence." Michalson, ed., *Christianity and the Existentialists,* pp. 133f.

of a period in a unique way" and pointing to "a self-interpretation of man" and "the ultimate concern of a human group or period."[22]

The theological importance of the ability to read style now becomes apparent. By being able to read the style of a particular group or period one is able to discover its most immediate expression of religious substance, of the experience of ultimate depth which is manifest both through the subjectivity of the creators and through the objectivity grasped in the creations of that period.[23] By discovering this concrete unity of depth and structure one is able to make a correlation between direct religious expressions of depth and other cultural forms. At a time in history when men have lost an immediate relation to mythical or prescientific expressions of depth, they can understand such expressions and still be culturally creative if they can relate them to the experience of depth embedded in present cultural forms.

Tillich thus analyzes three main forms of culture—language, art, and philosophy. Language, he says, is the basic cultural creation, the expression "of man's freedom from the given situation and its concrete demands."[24] If religion is the substance of cultural creation, then religious language is not a special or supernaturally received language, but human language used to express and communicate ultimate concern, either directly as in myth and symbol or indirectly through its style. Language is not holy itself, but it can become "holy for those to whom it expresses their ultimate concern from generation to generation."[25] Furthermore, if the style of any cultural form expresses an age's ultimate concern, then the style of a language as actually used is the place to look

22. *Theology of Culture*, pp. 42, 70.
23. "If you want to know what is the ultimate self-interpretation of a historical period, you must ask, 'What kind of style is present in the artistic creations of this period.' " Michalson, ed., p. 133.
24. *Theology of Culture*, pp. 42, 47. Cf. *ST*, 1, 170.
25. *Theology of Culture*, p. 48. Cf. his "The Word of God," in *Language: An Enquiry into Its Meaning and Function*, ed. Ruth Nanda Anshen, Science of Culture Series, 3 (New York, Harper & Brothers, 1957), pp. 122–33, esp. pp. 123, 125, 127.

for religious substance or ultimate concern. It is perceived indirectly since it is a quality suffusing the whole situation rather than a part or aspect of the object or subject; but when uncovered, this expression of depth provides an intermediate step to correlating language as a cultural form with language used religiously. Tillich does not provide examples of such linguistic analysis— apart from what is done in the *Systematic Theology*—in as rich a measure as he does for artistic styles in painting. But one such example can be found in contemporary literary style, with its characteristics of economy and irregularity.[26] No writer sensitive to the present era is able to write in a highly decorative and expansive style and still be honest with himself. This stylistic fact is interpreted theologically when it is correlated with such religious language as that which speaks of the hiddenness of God. It is an indirect cultural expression of the same experience of fragmentation or meaninglessness that, in direct religious experiences, is embodied in such symbols as the hiddenness of God.

Tillich's analysis of artistic styles proceeds along the same lines, although it is richer in illustrative examples.[27] All styles, according to Tillich, can express ultimate concern.[28] Thus, in an *imitative* style, as seen in a landscape or portrait, the ultimate is present as "the hidden ground" or the "depth of meaning" in the whole work. In a *subjective* style it is present in the "state of being grasped by the power of being and meaning." In an *idealistic* style it is present as the "potential perfection" which is anticipated and expressed. In a *realistic* style it is present as the "divine–demonic and judging background of everything that is."[29] An *expressive* style is closest to religion because it is the most direct representation of the ultimate itself. Its characteristic

26. See Paul Tillich, "The Lost Dimension in Religion," *Saturday Evening Post*, 230 (June 14, 1958), p. 78.

27. See his "Existentialist Aspects of Modern Art," in Michalson, ed., pp. 128–47.

28. *Theology of Culture*, p. 72.

29. Each of these styles is, first of all, a stylistic element, but in certain paintings certain elements become predominant and determine the style of the whole.

is to disrupt the "naturally given appearance of things" in order to express the dimension of depth, "the ground and abyss in which everything is rooted."[30] Reality is ordinarily experienced within the subjectival–objectival relation—reality is what is experienced by someone. Expressive art disrupts that structure not by destroying objective reality, but by transforming it in such a way that an ultimate depth becomes manifest in the work of art and in ourselves as we behold it. It is, therefore, "essentially adequate to express religious meaning directly, both through the medium of secular and through the medium of traditional religious subject matter."[31] Because of its capacity to express religious meaning directly, expressive art resembles myth and ritual. Its artistic form serves the purpose of pointing to a substance beyond form and content. Myth and ritual in their way and expressive art in its way combine elements of structure in such a way as to point directly to the depth of the structure. Thus, an expressive work of art is for esthetics what myth is for knowledge and ritual for morality.

In the context of the relation of art and religion, the simplest classification of works of art which Tillich uses is based upon "four levels" of the relation of art to religion.[32] First, there are works in which ultimate concern is only indirectly expressed. The style and content of such works are "secular."[33] Second, there are works which have nonreligious content combined with a style that is religious. They deal with "secular" things or events, but they do so in such a way that the style of presentation contains a period's answer to the question of ultimate meaning. Third, there are works which have religious content and secular style. Examples of this group would be Renaissance paintings of the Holy Virgin and the Holy Child. Finally, there are works in which the content and style are both religious. In some periods of history— and Tillich suggests that perhaps the mid-twentieth century is

30. *Theology of Culture*, p. 74.
31. Ibid., p. 73.
32. In "Existentialist Aspects of Modern Art," Michalson, ed., pp. 128–47.
33. Even in this case, however, the style would be indirectly religious.

such a period[34]—this kind of religious art is not possible. In relation to this classification of types of art, the expressive style would characterize the second and fourth classes.

The way in which a theologian makes use of artistic works becomes clear when one looks at specific examples of Tillich's dealings with art. The kind most removed from direct religious expression is, of course, the one which has neither overt religious content nor directly religious style. Tillich adduces Jan Steen's "The World Upside Down" as one work of that type and Rubens' "Return of the Prodigal" as another.[35] He came upon the first of these two in the course of a visit to the National Gallery in the early 1950s as preparatory work for a study on religion and art. He reports that, although he had gone with the intention of looking at religious paintings, he found himself attracted by Steen's "The World Upside Down," which had no ostensible religious content or style. The reason was that, even without an ostensible religious character, the painting did indirectly express an ultimate interpretation of human existence; it expressed "power of being in terms of an unrestricted vitality in which the self-affirmation of life becomes almost ecstatic."[36] A brief analysis of this description of the painting shows exactly how it is drawn into a theological correlation. To say that a painting expresses "power of being" is to discover a cognitive counterpart to its esthetic form of expression. Even more than that, it is to discover the cognitive counterpart in the sphere of the ontological, for the term "power of being" is a metaphorical expression for the concept of being-itself. Moreover, since "power of being," or "being-itself," refers to the same dimension of reality as expressed in religious symbols—the dimension of depth—the cognitive statement of the meaning of the artistic work makes it available for correlation. Another connection is provided when Tillich formulates the substance of the painting as the "unrestricted vitality in which the self-affirmation of life becomes al-

34. "Existentialist Aspects of Modern Art," Michalson, ed., pp. 134, 144.
35. Ibid., p. 135.
36. Ibid.

most ecstatic." An ecstatic self-affirmation of life is itself a religious experience. The whole circumscribing phrase is a statement of what is directly expressed in such religious symbols as "the holy, living God."

From an experience that is esthetic we have moved to one that is religious. An artistic appreciation of a secular painting leads to an artistic experience of the dimension of depth. When translated into cognitive terms, this makes possible a connection with the cognitive symbols of revelation. The result of the whole process is that the work of art and the religious symbols give meaning to each other. What is meant by the religious symbol, "the holy, living God," can be communicated esthetically by the painting; what is meant by the painting can be communicated religiously by cognitive symbols.[37] Exactly the same procedure can be used with any painting that a viewer can appreciate. But the number of steps from the esthetic to the religious would be fewer in cases where the painting is religious in content and style.

A third main form of culture is philosophy. Like language and art, it too expresses a substance and has a style.[38] In asking how the depth dimension of reality and ourselves is manifest in the philosophical work of a period, a theologian again enters upon an analysis of style. Our age, Tillich thinks, can be characterized by a movement and a protest.[39] The movement is that of the spirit of industrial society, and the protest is that of the spirit of existentialist analysis. The spirit of industrial society (which Tillich also occasionally calls the spirit of self-sufficient finitude or the bourgeois spirit) is characterized by a concentration "of man's activities upon methodical investigation and technical transformation of his world, including himself,"[40] which brings with it the

37. The steps by which the move is made from the esthetic to the religious would themselves be at the level of second-order theological reflection. See above, p. 76.

38. *Theology of Culture,* p. 71, refers to Dilthey's classification of philosophical styles: subjective idealism, objective idealism, and realism.

39. Ibid., p. 43. Cf. *The Religious Situation,* tr. H. Richard Niebuhr, (New York, Meridian Books, 1956).

40. *Theology of Culture,* p. 43.

loss of the dimension of depth "in his encounter with reality." In other words, "the system of finite interrelations which we call the universe has become self-sufficient." The spirit of existentialist protest resists self-sufficient finitude; it endeavors to open the structure of being to its depth. In relation to other philosophical styles existentialism is analogous to expressionism in art.[41] It disrupts the ordinary subject–object structure of being, in which man manipulates his world and himself as a collection of objects. It criticizes "the identification of Reality or Being with Reality-as-known, with the object of Reason or thought." Neither idealism nor naturalism is able to protest against the spirit of industrial society because both of them "are creations of that spirit"; they are alternatives within the scheme of an unbroken subject–object structure. Idealism emphasizes the subjectival side and naturalism the objectival side of it, but they do not open the structure to its own depth. Moreover, theology today cannot make direct use of either of them as a tool for its self-expression because "neither of them expresses the contemporary culture."[42] The style of philosophizing which gives expression to the dimension of depth in the present age is existentialism, because it knows how to disrupt the structure.

Interpreting existentialism theologically thus involves the same kind of correlating work as does interpreting language and art—namely, that of showing how existentialism's philosophical form gives expression to the depth beyond the self–world structure. It involves the further task of relating this cultural expression of depth to the directly religious expression of it as found in the Christian tradition. Christian theology, Tillich says, cannot use the material of existential analysis by "simply accepting it" but must confront it "with the answer implied in the Christian message" or with the "symbol in which Christianity has expressed its ultimate concern."[43]

Existential analysis is for philosophy what expressionism is for

---

41. Cf. "Existential Philosophy: Its Historical Meaning," ibid., pp. 76–111.

42. Ibid., pp. 77, 48.

43. Ibid., p. 49.

art. It is the style of philosophical thinking which expresses the dimension of depth, and which therefore provides the readiest point of contact with religious symbols. Tillich's actual work again illustrates this fact.[44] His analysis of anxiety, as distinct from fear, points to an experience of something beyond the subject–object structure. In fear man is related to some definite object. In anxiety, however, he experiences not an object but his own finitude. To analyze anxiety philosophically one must use terminology which normally expresses the structure of being in order to express something beyond the structure, for the experience of anxiety is of such a character that it involves a breaking of the subject–object relation. To be anxious is to have experienced a "nothing" that breaks in upon oneself and one's world. This existential experience is, in the contemporary world, an encounter with what is beyond the ontological structure of self and world.

Language, art, and philosophy are forms of culture with which Tillich correlates the symbols of Christian tradition. There is a fourth cultural area which might be drawn into the same procedure, although Tillich does not do so. This is the sphere of the mythological, if mythology (as distinguished from myth) is regarded as a form of responsively apprehending the structure of reality.[45] That is to say, if there is a basic man–god mythological structure, corresponding to the self–world ontological structure, then there is a mythological expression of depth which corresponds to existentialism in philosophy or expressionism in art. It presents theological reflection with the task of correlating the mythological structure with religious symbols. (The mythical is as such religious. The mythological is a counterpart to the ontological and is only indirectly religious. This is not a distinction made by Tillich, but, as I sought to show in Chapter 3, it is im-

44. See Paul Tillich, "Existential Analysis and Religious Symbols," in *Contemporary Problems in Religion,* ed. Harold A. Baselius (Detroit, 1956). A German translation of it appears in *GW, 5,* 223–36. Other examples are in *ST, 2.*

45. See above, p. 87.

plicit in the structure of his thought.) In such a mythological structure the emergence of exclusive monotheism represents an expression of depth. The god of exclusive monotheism is still mythological insofar as he is an opposite of man, for as an opposite he is still part of the man–god structure. But he transcends the structure insofar as the monotheism is radical or exclusive, for exclusiveness removes him from that position of polar opposition to man. This form of monotheism, therefore, raises a question for theological reflection which corresponds exactly to the one posed esthetically by expressionism and ontologically by existentialism: How is a mythological expression of depth (as the one god) related to the directly religious expression of depth? Exclusive monotheism, mythologically expressed, serves as an intermediate step in relating the mythological structure with directly religious expressions of depth.

Since this form of relating structure and depth is not part of Tillich's own work, nor even included in his expressed intentions, I shall end its discussion with these few suggestions and a formula which would make its execution possible and consistent with Tillich's other works: if ontological concepts are made theonomous—i.e. related to religious symbols of depth—when they are predicated of God, then the mythological gods would be made theonomous (or "ontonomous," to preserve the parallel in terminology) when they are conceived of as expressions of elements in the structure of being-itself.

CHAPTER 6

Question and Answer

Thus far reflection and doubt have been analyzed, together with the correlations deriving from them, by reference to the elements of subjectivity and objectivity in the fundamental structure. The present chapter takes up a description of the problem that accords with Tillich's usual description of his method. He normally describes his theology as a correlation of existential questions with theological (religious) answers. Since "the answers implied in the event of revelation are meaningful only in so far as they are in correlation with questions concerning the whole of our existence, with existential questions," the procedure of systematics must be to analyze the human situation out of which the questions arise and to "demonstrate that the symbols used in the Christian message are the answers to these questions" (*ST, 1,* 61f.). "Demonstrate" is perhaps too strong a term. What Tillich actually does is to place the symbols properly, so that anyone can know what is being said by them. He does not try to prove that they are true. The truth of symbols cannot be, and need not be, "proved." Their truth is their power to lay hold of and transform those for whom they are symbols; it is their capacity to express and communicate ultimate concern. To the extent that a symbol does express an ultimate concern it has truth; to the extent that the concern it expresses is truly ultimate—independently of whether it is at any given time or in any given group acknowledged as ultimate—it *is* true.[1]

How the correlation of question and answer relates to reflection and response or to correlations of structure and depth can be seen if we take into account the character of an existential question, for

1. Cf. *ST, 1,* 240.

what is correlated in systematics are existential questions and symbolic answers. Questions have the characteristic of pointing beyond themselves, as do symbols. Like every question, an existential question is a movement disrupting the object to which it is directed. A question shakes the given structure of the reality with which it is dealing. In this way it is a basic form of critical reflection. In asking a question about this or that, we are calling into question the thing's objective givenness. An existential question disrupts the whole structure of finite being. It is not directed at objects or the whole of objectivity, but to what is experienced in "the anxiety in which [people] are aware of their finitude, the threat of nonbeing." (*ST, 1,* 62). It opens the structure of being to that which is beyond it—its depth, as "abyss" or "ground."

The fact that the question is an existential one implies, moreover, that we do not entertain or theoretically construct it at will. It presses upon us—a fact which Tillich expresses by saying that there is "an unconditional element in the very act of asking any question" (*ST, 1,* 208). An existential question takes hold of us unconditionally; like an objectival subject it engages our attention and elicits our response. We do not decide to entertain it, it comes upon us; it is not subject to our conscious control, it overtakes us. In other words, it is an expression of the power of negativity in the structure of being, which calls into question the being of everything finite. Its proper object is "nothing." It is the negative form in which the depth of being lays hold of us, as that to which we are directed and for which we must seek. It arises from the possibility of not being at all.

In Tillich's usage "question" does not refer, of course, primarily to a grammatical form. It is an act, a distinctive movement of the self[2] in which the self is both agent and responder. In an existen-

2. Cf. *GW, 4,* 107. On the nature of questioning, see further Martin Heidegger, *Sein und Zeit* (Tübingen, Max Niemeyer Verlag, 1963[10]), pp. 5ff., Gerhard Noller, *Sein und Existenz: Die Überwindung des Subjekt- Objektschemas in der Philosophie Heideggers und in der Theologie der Entmythologisierung* (München, Christ Kaiser Verlag, 1962), pp. 15ff., and Gadamer, *Wahrheit und Methode,* pp. 283ff., 344ff., 351ff. "Das Aufkommen einer Frage bricht gleichsam das Sein des Befragten auf. Der Logos, der dieses

tial question our very subjectivity and the very objectivity of the world are disrupted or called into question. Here is the point of contact with an answering symbol. Symbols and questions are both subjective and objective; they both point to the depth beyond the structure. Thus, the "question implied in finitude" refers to a movement of finitude (i.e. any man) in which it relates to what is beyond it, and the symbol that "answers" it refers to the fulfillment of that same movement. The self in its world first looks beyond itself in the form of a question: What is beyond the polarity? This question is implied in finitude itself because finitude is a unity in which being is limited by nonbeing and in which every polar element is limited by its opposite. In essential finitude the question is always answered (*ST, 1,* 252);[3] in "fallen" finitude the question can be asked without being answered, and an answer can be present without having a question to which it relates. An unanswered question and an answer unrelated to any real question reflect the state of fallenness rather than that of essential finitude. But the question-and-answer relation itself is implied in the polar structure of finite being.

The way in which the question–answer correlation is related to the previous discussion can then be stated in four points: Questioning is a basic form of critical reflection; receiving answers is a basic form of distancing response; existential questions and religious answers are movements in which the subject–object structure is opened to its depth, in one case as abyss, in the other as ground; in both cases all elements of subjectivity and objectivity are involved. The correlation of questions and answers is, therefore, a recapitulation of the problems of reflection and response, subjectivity and objectivity.

The question–answer conception of correlation is not only a signature of the whole method of systematic theology;[4] it is also

---

aufgebrochene Sein entfaltet, ist insofern immer schon Antwort" (Gadamer, p. 345).

3. Hence, contrary to Guyton B. Hammond's thesis in *Man in Estrangement* (Nashville, Tenn., Vanderbilt University Press, 1965), p. 20, the root of correlation is in finitude itself, not only in existential self-estrangement.

4. Tillich's last public address, however, suggests a method for constructing

the most direct expression of two periods in Tillich's own experience. The First World War—and specifically the Battle of Champagne in 1915—shattered both his way of thinking philosophically and his own expectations concerning human possibilities. He says of this four-year experience that it opened "the abyss" for him and his generation so much that it could never again be closed.[5] Thereafter Tillich's theology and philosophy had to take account of it. What can be grasped philosophically, and what can only be expressed theologically? At what point does philosophical thought reach the limit of its capacity, and at what point does theology reach its limit and make a juncture with philosophy? Tillich refers to his *Religionsphilosophie* as the work in which he endeavors to formulate an answer to that question.[6] He does so by interpreting the experience of the abyss and the idea of justification through faith as the points marking the boundary between philosophy and theology. They represent the limits of philosophical conceptualization. His *System der Wissenschaften,* which already has been discussed, and his contact with Heidegger's existential philosophy, which is reflected in the *Courage to Be* and in the *Systematic Theology* (especially in Parts 2 and 3), are two further stages of this development.[7] Here, as in all of his work, Tillich's thinking is closely interwoven with his experience. In the conception of the questionability of the structure of being he formulates the experience of the catastrophe of the war. To German intellectual leaders, who were schooled in philosophical idealism, the outbreak of this war was tantamount to an occurrence of something impossible. All of the leading theologians—Barth, Brunner, Bultmann, Gogarten, Hirsch—registered the same shock at its outbreak. This fact is worth mentioning simply because it has no exact equivalent outside the

---

a theology in more direct contact with the history of religions. See Paul Tillich, "The Significance of the History of Religions for the Systematic Theologian," in *The Future of Religions,* ed. Jerald C. Brauer (New York, Harper & Row, 1966), pp. 80–94.

5. *Auf der Grenze,* p. 39. (*Boundary,* p. 52.)

6. Ibid.

7. Ibid., pp. 41f. In Heidegger's philosophy Tillich thought he saw an example of "theonomous" philosophizing.

European continent. It is true, of course, that theology among English-speaking peoples was impressed by the catastrophe of the wars in this century, but it was not so severely shaken in its foundations because it was never as fully involved in the disaster. In part this was due to the more cloistered position of theology in lands outside of Germany, and in part it was due, especially in the United States, to the denominational fragmentation of theological work that prevailed until quite recently.

The First World War provoked a fundamental reorientation of thought and life for Tillich because it presented in an unforgettable way the questionability of being at all. It shook the self-evidence of being with a question that needed an answer, by confronting men with a negative power greater than themselves and their known world. The catastrophe which the war brought was not simply that it exposed a miscalculation about human possibilities in a historical situation, but that it shattered convictions concerning the ultimate character of the power in which men and all beings were grounded. It raised the threat that being human—or that being at all—was an ultimately self-defeating activity.

If Tillich's experience of the First World War was an exposure to sheer abyss—to the unanswered question of the meaning of being at all—his experience of the 1920s was an answer to this question. The war had shattered self-sufficiency, but in the 1920s a new current of expectation made its way through the German intellectual world. The work of this decade was attended by the excitement of a new era, an excitement amply documented in Tillich's writings from this period. The Heidelberg philosopher, Hans-Georg Gadamer, says that the mid-twenties in Marburg were the beginning of an "exciting era of philosophical and theological discussion" ("spannungsvolle Epoche philosophisch-theologischer Auseinandersetzung").[8] Thus, the First World War and

8. "Martin Heidegger und die Marburger Theologie," in *Zeit und Geschichte: Rudolf Bultmann zum 80. Geburtstag,* ed. Erich Dinkler (Tübingen, J. C. B. Mohr, 1964), p. 479.

the 1920s provide the experiential background for the questions and answers formulated in Tillich's *Systematic Theology,* and more generally for the correlation between the activity of questioning and of being answered. Tillich has three main forms of the question (being, existence, life) and three main forms of the answer (God, the Christ, Spirit). These three determine the divisions of the *Systematic Theology,* since the question of reason (*Systematic Theology,* Part 1) is an aspect of being, and the question of history (*Systematic Theology,* Part 5) an aspect of life.

In the first form of correlation, "being" is the question and "God" is the answer. What is meant by "being" in this context is the structure of finitude, and what is meant by "God" is the depth of that structure. Thus, the question of being[9] is the question, What is beyond the polar structure of subjectivity and objectivity? The answer is, God is that which is beyond the structure. To put the relation in these terms, however, is to give only a general theoretical form to a correlation that is existential and religious. The question of being, however it is theoretically formulated, is man's own questioning concerning the foundation of his finite being. It is asked in anxiety and answered with courage, regardless of the theoretical form in which it may be put.

The question of what is beyond the finite structure arises in three ways. First, it arises out of the fact that the structure of being has within itself an unconditional element, that is to say, an element which is not subject to the structure. The traditional ontological arguments for God serve to disclose this unconditional element. Second, it arises from the element of nonbeing in the structure of being. This element also is not part of the subject–object structure, and it too points beyond the structure. The traditional cosmological arguments for God serve to disclose the pres-

9. The "question of being" and the "question of God" are synonymous expressions in that they designate the same question of the unconditional. But, strictly taken, the first is in the mode of reflection, and the second in the mode of response.

ence of this element in the structure of being. Third, it arises from the polarities implied in the ontological structure. The polarities, which are balanced in the whole, are threatened by disruption when they draw apart from each other. The disruption of the structure is experienced as a threat to our being at all. This threat, like the element of the unconditional and the element of non-being, comes from beyond the structure and raises the question of what "precedes" the polarities of being. The function of the traditional teleological arguments for God is to disclose this threat to the unity of the polarities of being. Since Tillich takes the cosmological and teleological arguments under the one heading of the *necessity* of the question and the ontological arguments under that of the *possibility* of the question, these three ways can be reduced to two by saying that the question of being arises from an experience of an *unconditional* element and a *threatening* element in man's act of being himself in his world. Man *can* ask the question because there is an unconditional element in the structure; he *must* ask it because the structure—by which he himself is constituted—is threatened.

Theological correlation connects the ontological question with its religious answer. Both the question and the answer are at hand, one of them in the human situation universally and in such theoretical forms as the arguments for God, and the other of them in the basic symbols connected with the doctrine of God. To interpret material from the doctrine of God a theologian must find the ontological question to which the symbols are addressed. In doing so, he is connecting the acts in which man reflects his own being with the acts in which he responds to the power that sustains his being. This procedure is most clearly illustrated by Tillich's treatment of the categories of finite being and thinking, four of which he finds theologically important—time, space, causality, and substance. What is the form of the question they imply, and which symbols from the doctrine of God answer them? Tillich analyzes them both from the "inside" (from the standpoint of the way the human self experiences them inwardly) and from the "outside" (from the standpoint of their structural character).

Viewed from the outside, time, the "central category" of finitude (*ST, 1,* 193f.), has both positive and negative characteristics. The temporal process brings forth the new and has creative character, but it also takes away the old and has destructive character. This double character raises the question of the ultimate meaning of time. What lies beyond the polarity of creativity and destructiveness? No answer to this question can be derived from the analysis itself; ontology can only "state a balance" of the two sides.

Viewed from the inside, the positive and negative characteristics of finite being are "courage" and "anxiety." As an ontological concept, courage is the inside designation of "being," and anxiety is the inside designation of "nonbeing." With respect to the category of time courage is the courage to affirm the present and anxiety is anxiety in the face of transitoriness (the past and the future). "In the anxiety of having to die, not in the fear of death, nonbeing is experienced from 'the inside.' " The balance between courage, which affirms temporality, and anxiety, which tries to avoid temporality, raises the question of how such courage is possible. Man "must defend his present against the vision of an infinite past and of an infinite future; he is excluded from both. Man cannot escape the question of the ultimate foundation of his ontological courage" (*ST, 1,* 194). He experiences the infinity of the past and future in anxiety, yet he can courageously affirm the present. On what grounds does he do so? What lies beyond the balance of courage and anxiety?

The religious symbol connected with this form of the ontological question is the symbol of the eternity of God. To understand what is meant by the statement, "God is eternal," one must relate this symbolic statement to the question of the foundation of ultimate courage and the ultimate meaning of temporality. The symbol itself, moreover, *is* the answer to the question; it is not a description of, or a reference to, the answer. As Tillich puts it, "faith in the eternal God is the basis for a courage which conquers the negativities of the temporal process. Neither the anxiety of the past nor that of the future remains" (*ST, 1,* 276). When, in spite of his anxiety over the past and future, a man says that he can affirm the present because God is eternal, he is expressing a decision concerning what lies beyond the balance of creation and destruction and of courage and anxiety which categorically expresses his finitude.

Thus, under the category of time, the question of being is, "What is the ultimate meaning of temporality (i.e. is it creativity or destructiveness or something else?), and what is the ultimate source of courage?" The answer, "God," is conveyed by the symbol of the eternal God. His eternity is the meaning of temporality as well as the source of temporal courage. It can serve, therefore, as a negative criterion. Whatever is not able to provide the courage to face the anxiety of temporality is not divine—"only that is divine which gives the courage to endure the anxiety of temporal existence" (*ST, 1,* 274). Conversely, whenever the invocation "eternal God" expresses or produces courage to face temporal anxiety, it expresses or produces the experience of eternity. Accordingly, the questions and answers involved here could be stated thus: What lies beyond the balance of creativity and destructiveness? God, who is eternal, who takes negativity into creative power. How is the courage to be finite possible? There are symbols (such as "eternal God") which convey that courage. Why do we say "God is eternal"? In order to express and convey the power to overcome anxiety and the threat of destruction.

An analysis of the category of space discloses a similar question to which symbols from the doctrine of God are answers. Ontological space includes not only physical location but also "a vocation, a sphere of influence, a group, a historical period, a place in remembrance and anticipation, a place within a structure of values and meanings" (*ST, 1,* 194). It has positive and negative meanings, as does time, because every given space can be lost. Anxiety about having to lose a space is balanced by courage to affirm a present, limited space. This balance implies a question: How is the courage to affirm it possible? "How can a being which cannot be without space accept both preliminary and final spacelessness" (*ST, 1,* 195)? How can man accept his finitude as it is expressed in the category of space? The religious symbol which answers this question is the omnipresence of God. It overcomes anxiety and provides courage. "In the certainty of the omnipresent God we are always at home and not at home, rooted and uprooted, resting and wandering, being placed and displaced, known by one place and not known by any place. And in the certainty of the omnipresent God we are always in the sanctuary" (*ST*, *1*, 278). Tillich's language in this quotation is closer to primary religious language than to theological reflection. To put it more exactly, it is a fusion of religious and theological language, for it simultaneously speaks about symbols and has symbolic power.

Finally, an analysis of the categories of causality and substance discloses a parallel question to which the symbol of God as the "creative ground" is the answer. In the category of causality the ontological question is, "How can a being who is dependent upon the causal nexus and its contingencies accept this dependence and, at the same time, attribute to himself a necessity and self-reliance which contradict this dependence" (*ST*, *1*, 197)? In the category of substance it is, "How can a finite being, aware of the inescapable loss of his substance, accept this loss"(*ST*, *1*, 198)? To say that God is the creative ground of being is to express the ultimate source of the courage to face the contingency and accidental character of finitude.

In short, the question of being is the question of how it is possible for a finite being to accept his finitude, which is identical in content to the question of what lies beyond the polarities of the structure of being. The answer to the question is the power which makes it possible to do just that—to accept finitude. This power is symbolized in "God," or "the omnipotent God," which gives the "first and basic answer" to the question implied in finitude (*ST*, *1*, 273). If we formulate this point in relation to the three ways in which the question of being arises,[10] we can say that the unconditional as a question lies at the end of the ontological argument and the unconditional as an answer is the symbol "God," that nonbeing as a threat to finite being lies at the end of the cos-

10. See above, pp. 141f.

mological argument and that an answer to that threat is "God," and that the possible end of meaning is at the end of the teleological argument and the answer to that end of meaning is "God."

Tillich's ontological analysis, as seen earlier, works at four different levels—the basic structure, the ontological elements, the relation of essence and existence, and the categories of finite being. The categories have been used for a specific illustration of the correlation of question and answer, but the other parts of the analysis are related to "God" in a similar way. Thus, from the ontological elements of freedom and destiny, dynamics and form, individuality and participation, a question arises, because the polar relation, in which each element is balanced by its opposite, is threatened by any disturbance of the balance. Accordingly, there are forms of anxiety corresponding to the threat experienced in the polarities, and there are answering symbols from the doctrine of God. The power to face anxiety about the loss of freedom and destiny is provided by the symbol of God who is his own freedom and destiny (*ST, 1,* 248f.). The power to face anxiety about the loss of individuality or community (participation) is provided by the symbol of God who is a personal God and also the *parousia*—the universal participant (*ST, 1,* 245). The power to face anxiety about the loss of dynamics or form (vitality or intentionality) is provided by the symbol of God who is living, that is, who unites a negative or dynamic moment (*Ungrund,* first potency, meonic freedom) with a positive or formal moment, possibility with fulfillment, vitality with intentionality (will with intellect) (*ST, 1,* 246f.).

The question implied in finitude can be formulated in another way. Instead of asking, "How is it possible to accept what I am?" one can ask, "What is the meaning of my being finite?"[11] The question cannot be answered conceptually because every concept is formed and operative within finitude. It can be answered only symbolically, and the answer to it is contained in the symbol of God the creator. "The doctrine of creation . . . answers the ques-

11. Cf. *ST, 1,* 252. Not, as Nörenberg, *Analogia Imaginis,* p. 81, suggests: What is the *cause* of my finitude?

tion implied in man's finitude and in finitude generally. In giving this answer, it discovers that the meaning of finitude is creatureliness" (*ST, 1,* 252). The situation of creatureliness is the question to which divine creativity is the answer; the meaning of finitude is that man is related to a ground beyond the polar structure. The symbol of God the creator embodies the meaning of finite being as well as the power to accept finitude. If the first answer to the question of being is the power (embodied in symbols) which makes it possible to accept one's finitude, the second answer to the question of being is the meaning (embodied in symbols) which illuminates the situation of finitude. "God is the omnipotent creator" is a symbolic combination of the two answers.

The various aspects of the doctrine of creation express facets of creatureliness and finitude. Insofar as finitude is not only structure-rooted-in-ground but also a mixture of being and not-being, the symbolic answer to its meaning is given when one says God created the world ex nihilo. Again, to say that God sustains or preserves the world is to express "faith in the continuity of the structure of reality as the basis for being and acting" (*ST, 1,* 262). The certainty that finite meaning is fulfilled is expressed in symbols of God's directing creativity (providence) (*ST, 1,* 270).

In summary, the question of being is a movement in which man turns to the source of his courage and the meaning of his being. The answer of God is a movement in which he receives the power to be finite in spite of the threat of nonbeing (courage prevails over anxiety) and the power to see an ultimate fulfillment of his being (meaning prevails over meaninglessness). Theology interprets the symbols of the doctrine of God so as to show how they embody that power. It mediates between the philosophical analysis and the religious symbol by showing the points at which they touch. A philosophical analysis of being yields the question, "What does it mean to be finite?" The religious answer to this question is embodied in the symbol, "God has created all things visible and invisible." In close juxtaposition the question and the answer are scarcely appropriate to each other. "What does it mean to be finite?" does not seem to be answered by "God creates all things." But theology provides a mediation between the question and the answer by showing how the question emerges from an analysis of the structure of being and how the answer is related to the structure. An ontological analysis points to, but can never grasp, being as such; it remains in undecided oscillation between the element of being and the element of not-being in finitude. Does being prevail over nonbeing? Is the ultimate meaning of finitude fulfillment or destruction? These questions cannot be answered by analyzing the structure in which the positive and the negative are both present. But the religious, symbolic statement, "God creates all things," is interpreted as an answer to this question when theology identifies "God" with the power to be. It is a symbolic way of saying that the ground in which finitude is rooted is one which does not destroy but fulfills the finitude of the creature. To say, "I am created," and to say, "I am finite," are not equivalent. The first statement is a religious answer to the question implicit in the second statement. It says not only that I am finite but that my being finite has an ultimate meaning, and it *actualizes* that meaning.

In Tillich's exposition the doctrine of God concludes with another question, which provides a transition to the analysis of existence and the symbols of the Christ. The doctrine of God concludes with a "quest for a doctrine of existence and the Christ," because the possibility of using the central symbols "Lord" and "Father" to express God's holy power and holy love "without rebellion or submissiveness" is "provided for us by the manifestation of the Lord and Father as Son and Brother under the conditions of existence" (*ST, 1,* 289). Existence implies the quest for new being. It is fallen or self-destructive finitude—finitude turned against itself. It moves not only toward its ground and abyss but toward its restoration. It asks not only for the source of courage but for the healing of distortion. To exist means to "be" in such a way that the polarities of the structure of being oppose rather than support each other, and this opposition leads to a situation of distortion, self-destruction, "estrangement." Here the answering symbols convey the presence of new being.

In Part 3 of the *Systematic Theology*[12] Tillich deals with "Existence and the Christ." He moves from the quest for healing to the symbol which embodies and conveys the healing. In the question of being, one asks how to sustain the polarities which constitute finitude; in the question of existence, one asks how to restore conflicting polarities to their state of balanced tension. In existence finite being works against itself because it is separated from its ground. The question is, "How can it be reunited with its ground?"

In selecting material to use for analyzing this question, Tillich departs from his usual procedure. He opens the question with reference to a symbol rather than with a philosophical analysis. The symbol of the fall is an expression of man's existential predicament, of the question that is man himself. What is initially startling in this procedure is the fact that the symbol of the fall and the symbol of creation do not appear to express the same kind of thing. The symbol of creation is part of the *answer* to finitude; the symbol of the fall is part of the *question* of existence. How can one account for this fact? Can a religious symbol[13] express the question as well as the answer?

There are, I think, two ways of accounting for Tillich's procedural variation here. First, in the history of thought the question of man's existential predicament was expressed in symbols before it was conceptualized. Existentialist analysis produces the same result as the symbol of the fall—a disclosure of man's predicament—but the symbolic expression was not translated into conceptual terms before the rise of existentialism.[14] With the help of existentialist analysis, which Tillich calls the "good luck" of theology, man's predicament can be conceptually analyzed.

A second way of accounting for the procedural variation is to

---

12. Which makes up Volume 2 of the three-volume *Systematic Theology*.

13. In *ST, 2,* 30, Tillich refers to it by such phrases as the "Christian symbol [of] the Fall" and "religious symbolism."

14. Cf. Paul Ricoeur, *Fallible Man,* tr. Charles Kelbley (Chicago, Henry Regnery, n.d.), p. 12, where reference is made to the successive transpositions en route from myth to philosophy.

point out a parallel between creation and the fall that is not immediately apparent in Tillich's topical arrangement. If creation symbolically answers the question of what it means to be finite, the
fall symbolically answers the question of what it means to exist; that is to say, it is in part an *answer* to the meaning of
existence. Creation expresses the meaning of finitude by embodying the eternal power of being. The fall expresses the meaning of
existence as a disconnection of finitude from its ground; to exist
means to be separated from God as well as from essential finitude.
But this symbol[15] is different from the symbol of creation in that
it expresses an answer which is a further question. To exist means
to be estranged, but to be estranged means to look for reconciliation.

The question implied in existence is how a man can actually be
what he essentially is. "He asks it, whether or not he is vocal
about it. He cannot avoid asking it, because his very being is the
question of his existence" (*ST*, 2, 13). No man is what he
could and should be. Every man is related to his essential being
as to that which has been "lost." The fact that he *must* ask about
what it means for him to be human indicates that he has lost
his essential being; the fact that he *can* ask about it indicates that
he has not lost it altogether. Here is an existential parallel to the
two types of argument for God. Man must ask about God because
of the threat of nonbeing in the ontological structure; he can ask
because of the presence of an unconditional element in it. He
must ask about his true being because he has lost it; he can
ask because he has not lost it altogether. Just as the depth of
being appears as a question (being-itself) and also as an answer
(God), so the essential being of man appears as a question (the
quest of existence) and also as an answer (the Christ). Similarly,
just as the question implied in finitude is answered by the symbol
of "eternity," so the question implied in existence is answered by
the symbol of "forgiveness" (*ST*, 2, 15), the New Being. If finite

15. Like other symbols of the meaning of existence: "sin," "condemnation," and "wrath of God." *ST*, 2, 49, 76, 78.

man asks, "How can I be what I am?" existing man asks, "How can I become what I essentially am?"

The question implied in existence arises from the split between essential and existential being. It is not directly the question of the ground of the structure of finite being, but the quest for a power that can undo the destructive tendency in the structure. Under the conditions of existence the structure of finitude becomes a "structure of destruction" (*ST*, 2, 71). Thus, the existential counterpart to the essential balance between nonbeing and being is the balance between destruction and healing; "structures of destruction . . . are counterbalanced by structures of healing and reunion of the estranged" (*ST*, 2, 75). What essentially is finitude, existentially is evil—it is both destruction and estrangement; "the transformation of essential finitude into existential evil is a general characteristic of the state of estrangement" (*ST*, 2, 68).

This transformation can be followed through the whole structure of being. The polar balance of self and world in the basic structure is broken as the self fails to bring its drives into a unity and loses its "determining center." It is split within itself and has no unified "world" over against it. "In extreme cases the complete unreality of one's world is felt; nothing is left except the awareness of one's own empty self" (*ST*, 2, 61). The polarity continues to be a polarity even in existence, because anything that disrupts one side also disrupts the other; but it is destructive.

What happens in the basic structure happens also in the elemental polarities of individuality and participation, dynamics and form, and freedom and destiny. In essential being, freedom and destiny are in polar balance, "rooted in the ground of being, i.e., the source of both of them and the ground of their polar unity" (*ST*, 2, 62). In existence, freedom becomes arbitrariness, by not relating itself to "the objects provided by destiny" (*ST*, 2, 62), and destiny to the same degree becomes mechanical necessity. In essential being, dynamics and form are in unity; in existence, dynamics is "distorted into a formless urge for self-transcendence," and the form "becomes external law" (*ST*, 2, 64). In essential being, individuality and participation are in unity—"the more individualized a being is, the more it is able to participate" (*ST, 2,* 65). In existence, the two are separated; the individual is shut within himself and unable to participate. "He falls under the power of objects which tend to make him into a mere object without a self. If subjectivity separates itself from objectivity, the objects swallow the empty shell of subjectivity" (*ST, 2,* 65). The sheer destructiveness of the situation is shown precisely here. The polarities cannot be destroyed nor can they be restored; they are in a state of constant self-conflict.

The transformation of finitude into destructiveness also takes place in the categories of time, space, causality, and substance. The category of time can be used to illustrate all of them. Finitude is essentially a unity of being and nonbeing, but existentially it is a destructive mixture—nonbeing prevails over being. This happens by a divorce from the ultimate power of being. In existence the categories are not related to their ground; they "control existence" themselves. Man reacts to this control first by resistance and then by despair (*ST, 2,* 68). He resists by trying to deny his finitude, but since he cannot really deny it, he despairs. This process appears in his relation to time. Essentially time bears the double character of creativity and transitoriness, but its ultimate meaning is creativity as rooted in the eternal ground. When time is estranged from that divine ground, transitoriness predominates over creativity; without the "eternal now" time is experienced as "mere transitoriness without actual presence" (*ST, 2,* 69). It is seen as a demonic power which destroys what it creates and which must be resisted. Man resists transitoriness by trying to overcome it or oppose it. He cannot accept it because he sees it as a hostile power with which his own destiny is at irreconcilable odds. Yet he cannot succeed in his resistance since he does find himself temporally limited, whether he assents to it or not. This is what produces his despair—he must resist (because transitoriness is hostile to his being) but he cannot succeed (because transitoriness overtakes him eventually). He can neither give up resisting nor succeed in it. "It is not the experience of time as such which produces despair; rather it is defeat in the resistance against time" (*ST*, *2*, 69). Resistance to transitoriness results from what man essentially is, for, though finite, he does belong to the eternal. Inability to resist successfully or to accept temporality results from his estrangement, for, estranged from the power of the eternal, he has no way of taking temporality into himself. "His existential unwillingness to accept his temporality makes time a demonic structure of destruction for him" (*ST*, *2*, 69).

The other categories of finitude express the same predicament. The mixture of being and nonbeing, which constitutes finitude, must be rooted either in the power of being or of nonbeing. When it is estranged from its unity with being-itself, finitude appears to be rooted in nonbeing. The power to which it is ultimately subject is demonic, perpetually self-destructive, as the very concept of nonbeing suggests. Nonetheless, man cannot give himself over to the demonic; he cannot accept sheer negativity as ultimate because such an acceptance contradicts what he essentially is—rooted in the power of being. If he accepts it, he loses himself; if he resists, he also loses himself; but he cannot succeed at losing himself either. "Despair," Tillich says, "is the state of inescapable conflict. It is the conflict, on the one hand, between what one potentially is and therefore ought to be and, on the other hand, what one actually is in the combination of freedom and destiny. The pain of despair is the agony of being responsible for the loss of meaning of one's existence and of being unable to recover it"; it is symbolized in "the wrath of God" and "condemnation" (*ST*, *2*, 75, 76, 78). In a situation, therefore, where part of him —his finitude—appears demonic, man must resist it even though he cannot succeed. This state of being hopelessly divided against himself is the state out of which the quest for new being arises. It is the quest for that which will deliver him from the despair from which he cannot deliver himself (*ST*, *2*, 8off.). The answer which the New Being brings to man is the power to accept finitude paradoxically—to find his being in his existential self-destructiveness. The paradoxical meaning of new being is that the apparent destruction involved in existence is salvation.

Here theology interprets the being of Jesus as the Christ as an answer to the quest for salvation. As in the other phases of correlation, theology does not argue from the question to the answer but interprets the answer received in relation to the quest in which a man is actually engaged. "Participation, not historical argument, guarantees the reality of the event upon which Christianity is based. It guarantees a personal life in which the New Being has conquered the old being," Tillich writes in connection with the problem of the historical Jesus (*ST*, 2, 114).[16]

To the quest for the New Being the answer is the reality of Jesus as the Christ. At some time in the past a man lived, whose freedom and destiny overcame the self-destructive conditions of existence. In history a man appeared who, unlike all other men, was an actualization of man in his essential humanity—that is to say, in his unity with the divine ground. He appeared in history, under the conditions of existence, participating in them and yet not overcome by them. In what way is this man an answer to the quest for new being? How does the fact that he overcame estrangement from within answer our quest? It does so in theoretical or abstract terms, because this one man is also the being in which we participate. He is new *being,* not only one person among others; he is new being, not only *a* new being. To put it thus merely gives a description of the fact that he is the answer to the quest; it does not convey the transforming power of the answer—it *is* not the answer. The answer *is* something else, not a statement but a "picture." "The power which has created and preserved the community of the New Being is not an abstract statement about its appearance; it is the picture of him in whom it has appeared. . . . Through this picture the New Being has power to transform those who are transformed by it" (*ST*, 2, 114). This picture depicts a personal life which undergoes all the conditions of existence but nonetheless conquers the estrangement of existence and maintains unity with the divine ground (*ST*, 2, 135).

16. Cf. "New Being is essential being under the conditions of existence, conquering the gap between essence and existence" (*ST*, 2, 118f.).

What enables the picture to be the answer to existence is its transforming power. The fact that it has this power implies what Tillich calls an *analogia imaginis,* an analogy between the picture and the actual person it pictures.[17] That is to say, its having such transforming power does not guarantee that the details of the picture correspond exactly to the details of the actual person portrayed, but it does guarantee that the whole picture is "an adequate expression of the transforming power of the New Being in Jesus as the Christ" (*ST, 2,* 115).

Thus, theology correlates the biblical picture with the question of existence. The picture *is* the answer insofar as it has transforming power, and theology connects it with that which is to be transformed. But theological reflection does more than connect; it also seeks to clarify how, and perhaps why, this picture is the answer that it is. This phase is brought out when Tillich explains why Christianity could succeed where the mystery cults and Gnostic visions could not (*ST, 2,* 151). He says that, unlike those cults and visions, the biblical picture of Jesus was that of a unique event, in all of its individuality and concreteness, yet with universal significance. A real individuality "shines through all his utterances and actions," and within that individuality his "universal significance" appears. Not only is he an interesting, unique man, but he bears a relation to existence universally, a relation which receives its foremost expression in the two symbols of the cross and the resurrection. The cross expresses his subjection to existence, the resurrection his conquest of it.

The fact that theology can engage in this sort of reflection illustrates the independence of our acts of questioning and of being answered. For a correlation, in contrast to a unifying synthesis, implies an irreducible polarity in our questions and answers, or in our criticizing and our responding. If the picture of Jesus as the Christ simply *is* the answer in the sense that it comes upon a man with the power to transform his existence, then comparing this answer with other possible answers seems to be idle and irrele-

17. Klaus-Dieter Nörenberg uses this phrase as a title for his study of symbols in Tillich. See N. 11, above.

vant.[18] Furthermore, if the picture is effective only for those who receive it as an answer, how can any comparison of it with other answers ever do more than simply restate the fact that the picture *is* the answer because it *comes* to someone as such and for no other reason? Can we ever state why this particular picture rather than another is effective? Tillich's explanation implies that we can, at least within limits. It is possible for us to see that something should be—and theoretically is—an answer even if we do not experience it as an answer.[19] Thus it is theoretically possible to see that the biblical picture of Jesus as the Christ was victorious over the answers of the mystery cults and Gnosticism because of its concrete and universal traits. The criterion implied in this theoretical judgment is that no picture could answer the question of existence if it were not that of a man who existed and represented existence universally.[20] But we would not be able to formulate such a criterion if the question were completely determined by the answer. The existential quest can arise independently of an answer to it, and the answer can come independently of a formulated question. Only when the question and answer respond to each other, or are adequate to each other, can a picture which comes as an answer continue to be received as an answer and a question which is formulated as a question continue to be a real question.[21]

Both finitude as such and existence as such are abstractions from actual life. In the life-process there is a mixture of what is

18. As Barth has often said.

19. Cf. *ST*, *3*, 369.

20. Similarly, Tillich can say in *ST*, *3*, 392, that the symbol "Kingdom of God" *would have no justification if* history meant a sacrifice of individuals altogether.

21. A word might be said here about formulations such as the christological dogmas. They are, in the first place, conceptual translations of the biblical picture. But they, as well as Tillich's reformulations, serve a "protective" purpose, protecting the substance of the symbols but not replacing them with conceptual counterparts. In Tillich's method of correlation this would mean that they guard the symbolic character of the answer (the biblical picture) as well as the conceptual character of the question derived from an analysis of existence.

essential and what is existential. Accordingly, its question combines those of being and existence. In the correlation of life (including history) with the Spirit (including the Kingdom of God), the question asks both for the source of our possibility to live and for unambiguous life. If the question of finitude is, "How is courage possible?" and the question of existence is, "Where is new being?" then the question of life is, "How is life possible and where is unambiguous life?"

The answer to how life is possible is expressed in symbols of the Spirit; the answer to where unambiguous life is found is given in Spiritual acts. Unambiguous life is possible because the Spirit transcends and unites the subjectival and objectival; and wherever the split between the polarities is ecstatically transcended, the Spiritual acts are found. This point can be illustrated by cognition and speaking. Knowledge can reach its object, in spite of the distorting effects a subject has upon the object in the act of knowing it, when the Spirit relates them to each other so that the objectivity and the subjectivity of each is preserved in a higher unity—not a homogenization of the two but the manifestation of their depth. Language can express a union of the speaker with reality when it is the Word of God—that is to say, when it is an act in which the Spirit relates the speaker to the object spoken of, in such a way that he who speaks and what he speaks of are united in the depth of both. As Spiritual language, the Word of God expresses the truth of the speaker as well as the truth of the reality of which he is speaking.

The answer of the Spirit is distinguished from false answers which endeavor to bridge the gap between subject and object by sacrificing one of them to the other. The ambiguity of knowledge can be overcome only in an act that preserves the polarity at the same time it transcends it in an ultimate unity; such an act is Spiritual knowledge. The ambiguity of language cannot be overcome by attempts to use it to give a purely objective representation of objects or to construe it purely as a product of subjective activity. It can be overcome only in acts of speaking in which subjectivity reaches objectivity through the depth of both of them. Neither the subjective nor the objective can be canceled. Even in denying subjectivity, we cannot escape the fact that by making the denial we are exercising a subjectival subjectivity; and in denying objectivity, we cannot escape the fact that if the denial is to make sense at all it must be a denial of an objectival something. Where both are included and transcended, the language is Spiritual.

As acts of the Spirit, knowledge and speaking are a creative unity of several elements, for at one and the same time the subject who is knowing or speaking is also getting known and spoken. First, the subject is not only the agent of his conscious action but also the bearer of the Spirit, who is the Agent acting through his action.[22] Second, he is engaged not only in knowing an object but also in being known by that object (an objectival subject), because the Spirit acts through the object upon the one who is the subjectival subject. Third, the object which is being known or spoken of is not only a single object but the representative of objectivity as such. The Spirit manifests itself as the depth of objectivity in the object. Thus, Spiritual knowing or speaking is a dynamic unity of all these factors. The subject is a subject but also the bearer of subjectivity as such; the object is an object but also the embodiment of objectivity as such; the subject is a subject for an object as well as an object for that subject, and the object is an object for the subject as well as a subject for that object; and in all of this the Spirit manifests itself to itself.

Let us follow this theme further. Knowledge is ambiguous because it misses as well as reaches its object. Tillich refers to this as "the split between subject and object" (*ST, 3,* 70), which is both the precondition and the negative power in all knowledge. The aim and achievement of the cognitive act are always discrepant. It aims at a knowledge of reality objectively, independently of its relation to the knowing subject. It actually achieves a knowledge of reality which is conditioned by factors proceeding from the subject. Tillich cites four examples of this fact.

22. Nörenberg, *Analogia Imaginis,* p. 127, puts it correctly: "Die Ekstase bedeutet ein Durchdringen zum göttlichen Selbst in der Weise, dass, wenn Gott *für uns* auch Objekt ist, er doch nicht aufhört, *in uns* Subjekt zu sein" (italics added).

The first is what he calls the "ambiguity of observation." Observation is the basis of all knowledge, and even at this very basis the ambiguity is already apparent. The observer "wants to regard the phenomenon as it 'really' is" apart from the observation, but in the act of observing the observer also changes the object observed. The result, therefore, is not the " 'real' but encountered reality," which "from the point of view of the meaning of absolute truth" is "distorted reality" (*ST, 3,* 70). This fact, Tillich notes, has always been obvious in philosophy, the humanities, and history; but recently it has become obvious also in biology, psychology, and physics.[23]

This is an ambiguity in the sense that the structure presupposed in knowledge is also the structure that distorts it. In order to know an object the subject must be a subject. Without this basic polarity there would be no such thing as an act of knowledge. Nonetheless, this very structure also results in the consequence that the subject can never completely overcome the gap between itself and the object; it cannot get at the object as it really is but only as it is known. The actual result of the cognitive act is a mixture of the subject and the object.

The term "split," which Tillich applies to this relation, may be misleading. The ambiguous mixture of subjectivity and objectivity in knowledge partially suggests the very opposite of a split—namely, that the subject cannot keep its subjectivity out of the object. If it were able to withhold the formative influences of its subjectivity, it would be able to see the object in its pure objectivity. But Tillich interprets the ambiguity as resulting from the fact that the subject cannot get close to the object itself—hence the term "split," rather than "confusion." If a subject could get close to the object in its pure objectivity, the resultant knowledge, even though it would still be knowledge of an object by a subject, would not be an ambiguous mixture of subjectivity and objectivity but a polar union of them. The knowing subject would be purely subject at the very moment in which the object were purely object, and the two would be in union by virtue of the ground manifest

23. Cf. Noller, *Sein und Existenz,* p. 9.

in both of them. This, however, is the same as saying that the "split" between subject and object characterizes the distorted structure of finite being under the conditions of existence. Insofar as they express the structure of being, subject and object are united in their common ground. Insofar as they express a distortion of that structure, they can achieve their essential polarity and union only by being "healed." The question is, "In what acts is this ambiguity overcome so that the polarity is 'healed' and again transparent to its ground?"

What is true of observation is also true of the other three illustrations Tillich uses—abstraction, forming conceptual patterns, and argumentation. Each of them not only grasps reality but changes it in the grasping.

The same "split" between subject and object is manifested in language. Language not only creates a universe of meaning, and thereby liberates man from an environment, but also "separates the meaning from the reality to which it refers" (*ST, 3, 69*). The mind uses words to grasp objects and in so doing "opens up a gap between the object grasped and the meaning created by the word" (*ST, 3, 69*). Language is ambiguous because in "transforming reality into meaning it separates mind and reality." Where mind and reality stand over against each other without embodiment in language, they are not "split." But the creation of meaning (by which life attains the dimension of spirit) splits the two, since what is embodied in the word is not the reality itself but reality as apprehended. The ambiguity is reflected in many ways, and among the examples Tillich cites are those cases in which language is used in disregard of reality (as in flattery, polemics, intoxication, or propaganda) and those cases in which it is used perversely for the opposite of its essential function (to hide, distort, or contradict rather than to disclose reality).

Like knowledge, language is ambiguous because the act which discloses reality, by embodying it in linguistic meaning, is also the act which hides and distorts it. What then is beyond the split? This is the question which the ambiguity urges on man. Out of the experience of ambiguity the quest for unambiguous life arises, a quest for "a life which has reached that toward which it transcends itself" (*ST*, *3*, 107), a quest for a language which "not only grasps encountered reality" but "is itself reality beyond the split between subject and object" (*ST*, *3*, 70).

Tillich calls the act in which this split is overcome "ecstasy." In an ecstatic experience subject and object are not dissolved into each other but are taken into a union that transcends the "subject-object scheme" (*ST*, *3*, 119) but preserves both subjectivity and objectivity. For Tillich the best example of an ecstatic experience is prayer. In every "serious and successful prayer" a man speaks to God and insofar makes God objective. At the same time, however, God is experienced subjectivally. Prayer, therefore, ecstatically transcends the polarity of subjectival and objectival elements in experience. "We can only pray to the God who prays to himself through us. Prayer is a possibility only in so far as the subject-object structure is overcome; hence, it is an ecstatic possibility" (*ST*, *3*, 120). It includes, as does every ecstatic experience, three sets of correlata—subject and object, subjectivity and objectivity, structure and depth. In transcending the subject-object structure, it reaches the depth or ground of that structure. God, who is the genuine object of prayer, manifests himself subjectivally and objectivally.

Accordingly, Spiritual or ecstatic knowledge differs from "ordinary" (that is, taking place within the subject-object scheme) knowledge in the same way that prayer differs from ordinary dialogue among persons. In an ecstatically cognitive act, the knower not only knows something but is also known—a depth of meaning is experienced objectivally as well as subjectivally. Tillich can therefore say that when God spoke to the prophets "he did not give them new . . . facts, but he put the facts known to them in the light of ultimate meaning" (*ST*, *3*, 127).

Religious or symbolic language differs from ordinary language in the same way. Words which are religious symbols have an ecstatic character. They not only embody an object in meaning but also express the depth both of the objectivity which they grasp and of the subject who uses them. Language becomes the Word of God—that is, religious or symbolic—when and if it mediates the Spirit and has the power to grasp the human spirit (*ST*, *3*, 124). Any word that strikes the human mind in such a way as to create ultimate concern is the Word of God.

Reduced to formulas, the question and answer of life as illustrated by knowledge and language can be stated in the following way. How is unambiguous knowing or unambiguous speaking possible? Because in every finite act of knowing, the Spirit is knowing himself. Where is unambiguous knowledge or unambiguous language to be found? In Spiritual knowledge or Spiritual language, where the acts of knowing or speaking open the depth subjectivally and objectivally. In actual life the answer appears only fragmentarily, only in small areas of life, only now and then, here and there, not continuously and not extensively. But when it does appear, it is unambiguous.

CHAPTER 7

Final Reflection and Doubt

Our central problem—"What certainty can historically conscious thought discover?"—was defined at the beginning of this study, without any special attention to the ways in which Tillich himself formulated it. This present chapter will look at the essays and themes in which Tillich addressed the problem directly.

The cardinal problem for reflection and doubt, for grasping objectivity and responding to power, is posed by the fact that all acts of a subject toward the objectival are historically conditioned. There is no absolute or indifferent position from which a subject can approach the objectival sphere; every position is in part the expression of an ungraspable perspective. Tillich notices that the philosophers (Hegel, Schelling, Nietzsche) who recognized this fact so clearly in the nineteenth century were unable to solve the problem it raises. They recognized the historical conditioning, the perspectival element, in all thought—except their own. They spoke and thought as though they themselves occupied a position beyond historical conditioning. But even though they failed to solve it, the problem they recognized is real and important. What does it mean for knowledge that it is impossible for any man or group of men to gain a perspective upon their own perspective? Does it mean that there can be no certainty at all in knowledge of reality? This question is most acute when it concerns knowledge of what our ultimate concern is. To be mistaken in knowing what is the ultimate reality is to misunderstand and to lose the meaning of one's own being and of being at all; it is more than an error about fact. This is the peculiar pathos of all religious cognition, that truth is salvation and falsehood is loss.

Tillich's statements of this problem and his way of addressing it can be arranged in three steps. First, he sets forth the thesis that every act of cognition is historical, implying a decision in view of the unconditional. Second, he undertakes to justify a given interpretation of history (specifically, the Christian interpretation), for it is in the interpretation of history that historical conditioning turns full-circle upon itself and gives the problem of certainty its final form. We have to do here with a historically conscious interpretation of reality known by historical consciousness. Third, he addresses himself to the problem of the risk of faith, as it is expressed in a decision made unconditionally in view of the unconditional.

In an essay from 1926, "Kairos und Logos,"[1] Tillich makes a basic distinction between two lines in the development of philosophical thought since the sixteenth century. One line, represented preeminently by Descartes and Kant but also by Nicholas of Cusa, Spinoza, Bacon, Hume, and positivism, is occupied primarily with methodological concerns and is closely connected with the rise of modern science. The other line, symbolized by the name Boehme and carried on by the later Schelling, Hegel, Schopenhauer, Nietzsche, and *Lebensphilosophie,* is occupied chiefly with the stance of the subject in the act of knowing; it retains a metaphysical interest independent of modern science. The first line endeavors to understand the world, either by an intuitive–descriptive method as in historical sciences or by a reflective–explaining method as in natural sciences. The second line is interested in the world not primarily as cosmos, but as creation, conflict, and destiny. The first line is interested in the form of everything that is, the second line in the form-creating process itself. The difference between them is focused in their attitude toward time. For the first line time comes into play either not at all or only as sequence. For the second line it comes into play as "qualitatively filled" time, that is, as moments which are "creation and destiny," or *kairoi.* This difference leads Tillich to designate the first kind of thinking as "thinking in the atemporal logos" and the other as "thinking in the kairos." The significance of the

1. Reprinted in *GW, 4,* 43–76. Translated in *The Interpretation of History* (New York, Charles Scribner's Sons, 1936), pp. 123–75.

second line derives from the fact that it has seen something which is true of *all* knowledge, an aspect which the first line overlooks. *All* thinking is at bottom a thinking in kairos.

The logos, Tillich says, always appears in a kairos, "der Kairos bestimmt den Logos" (*GW, 4,* 50). That is to say, truth never stands there pure or naked; it is always there only as asserted by someone, whose act of asserting it also conditions it. To know the full truth of anything, therefore, requires that one pay attention not only to the logos, or the objectival side, but also to the kairos, the subjectival side. To state it more exactly than Tillich does: every truth has, objectively, a form and a content and, subjectively, a perspective and an act. All of these aspects must be taken into account. The act of assertion is made from a perspective, which is partly a free choice and partly historical conditioning on the part of the subject; and what is asserted unites elements of form and content. The logos, then, embraces the form of what is asserted and the (neutral) subjectivity of the act of asserting, whereas the kairos embraces the material of what is asserted and the perspective expressed in the act of assertion. Perspective is to the asserting act what material is to the asserted form.[2] The creative unity of logos (the form of the objectival, the act of the subjectival) and kairos (the material of the objectival, the perspective of the subjectival) is called "concrete decision." Hence Tillich can say that a decision is a position taken over against the unconditional, which is a matter of freedom and destiny and is the source from which knowledge as well as action proceed (*GW, 4,* 57); the creative unity of logos and kairos represents an emergence of the element of "depth," or the "third dimension," in knowledge. It is conveyed through knowing, but it is not the object of the act of knowing; it emerges subjectivally as well as objectivally, through the knower as well as through

2. Actually, Tillich's usage in "Kairos und Logos" does not entirely coincide with these distinctions. Sometimes "decision" seems to mean the perspective of the act, and "kairos" then means the creative unity of logos and decision. At other times, in accord with the title of the essay in question, "kairos" means the perspective of the act, and "decision" then means the unity of logos and kairos. I follow the latter usage here.

what is known. Accordingly, the notion of decision is related to Tillich's ideas of "style" and "norm" in other contexts. That is to say, a "concrete decision" is a historical embodiment of religious substance. Its verification, like that of styles or norms, is not based merely upon logical or kairical criteria but is its creative or destructive power. A true "concrete decision" has living power; a false one either has no power or has only destructive power.[3]

The decisional character in the knowledge of truth is indicated in several ways. One is the fact that any man's range of interest in things is limited. There are some problems, even perennial ones, which do not engage his attention at all; there are others which engage it only peripherally. Again, a limitation is apparent in the fact that not everything can be said everywhere and at every time. There are things which, though formally and materially true, work destructively when they are spoken or thought in given historical situations. For example, there are times when a no, which is only (but always) half the truth of the logos, must be spoken without a yes; and there are other times when it must remain unspoken.[4]

The distinction between logos and kairos is reflected in what is usually expected of a theoretician in contrast to a practitioner. The former is expected to disregard the kairos, the latter to disregard the logos. Yet this is a mistaken division in Tillich's view, because the kairos can never be excluded. The theoretician, as well as the practitioner, is involved in a concrete decision which embodies kairos and logos together. It has been thought that the attitude of a theoretician should be—to use Tillich's formulation—"asceticism" toward the kairos (historical situation, depth of life) and "eros" toward the logos (pure form), and the practioner's should be "asceticism" toward the logos and "eros" toward the kairos, the moment of destiny. A practical man should be in touch with the

3. Cf. *ST*, *1*, 105.
4. Cf. Tillich's reply to Barth, in which he says: "Der Begriff des 'Kairos' bedeutet für mich, dass man nicht zu jeder Zeit jedes sagen und tun kann, sondern dass jede Zeit die Aufgabe hat, den ewigen Sinn aller Zeit aus ihrem Leben und in ihren Worten neu zu schöpfen." "Antwort," in *GW, 7,* 240.

concreteness of the situation in which he is working; a theoretical man should disconnect himself from historical concreteness and address himself to what is generally true. (For clarification one should note that a practical concern with situations does not mean prudential application of general principles to specific cases —a practitioner is not the same as a technician—but a concern to bring out the depth of the situation. A pastoral adviser, for example, counsels someone not with the aim of discovering how to apply a general rule to this specific case but in order to bring about a creative unity of the man's own freedom and destiny.)

However, to associate the theoretician with the logos alone is to mistake the fundamental cognitive situation, for theory too expresses "concrete decision." There is no such thing as an "akairic" subject even in theoretical work. This fact may be hidden in disciplines where subjective conditioning is methodologically excluded as much as possible or in cultures where personal individuality is minimal, but implicitly it is always present because it is contained in the ontological structure itself. It comes to light in disciplines which reflect an interpreting perspective and in societies where personal individuality is acknowledged. Thus the decisional aspect remained largely unnoticed in ancient Greece or in the medieval West because the forms of both of these societies were stable and static.

A decisional element did appear at one point in the medieval understanding of cognition, namely, in the distinction between what is known naturally and what is known supernaturally. This distinction implied that a conditioning perspective, and not merely a formal activity, is found in a subject's act of knowing. What a Christian could know as a member of the community of grace was more than what a non-Christian could know—and he could know it because of where he stood. But the decision which separated the two spheres was not, in the medieval understanding, operative *within* them. Within each of the two divisions marked by the distinction between natural and supernatural every subject was in the same position. Those who received revelation were in a different cognitive position from those who did not, but not from others who had also received it. Among recipients of revelation every subject occupied a nondistinctive (akairic) position toward the object of revelatory knowledge. Knowledge within the two divisions could be modified by differences in natural or supernatural abilities, but there was no perspectival modification.

Protestantism and humanism historically put things on a different footing because their emergence presupposed a recognition of "concrete decision." If the Protestant reformers called for a decision even with regard to the content of revelation, they abolished the medieval significance of a distinction between natural and supernatural knowledge. They eliminated the notion that *within* the sphere of Christian reception of revelation the subject is nondistinctive, or akairic. The division which medieval thought had made *between* natural and supernatural became for Protestantism a division *within* them. Each man now expressed an individual perspective in his own knowing. Humanism introduced the same individuality into natural knowledge, and thus Protestantism and humanism together exposed the element of historical decision in the whole sphere of knowledge, supernatural as well as natural. At least implicitly, they recognized that a subject is not a pure receiver but also a conditioner of objective forms and contents.

Nonetheless, this implied recognition and the question related to it remained unformulated for a long time. And those who did formulate it—Hegel, Marx, Nietzsche—were unable to solve the question it raises. Cognition shares in the ambiguity or *Zwiespalt* of the actual world, not just in the sense that there is a tension between formal and material aspects in an object, but in the sense that there is a mixture of yes and no in the perspective and act of the subject, as well as mixture of positive and negative forces in the form and content of the object. But if every actual knowledge is ambiguous—partially creative and partially destructive as it combines affirmative and negative elements in a unity of perspective, act, form, and content—then is there any certainty in knowledge at all?

First of all, can one even know with certainty that all knowledge is ambiguous? Tillich recognizes the force of this question and undertakes to answer it directly (*GW, 4,* 73ff.). The doctrine of the decisional character of knowledge, he says, courts the same objection as does any notion of the relativity of knowledge. On one hand, if the knowledge that knowledge is decisional is itself a matter of decision—or, stated differently, if the claim that all knowing reflects a perspective is itself the reflection of a perspective—then the judgment that knowledge is ambiguous is itself ambiguous. If this judgment about knowledge is ambiguous, however, then knowledge may not be ambiguous after all. Thus the judgment is self-defeating. On the other hand, if it is not ambiguous, then there is one exception to the ambiguity of knowledge, and not all knowledge *is* ambiguous. Again the judgment defeats itself. Finally, if one says that every judgment is ambiguous save one (namely, the judgment that they are ambiguous), is not the exception quite arbitrary?

The solution to this problem, Tillich continues, can only be that the judgment that all knowledge is ambiguous does not belong to the sphere of judgmental knowledge at all. Rather, it is an expression of the relation of knowing to the unconditional, an expression of a central metaphysical attitude (*Haltung*). "A judgment which is removed from ambiguity, a judgment of unconditional, unambiguous truth can only be the fundamental judgment concerning the relation of unconditional and conditional elements itself" (*GW, 4,* 73). It is not properly a judgment but the "metaphysical meaning" (*Sinn*) of all judgments, expressing the standpoint of "gläubiger Realismus," that is, of the relativism that overcomes relativism (*GW, 4,* 74).

But how does one justify expressions of metaphysical meaning? *That* he must make decisions might be beyond the realm of decision itself for man—the necessity to decide is his destiny. Yet he does decide about the meaning of his having to decide—whether it is demonic or gracious—and this raises the question of how to justify one decision rather than another. The decision whether being human is ultimately destructive or creative may not be one decision in a whole series. But how does one justify it if it is the quality inherent in all decisions and destinies, expressed in the act of deciding (freedom) as well as in the object in view of which one decides (destiny)? If it is, in Tillich's term, a "transcendent decision," can it be justified or altered or criticized? Here the discussion "Kairos und Logos" leads into that of a "theological circle" in Tillich's later systematic thought.

One justification for "a theological circle" is its creative power. It is not verified as a single item of knowledge but as the power of a whole system of thought to illuminate reality and engage subjectival attention. However, this is not a sufficient answer because competing systems cannot be weighed against each other on that basis. The question, therefore, becomes preeminent when it deals with universal interpretations of history. Not only does the historical dimension so embrace all dimensions of being that an answer to its meaning is also an answer to the "universal meaning of being" (*ST, 3,* 350), but any interpretation of the meaning of historical being turns the problem of perspectival conditioning upon itself.

How does one adjudicate among competing historical interpretations, each of which has power to illuminate (for some people) and to engage attention (for some people)? Tillich addresses himself to this question in the *Systematic Theology* when he asks how it is possible to answer the question of the meaning of history (*ST, 3,* 349ff.). An objective answer is not possible, he says, in any "detached, scientific sense" because it is precluded by "the subject–object character of history" (*ST, 3,* 349). One can understand history only insofar as one is involved, as a subject, in historical action. The only way to understand the meaning of history itself—not of this or that particular history—would be to participate in historical action purely. But this is exactly the problem. Which historical activity actually is historical action itself? Which interpretation opens the true meaning of history? If activity is the key to understanding, then there are as many interpretations of history as there are types of historical activity. Which of them provides the meaning of history itself?

For particular groups the key is found in what Tillich calls their vocational consciousness. In Aristotle's *Politics,* for example, vocational consciousness is expressed by the contrast between Greek and barbarian; in Jewish prophetic literature it is the establishment of Yahweh's rule over all nations. Within its own circle, each vocational consciousness might be able to provide a universal interpretation of history. But how does one decide among the various types and the corresponding interpretations? A criterion is needed by which to judge which of the many interpretations is the true, or at least the truest, one; yet every criterion already expresses an interpretation, and the result is that, no matter which is selected as the key, it can be justified only because it has been presupposed. This, Tillich notes, is an unavoidable consequence of the "theological circle." Answers to ultimate questions are explications of a criterion but not demonstrations of its validity. The meaning of history and the criterion for judging that meaning are experienced in one and the same act—"the affirmation of the vocational consciousness in a definite historical group and the vision of history implied in this consciousness go together" (*ST*, *3*, 349).

If interpretations of history, and the criterion for judging the true interpretation, are derived from vocational consciousness, and if, for Christian vocational consciousness,[5] the meaning of history is the symbol "Kingdom of God," can one never ask the Christian theologian "*Is* this the true meaning?" If this question cannot be asked, the consequence seems to be that the only confirmation for the assertion is the fact that it is asserted.

Tillich does not want to stay at this point since he does grant the possibility of testing the Christian assertion on the part of a theologian (*ST*, *3*, 350). It must be possible, therefore, to ask, "*Is* the Kingdom of God the meaning of history as a Christian asserts?" This question is not taken seriously if one endeavors to reply to it by resignation to a circle of "commitment." It may well be the case—indeed such is implied in the very notion of "theo-

5. "In the Christian vocational consciousness, history is affirmed in such a way that the problems implied in the ambiguities of life under the dimension of history are answered through the symbol 'Kingdom of God'" (*ST*, *3*, 349).

logical circle"—that one does find the Kingdom of God an answer to the question of the meaning of history. But the fact that one finds it so, or that the whole Christian community finds it so, or even that the whole human race might find it so, still does not answer the question or remove its seriousness. Even if it were true —and, of course, it is not—that in all time past, up to the very moment of writing or reading this sentence, every human being had agreed, "The Kingdom of God *is* the answer to the meaning of history and of being universally," it would be no guarantee that tomorrow there would not be someone to demur. An absolute certainty cannot be provided by any number of finite instances, however large.

In other words, to say that interpretations of history are finally expressions of faith only pushes the question a step farther back. The Kingdom of God may symbolize the Christian answer, but there are people of other faiths for whom the symbol is not the answer. Thus, although one can validate an interpretation of the meaning of history, and of being universally, by reference to a theological circle based upon primary religious symbols, the question of adjudicating among those symbols still remains in force. One can still ask whether the religious symbol, Kingdom of God, by which a historical interpretation is ultimately justified, is truer than another religious symbol. And what if it is not? With this we come to the question of the "risk of faith."

Tillich's notion of the theological circle, upon which historical interpretation is based, cannot give a final answer to the question of truth. It leaves open the possibility that the circle may be a distortion rather than an expression of truth itself. We must therefore ask about the risk of being wrong in the reception of final revelation. As Tillich observes, a mistake with regard to revelation is not just an error but "heresy," in the sense that it expresses a turning away from "the true to a false, idolatrous concern,"[6] the consequences of which are destructive. Where final revelation is received, everything is risked.

6. *Dynamics of Faith*, p. 26.

For Christian faith the final revelation is Jesus as the Christ; "the Kairos which was fulfilled in him is the constellation of final revelation" (*ST*, *1*, 136). The risk implied in saying this can be expressed as a question, "What if this is *not* really final revelation?" Such a risk cannot be removed by reference to the claim that this revelation is final, for, as Tillich notes, the definition of what is final in revelation is itself circular—final revelation is final for those who receive it as final. Essentially *every* actual revelation is final (*ST*, *1*, 132) because the one who has received it as revelation has received it as an expression of the truth concerning his being and all being. In this regard Christian revelation is exactly on a par with any revelation. In claiming that the revelation given in Jesus as the Christ is final and unsurpassable, Christianity is claiming that through this event it has in fact received the revelation upon which it is founded. But every recipient of revelation will make an identical claim concerning what he has received. Do we have any way of determining whether the revelation received as final is indeed final? If we cannot know whether revelation is final, can we at least know that we do not need to know it? Do we have a way of testing which of the many claims to finality are genuine or of knowing whether any revelation is even final? Are they all genuine simply on the basis of their claim to be? Can one settle for an indifferent or a generous tolerance, an easy to-each-his-own?[7]

This last possibility seems to be ruled out by the character of final revelation. As revelation, truth is not only final for those who have experienced it as final but also universal in its significance, a criterion of all revelation, judging other revelations by reference to itself. It is not content to be indifferent to other experiences of revelation by other people; rather, it claims to be that toward which all revelatory experiences are driving. In the actual historical situation, therefore, we do not find reciprocal tolerance but competing claims of revelations, each of them judging others by itself.

7. Cf. *Dynamics of Faith*, p. 123, where Tillich asks: "Must the encounter of faith with faith lead either to a tolerance without criteria or to an intolerance without self-criticism?"

Again, the question of which one is really final cannot be answered by working out in advance a criterion of revelation and then applying it to the many actual revelations since the criterion of revelation can be derived only from what someone already considers to be final revelation. Christianity thus derives its criterion from what it considers to be final, namely, the manifestation of Jesus as the Christ. This process mirrors the "circular character of systematic theology" which is a "necessary expression of its existential character" (*ST, 1,* 135). But if this is taken as a starting point, can we, following Tillich's description, ever find it possible to overcome the viciousness of circularity, to discover not whether this or that is our conviction but whether our conviction is true? Can we reach a point where there is an answer to the question, "What if Christianity has been wrong in saying that Jesus is the Christ?"

Tillich's answer to this is twofold. In the first place, the affirmation that Jesus is the Christ moves in a theological circle and means only that those who have received final revelation through him have received it through him and not through another. It does not say anything about whether they were mistaken in what they considered to be final.[8] Neither the reception nor the criticism of a revelation can escape the circle. Receiving revelation—i.e. being grasped by a symbol or responding to a power acting upon the self —is correlative to criticizing revelation—i.e. reflecting what the revelation is. Thus, to be grasped by something as revelation and to judge that it is final revelation express the stances of the self toward the objectival, in one case as power (subjective) and in the other as object (objective). Both are still in the theological circle since the criterion by which the self judges is derived from the substance received.

The circularity is not broken by Tillich's description of the content of the affirmation that Jesus is the Christ. This content has two sides to it. On one side, to take the appearance of Jesus the Christ as revelation only expresses the foundation of Christian

8. Cf. *ST, 3,* 269.

faith, which is validated circularly, either concretely in the New Testament picture or abstractly as a principle. The abstract principle states that a revelation is final "if it has the power of negating itself without losing itself" (*ST*, *1*, 133). The concrete picture portrays a man who sacrifices himself as Jesus to himself as the Christ, one who negates himself without losing himself. "All reports and interpretations of the New Testament concerning Jesus as the Christ possess two outstanding characteristics: his maintenance of unity with God and his sacrifice of everything he could have gained for himself from this unity" (*ST*, *1*, 135).

On the other side, the principle or picture of final revelation is universally valid, the "criterion of every revelation . . . of every religion and of every culture, not only of the culture and religion in and through which it has appeared" (*ST*, *1*, 137). Though it is something that the Christian receives as a Christian, it is nonetheless meant to be valid for mankind and for being universally. Tillich is explicit on this point: "Nothing less than this should be asserted by Christian theology" (*ST*, *1*, 137; *3*, 367f.). And Christianity asserts it because Jesus as the Christ stands the double test of finality—unity with the ground of being and sacrifice of himself as Jesus to himself as the Christ. Similarly, in making its claim that it has the key to interpreting history, Christianity cannot "overlook the fact that there are other interpretations of history which make the same claim for another central event" (*ST*, *3*, 367). It is not enough simply to make the claim in daring faith; theology must also show that the question of history has not been answered by any of the other claimed centers. For this reason Tillich briefly surveys the possibilities and concludes that "the only historical event in which the universal center of the history of revelation and salvation can be seen—not only for daring faith but also for a rational interpretation of this faith—is the event on which Christianity is based" (*ST*, *3*, 368).

That the "rational interpretation" does not escape the circularity any more than daring faith does can be shown by the following consideration. Jesus stands the double test of finality, Tillich says. But could he do otherwise? If the criterion of finality is derived from him in the first place, under what conditions could he possibly fail to stand the test of the criterion? If the criterion of finality is what it is (unity with God, self-sacrifice) because it is derived from the New Testament picture of Jesus as the Christ, how could the New Testament picture of Jesus as the Christ possibly fail to meet the criterion? Again, a survey of possibilities shows that what Christianity claims for its interpretation of history is true, Tillich says. But if the survey itself has to be conducted within a perspective, has it done any more than justify a claim by presupposing it? It may show why a person thinks something to be true, but does it show that what he thinks to be true is true?

The questions, related as they are to one set of Tillich's formulations, seem only to confirm that a theological circle is vicious. The problem need not invalidate a systematic theology, if such a theology is taken as no more than a methodical exposition of the contents of the Christian faith for the Christian church, but it cannot be avoided once one asks the question of truth at large. And—at least indirectly—Tillich does face it when he gives his other, noncircular answer in his description of the life and death of religious symbols and of the significance of the symbol of symbols, the cross. In *Dynamics of Faith* he raises the question of the truth of faith and its criteria.[9] Since it is an expression of ultimate concern or of revelation, faith has a truth distinct from scientific, historical, or philosophical truth. But it does express truth and it does have criteria, which are of two sorts, corresponding to what Tillich calls the subjective and the objective sides. From the subjective side a statement or symbol is true "if it adequately expresses an ultimate concern."[10] For Christianity this would mean that the New Testament picture of Jesus as the Christ is true if it does mediate final revelation. If this is indeed the picture through which Christians have encountered the ultimate meaning of being, then the picture is true from the subjective side. From the objective side a symbol is true if its content is really what it claims

9. Pp. 95ff.
10. *Dynamics of Faith*, p. 96.

to be—ultimate. For Christianity this would mean that the symbol of final revelation, Jesus as the Christ, is objectively true if Jesus is indeed the Christ, not just because Christians consider him to be.

The subjective criterion corresponds to the criterion operative within a circle of faith. A symbol is true if it has the power "of expressing an ultimate concern in such a way that it creates reply, action, communication."[11] That the symbol of Jesus as the Christ is true within the Christian church means that it is capable of creating a reply to itself as ultimate, that it can engender action, and that it is capable of communicating ultimate concern to those for whom such concern has, as it were, faded. But the life of symbols is limited. Not only do those symbols which are effective for some people leave others unaffected, but those which in the past have moved people may cease to do so. This criterion, therefore, cannot answer the question whether the symbols to which someone has responded heretofore will continue to have engaging power, nor can it say whether the symbols which elicit response from Christians can also engage men everywhere. Both of these questions can be answered only if there is a way of determining whether the content of any given ultimate concern is truly ultimate.

This leads to the objective criterion. How does one tell whether the content of an ultimate concern is really ultimate, or whether it is idolatrous? Tillich answers again with the abstract principle that appears in his systematics: "That symbol is most adequate which expresses not only the ultimate but also its own lack of ultimacy."[12] The important question, however, is whether this principle is simply a restatement of what is concretely contained in the ultimate concern of a Christian—as the formulations of the *Systematic Theology* adduced above suggest—or something more. Tillich indicates that it is more when he writes, "The event which has created this symbol has given the criterion by which the truth of Christianity, as well as of any other religion, must be judged. The only infallible truth of faith . . . is that any truth of faith

11. Ibid.
12. Ibid., p. 97.

stands under a yes-or-no [yes-and-no] judgment." It contains a yes because it "does not reject any truth of faith in whatever form it may appear in the history of faith," and it contains a no because "it does not accept any truth of faith as ultimate *except the one that no man possesses it*."[13] If this is true, then the symbol of the cross is an objective criterion in the sense that its validity is independent of its derivation, and its truth can be tested outside the circle of its first efficacy. Of course, this does not mean that the New Testament picture does in fact communicate and express men's ultimate concern to all men everywhere, for obviously there are countless people who do not respond to this picture. What it does mean is that a person's acknowledgment of the final criterion does not depend upon whether he is responsive to Christian symbols.

How this can be so is suggested by Tillich's statements concerning the risk and the absolute certainty of faith. "The risk of failure, of error and of idolatrous distortion," he writes, "can be taken because the failure cannot separate us from what is our ultimate concern."[14] The absolute certainty and the absolute content of faith are that in relation to the ultimate we are always receiving and never giving, and that in the picture of the Christ the criterion against its own idolatrous abuse is given.[15] These statements formulate the experience of an absolute certainty which breaks through the circularity of perspective and content, a certainty which can be final not because it represents an unshakable conviction on someone's part but because it exposes knowledge of a reality which by its nature cannot be superseded. What this entails can be seen by a comparison with Hegel's absolute whole.

We can begin by taking note of the difficulty presented by circular systematic thought. Even if, as in Hegel, a system is able to take account of positive and negative content in a universal scope, it is frustrated by its inability to get a perspective on its own perspectival conditioning of that content. The final justification for its norms rests with the thinker who makes the construction. This problem

13. Ibid., p. 98. (Italics added.)
14. Ibid., p. 105.
15. Ibid., p. 104.

would be soluble if one could attain an absolute perspective on all perspectives and actually reflect the whole, but Hegel's system has shown that one cannot. Tillich, unlike Hegel, saw a different solution. One cannot reach an absolute perspective, but one can accomplish the same purpose by taking account of a perspective which radically negates the perspective expressed in the systematic thought itself. If it is possible to show that an affirmation which defines the systematic circle is not undermined by its negation, then the viciousness of the circularity is broken. In this case the perspective anticipates its negation by another perspective and thereby *anticipates all possible perspectives.* If such a point can be reached, Hegel's insoluble problem is attacked from a different direction and no longer remains insoluble in principle; the whole can be known, not by positive construction, but by anticipation of its negation.

Tillich's theological system can serve as an example. The theological circle is defined for him by the affirmation that Jesus is the Christ. The statement that he is the Christ means that he has been received as the Christ by the Christian church, and there is no way of validating the truth of the claim apart from that situation. It cannot receive any further justification because it does not need it (for those who accept it as ultimate) and it cannot be given any (for those who do not accept it as ultimate). The affirmation that Jesus is the Christ expresses a perspective from which everything else is seen and on which one cannot get a further perspective. But one can express its negation by taking the claim that Jesus is *not* the Christ as the definition of another, opposite, and, in its own circularity, equally ultimate perspective. The opposition between these two perspectives (which is an expression of historical ambiguity itself) can be transcended only if the affirmation and the denial confirm rather than destroy each other. If the affirmation that Jesus is the Christ and the symbol of the cross which stands behind it are indeed absolutely certain, and not just certain within a theological circle, then the act and content of the affirmation and the response and object of the symbol are of such a character that they include their own denials—they are not invalidated but confirmed by their opposites. That is to say, the claim that Jesus is the Christ would anticipate, and be supported by, the claim that he is not the Christ.

If the truth of a symbol generally is its power to elicit a free response from the self, the truth of the Christian symbol of the cross is its continuing power to elicit such free responses.[16] However, this cannot be its final, certain truth because there is no way of knowing whether it will continue to have such power and whether the man who does respond is closer to or farther from the ultimate truth than the man who does not. On the contrary, the symbol can be absolutely certain only insofar as it anticipates and includes the situation in which it does not have power to elicit free response. A person who has once been engaged by the symbol will then also know a truth that holds good even if he ceases to respond to this symbol in the future or if he encounters others who are not responsive to it. The circularity of symbol-response is broken from within. Similarly, if the truth of a fundamental principle is the fact that it can organize all content from the one perspective it expresses, then the truth of the Christian affirmation that Jesus is the Christ is its continuing ability to interpret the content of experience meaningfully. But this truth is not absolutely certain because there are other statements of perspective and there is no way of knowing which, if any, of the competing ultimates will turn out to be the real ultimate. The truth can be absolutely certain only if it anticipates its negation by another perspective in such a way that the negation will support rather than undermine what it says.

This sort of paradoxical point is what Tillich suggests by his references to an absolute certainty and absolute content of faith.[17] The content is absolute not because it expresses a theological circle but because it can break out of circularity. The paradoxical

16. Cf. Paul Tillich, "The Theology of Missions," in *Witness to a Generation: Significant Writings from* Christianity and Crisis (*1941–1966*), ed. Wayne H. Cowan (Indianapolis, Bobbs-Merrill Co., 1966), pp. 83–90.

17. Barth seems to reach the same point, though by a different route, in his *Christ and Adam: Man and Humanity in Romans 5*, tr. T. A. Smail (New York, Harper & Brothers, 1956), pp. 75, 77 ("the Jews, when they condemned Christ to a sinner's death, were in fact carrying out the good, right-

character of what is expressed in the cross, the revelation of Jesus as the Christ, is what makes the symbol "universal without being heteronomous" (*ST, 1*, 134), for it is able to allow its negators to be negators and to accept their truth even when it cannot see it as truth.

Thus, the position which is expressed epistemologically in self-transcending relativism, theologically in the idea of God beyond the God of theism, philosophically in "gläubiger Realismus," and religiously in the symbol of the cross, provides Tillich's first and final answer to the question of how it is possible to know for certain what the meaning of historical being, and of being universally, is. Historical being is characterized by the fact that every self, every man as he says "I," stands alone, always implicitly if not always explicitly, and unconditionally responsible for his assertion of what is true, and also by the fact that he may be wrong, that the "decision" implied in his knowing may be at bottom a decision against the truth. The answer to the problem this situation poses is that ultimate meaning is grace, paradoxically experienced and known. The fact that every man is unconditionally responsible and that he inevitably decides for or against truth itself is answered only by the paradoxical experience that even a denial of truth confirms truth itself; in other words, in one way or another every man lives in truth and therefore in grace. To reflect and respond to the object and presence named "Jesus as the Christ" is to know this certainty.

Such a paradoxical experience and the certainty it communicates is the root of courage for any man to stand alone in responsibility, without the excuse of human frailty or the consolation of his fellowmen, responsive to the unconditional as God and seeking the unconditional as being. Indeed, it would scarcely be possible for anyone sensitive to the possibility of idolatry and falsehood to be either a philosopher or a theologian if he did not have a way of answering the question, "What if theology is a

---

eous and merciful will of God"), and in his *Kirchliche Dogmatik, 2*, Pt. 2, (Zollikon–Zürich, Evangelischer Verlag, 1959) pp. 508–63, esp. pp. 557, 559.

denial of God and philosophy an affirmation of nothing?" Faith, Tillich said in a memorable passage,

> comprises both itself and the doubt of itself. The Christ is Jesus and the negation of Jesus. Biblical religion is the negation and the affirmation of ontology. To live serenely and courageously in these tensions and to discover finally their ultimate unity in the depths of our own souls and in the depth of the divine life is the task and the dignity of human thought.[18]

18. *Biblical Religion*, p. 85.

CHAPTER 8

Concluding Evaluation

In the preceding chapters the method of constructive analysis was used to examine Tillich's answer to the question which arose from speculative idealism in the nineteenth century. Where is the presence of God himself, and what object embodies being-itself? What presence or object can escape the dissolving power of critical reflection and doubting response? We noted that Tillich's solution resulted from his recognizing that such a presence and object is found only in a paradoxical reality. It cannot be found in a whole universe, since the man who constructs such a universe in a system of thought cannot be included in it himself. Neither can it be found in a sacral entity, such as a holy book, since there is nothing that permanently escapes being reflected or doubted. A second part of the solution resulted from Tillich's recognition of the correlation between a paradoxical presence and a paradoxical object, and between critical reflection and doubting response.

In both parts of the solution Tillich differs from speculative idealism. The late Schelling, who spoke of the self which posits itself as posited-by-another, came very close to this paradoxical and correlative conception.[1] Yet he was too firmly caught in the idealist form of speculation to notice that thought is not only reflective but also responsive. The speculative self can *posit* reality, it can even posit itself as having-been-posited (that is, it can posit its own contingency), but it does not *respond* to the presence of reality in an equally fundamental way. If responsive and reflective thinking are equally original, as Tillich recognized them to be,

1. See Schulz, *Die Vollendung*, p. 291: out of the ecstatic transcendence, in which it knows it cannot posit itself to itself, the self recognizes that it has "always already returned." Cf. pp. 55, 123.

then the self's relation to reality is not only one of speculatively mediating objectivity but also one of responding to power. Consequently, the circle of reflection must be left open because there is always a presence to which the self must respond when the presence discloses itself.

Tillich also differs from the "dialectical" theologians of the 1920s.[2] Dialectical theology must be credited with having discovered the alternative to speculative idealism, at least as far as the history of theology is concerned; it formulated a conception of the christological paradox and recognized that thinking is responsive as well as reflective. But Tillich was the one who recognized the *interdependence* of reflective and responsive thought, which led to the method of correlation. In the dialectical theologians, by contrast, one sees a constant tendency to subordinate objectifying thought to responsive thought. Such a subordination, however, ultimately incurs the same error as speculative idealism, only in an opposite way.

Thus, Hegel is the preeminent symbol of the idealist problem, because in his system there is no longer a gap between what one does think and what one ought to think, or between thinking and reality; there is no standpoint from which the absolute whole can be criticized; the whole just *is*. Barth quite rightly refers to such a system as a philosophy of self-confidence, which rests upon the full coincidence of the act of thinking and the content of thought —the "völlige Gegenwart des von ihm Gedachten in seinem Denken" and the "völlige Gegenwart seines Denkens in dem von ihm Gedachten."[3] But one runs into exactly the same problem if one simply inverts the relation between reflection and response, as Brunner does in *Die Mystik und das Wort* as well as in *Wahr-*

2. By dialectical theologians I mean not only the founders and editors of *Zwischen den Zeiten* (1922–33)—Karl Barth, Eduard Thurneysen, Georg Merz, and Friedrich Gogarten—but also such like-minded theologians as Emil Brunner and Emanuel Hirsch.

3. *Die protestantische Theologie im 19. Jahrhundert* (Zollikon-Zürich, Evangelischer Verlag, 1952), p. 349. Cf. Gotthard Günther, *Idee und Grundriss, 1*, p. 45, and passim.

heit als Begegnung, and as Barth does in the prolegomena of his *Kirchliche Dogmatik.*[4]

If the main objection to Hegel's system is that it allows no further perspectives—it is post-historical, in that sense—the same criticism can be directed at a theology in which a responsive relation to the God of the Bible is also post-historical. In an absolute speculative system one cannot distinguish between what I do think and what I should think about anything; the gap between essence and existence is eliminated. But can one distinguish in dialectical theology between the word to which I do respond and the word to which I should respond? Or is it not the case that if reflection is subordinate to an obedient response, then the fact that I do respond to a biblical word is itself the only warrant of its truth, just as the fact that I do think something is, in Hegel's absolute system, the sole and sufficient warrant of its truth? Barth and Brunner insist that our response to the biblical word must continually be corrected because it is never sufficient, but they have no way of saying whether the biblical word is the one to which we should respond in the first place. This is the exact counterpart to Hegel's speculative problem—the whole can correct the parts, but the whole is incorrigible; a response to the biblical word can be corrected by that word, but that word itself is incorrigible.

Whether this objection to the dialectical theologians would be sustained by a careful, constructive analysis of their work in detail is another question, of course. It is possible—and, with regard to at least one theme in Karl Barth, probable[5]—that such an analysis of these other men might disclose that they have in fact avoided the problem which seems to be entailed in this description of the structure of their systematic thought and in their explicit repudiations of speculative idealism. What is important for our present purposes is only that we note the alternative. We can subordinate

---

4. *Die Mystik und das Wort* (Tübingen, J. C. B. Mohr, 1924); *Wahrheit als Begegnung* (Zürich and Stuttgart, Zwingli-Verlag, 1938, 1963). See *Kirchliche Dogmatik, 1,* Pt. 1, par. 1–7.

5. Cf. my "Concepts, Symbols, and Sentences," pp. 513–27, esp. p. 522.

response to reflection and become absolutist in Hegel's manner if we take the search for truth seriously; or we can subordinate reflection to response and become exclusivist by subjecting everything else to our response to the biblical message, finally standing on an absolutist biblicism. Both choices demonstrate the same problem of historical limitation in systematic thought. The only way of avoiding Scylla as well as Charybdis is to make a correlative connection between two wholes—being and God, reflection and response. In this case, the systematic whole as constructed by reflection *can* be called into question, not by a further reflection but by a response to the thou of radical monotheism. Conversely, the thou to whom a total response is made can be doubted, though again, not through the power of another thou but by a reflection of being-itself. Thus, the objectival sphere is determined by the double activity of grasping its objectivity and responding to its subjectivity, so that the reflection of being-itself is correlative with, not subordinate to, the response to God. This correlation is possible because at a certain point reflection comes upon a reality that is objectivally paradoxical, and response is confronted with the paradoxical symbol of the cross. At these points everything is opened to its "depth."[6]

The best single illustration of how the two activities are interrelated is provided by the term which dominates Tillich's writings, "ultimate concern." A man's ultimate concern (his "faith") is both his being ultimately concerned (the subjective state) and that which elicits such concern (the objective reality). The question, "What concretely *is* my ultimate concern? What *does* concern me ultimately?" can be answered only by the symbol "God." If that symbol is not effective, there is no answer to the question. If there is no symbol of ultimate concern, one cannot say what a person's ultimate concern is. By various tests or experiences, one might discover relatively more and less important concerns for someone. A scientist—to use one of Tillich's examples—who, under a totalitarian regime, sacrifices his life or

6. In a positive sense depth is "ground"; in a negative sense it is "abyss."

his position rather than his integrity as a scientist shows that his scientific integrity is of greater concern than his position or his life. Of itself, however, the action does not show that his scientific integrity is his ultimate concern (even though Tillich—wrongly, I think—cites it as an example of the fact that some people who think they have no ultimate concern show, by such decisions, that they have). An ultimate concern must relate not only to a decision between life and death, integrity and self-betrayal, but to being and not being at all. This decision is never one among others.

Can one tell whether there is such a symbol of the ultimate? This leads to a second question, which is parallel to the first: "Is a given symbol ('God') a symbol of ultimate concern?" This question can be answered only by the concept of being-itself. That is to say, a symbol is a symbol of ultimate concern if its content is grasped as being-itself.

The correlative relation of reflection and response is clearly displayed here. "What is my ultimate concern?" is answered only if there is a symbol of the ultimate. "Is 'God' (or some other symbol) a symbol of the ultimate?" is answered only if there is a concept of being-itself.

The two terms and activities support each other, each one providing an answer to a question about the other. In actual reflection and actual response, however, we are not dealing with questions *about* the two but with questions *of* the two—that is, with questions that arise from each. Each of them has a limiting point which, when it is reached, shifts the activity into its correlative opposite. Our effort to grasp being-itself by reflection results in a perpetual question. We can never positively grasp it. Similarly, when we try to respond to God, we perpetually discover there is no objective reality which embodies him. The concept of being-itself and the symbol of God are thus the limiting points for reflection and response, beyond which the questions of reflection are answerable only by symbols and the symbols can be interpreted only by ontological concepts.

This is carried a step further as soon as we discover that the two limiting points are structurally identical. The point of juncture for reflection and response is the christological paradox. This paradox is a concept which expresses the ungraspability of being-itself and a symbol which embodies the utter transcendence of God. In a christological paradox—which, for Tillich's theology, is the New Testament's picture of Jesus as the Christ[7]—we have, on the one hand, an objectival reality that expresses being-itself. This means that it can be reflectively grasped only by a self-denying affirmation, that is to say, by a paradoxical concept. The reflecting subject grasps it, and his act of grasping makes it objectival; yet he grasps it as nonobjective. Thus the act is paradoxical. On the other hand, the paradoxical reality embodies God's transcendence. This means that it elicits a response which turns the responder away from the reality to which response is made. An obedient hearing of this person is an obedience that turns the hearer away from him as an objectively given person. A response to Jesus as the Christ is an obedience which is not fixed upon the historically given Jesus.

The structure of these two acts—grasping a paradoxical reality, responding to a christological symbol—is the same, so that whether I am grasping being-itself by means of a paradoxical concept or responding to God through the symbol of the cross (the picture of Jesus as the Christ) I am doing the same thing, although I have reached the paradoxical act in each case from two different directions. In reflecting being-itself I am referred to what is infinitely beyond every being, though present in all beings. In responding to God I am referred to what is infinitely beyond every symbolic reality, though present in all of them. In responding to God I am responding to the depth of the eliciting power that is in all symbols which elicit my response; in reflecting being-itself I am grasping the depth of reality that is in all the realities which I objectively grasp. Both of them designate the state of being ultimately concerned and the object about which one is ultimately concerned. A man is ultimately concerned when he tries to grasp

7. Above, p. 154.

being-itself or respond to God. The true object of that concern can only be a paradoxical something—it has to be christological rather than only theological or only ontological.

This single illustration focuses Tillich's distinctive contribution to systematic theological thought. If one asks whether it is a solution to the problem to which it is addressed, the answer must, I think, be affirmative. It does avoid the absolutism or exclusivism connected with systematics, and it does succeed in defining the presence and object which prevent ontology and theology from becoming nihilistic or arbitrary. This is what I have tried to show by my analysis of the various aspects of Tillich's solution.

In the course of the analysis we have also uncovered several points at which the limits of Tillich's systematic thought become visible. Such limits do not contradict the contention that Tillich did indeed solve the basic problem at issue; however, they do indicate the lines along which systematic theology must proceed if it starts where Tillich left off. These limits have been indicated along the way and will now be drawn together in several groups so as to give a more definite notion of their character and significance.

The first group of such criticisms is directed toward those aspects of Tillich's thought—and we are concerned with them only as they relate to the theme of reflection and response—where there is unclarity or incompleteness in his own statement. The unclarity can be eliminated if particular statements are interpreted by means of a whole constructive analysis. The incompleteness indicates points at which the thought, even on Tillich's own terms, needs to be developed further.

Thus, it was noted that behind Tillich's debate with Reinhold Niebuhr[8] on the role of ontological analysis there is a conception of ontology which involves it in something that might more traditionally be called theology. Specifically, when we are dealing with objectival subjects, we can treat them either as subjects to whom actions are ascribed or as subjects we encounter. This is the differ-

8. Above, p. 91, n. 58.

ence between "he" and "thou." We noted in this connection that, for Tillich, the area of ontology includes the ascriptive subject "he," but it does not include the encountered subject "thou." This means that ontology can and does include the things Niebuhr wishes to include in the historical and dramatic aspects of reality, but what is involved here is only a matter of including under ontology more than an analysis of the static elements of reality.

Tillich stated, in reference to a view of Martin Luther, that when we say the hidden power acting in the hand of the murderer is God himself, we are uncovering an ontological aspect in religion, for we are saying that God participates in the being of the finite subject who is performing the action. Our analysis of Tillich's thought allows us, however, to make just the distinction which is missing in his exposition at this point. If we speak not only of subject and object, as Tillich does, but of subjectival subjects and objects as well as of objectival subjects and objects, we can distinguish between "being" as the depth of objectivity and "God" as the depth of subjectivity on both sides of the relation. If "being" is peculiarly the province of ontology and "God" that of theology, then we are combining theological and ontological elements when we say that it is God who is acting in the agency of a finite being. The question is not whether ontology can grasp the free or unstructured aspects of reality, but what combination of ontological and theological elements expresses both the stability and negativity of being and both the agency of God, as the ultimate agent in all actions, and the power of God, as the one we encounter in all our encounters.

The difficulty with Tillich's thought here is partly that it requires clarification and partly that it requires further development. How are the ascriptive subject (God as the agent of actions) and the subject of encounter (God as the thou) to be related to each other? How is theology as the narrative of God's doing related to theology as the logic of the encounter between the self and God? Tillich's own exposition does not shed any particular light upon the question, nor is it an especially useful resource for solving the problems. But our analysis does make it possible to see where he fits in the general discussion.

A second instance where clarification is needed on a basic point in Tillich's thought was the case of the meaning of self as "I" and as "this individual being."[9] Here one must do more than notice that Tillich conflates two meanings in his ontological structure. As in the case of the ontological dimension of religion, which was just cited, there is in the mixture of "I" and "this man" an amalgamation of two types which should rather be kept distinct. An ontological analysis which includes the "I" precisely as first person belongs to one kind of thinking, which might be called "existential assertion." However, an analysis which involves the subject only as a subject, irrespective of its being subjectival or objectival, belongs to another kind of thinking; it is, like Tillich's whole analysis, a description rather than an existential assertion.

An existential assertion is a statement on the order of " 'I' fear it (him)," in which the subject of the statement is engaged also as the subject of the action it mentions. This is indicated by the quotation marks around "I," which denote the fact that it applies only when the statement is actually made by someone. By contrast, a reflexive description can speak of "the self" because the subject doing the analysis is not himself engaged in the action being analyzed; he is describing it from a cognitive distance. When I *speak of* the self and the world, I occupy a position of distance from what I am describing; when I utter the statement, " 'I' fear (hate, love, and so forth) something," as an existential assertion, I am engaged in the act stated in the sentence.

Preserving a distinction between existential assertions and reflexive descriptions would serve the purposes of systematics better than amalgamating them, since they do belong to different types. From this it follows that an exposition of the ontological structure, such as the one which runs through the three volumes of Tillich's *Systematic Theology,* should really be treated at two different levels—as a descriptive analysis of the constitutive func-

9. Above, pp. 24–28, 93. Cf. also pp. 116–18.

tions and objects of human endeavor, and as a set of basic forms
for existentially asserting being. It should include not only the
terms which describe the poles and elements of an ontological
structure but also the basic forms of existential assertion, in which
a first-person subject actually relates to his opposite as "world"
or as "thou."

A third instance where Tillich's exposition needs clarification
is the matter of the criterion of truth which is operative within a
circle of theological thought.[10] We noted that the circularity of
such thought means that the objective and subjective poles are
mutually interpretive. This implies, for example, that the picture
of Jesus as the Christ is recognized as the object of faith by a subject from whom the picture elicits a response of faith; it is not so
recognized apart from that response. If this is true, it poses a problem with regard to the criterion of truth, which Tillich seems to
answer in contradictory ways. On the one hand, he claims that
the truth of the Christian faith is universal and that its truth
should not be asserted dogmatically but shown apologetically. On
the other hand, he states that the criterion for determining whether
a religious truth is true is itself derived from the response of the
believer to it. If this is the case, the apologetic task seems to be
impossible. If the criterion of truth is taken from the circle of
faith, we can use the criterion to show the truth of something
only to people who are already of the faith. If we can show the
truth only to people who are already of the faith, the apologetic
task is both unnecessary and impossible.

A clarification of this problem in Tillich's thought has to be
based upon the nature of the universality and finality which appear in the criterion Tillich applies. Even though the criterion is
drawn from the material of the Christian faith, its validity is
recognizable theoretically by anyone, and hence its use is not dependent upon the circle of faith from which it is first taken. The
criterion states simply that a final revelation must be one which
in principle cannot be superseded; otherwise we can never know

10. Above, pp. 174f., 179.

what the future might do to it. A revelation is final only if it already includes, by anticipation, all possibilities in itself. It does this if it is self-negating in a double sense: it denies that the specific material expressing finality is itself a final expression, and it will hold good whether one affirms it or denies it. This clarification, however, does entail a consequence which breaks out of the structure of Tillich's systematics. This point will be taken up at the end of the present chapter.

A fourth instance where clarification is needed is the matter of relating the moral and the religious unconditionals.[11] The moral unconditional is defined as the unconditional claim which any other person makes upon me to be acknowledged as a person; the religious unconditional is the object which elicits my unconditional concern. The moral claim is what limits my objectification of the world. The one thing that can never become part of my objective world is the free subjectivity of another person. The religious symbol elicits a response of concern for my being or not being. It too can never become part of my objective world because it is a power to which I always respond but can never reflect. It is always a subject and never an object. In Christian theology this religious unconditional is the picture of Jesus as the Christ, for this picture is the reality which continues to elicit the free response of believers; its truth resides precisely in its power to do so.

What is the relation then between the person of Jesus in this picture and the person of any man? What is the relation between the power that any man has to limit my objectifying, and the power that this one man has? The picture of this one man Jesus and the presence of any man are both unconditional. How are they related to each other? One answer to this question is to say that the moral imperative is a formal unconditional, whereas the religious symbol is formal and contentual. What is acknowledged in any other person is only his pure subjectivity, the form of his freedom. What is acknowledged in the picture of Jesus as the Christ is the form and content of human freedom. If this is the

---

11. Above, p. 34. Cf. 95 and 101.

case, then what we face in another person is the fact of his personhood, and what we face in the picture of Jesus is that fact plus a concrete reality. Another person as a subject presents me with the form of objectival freedom; it is the form of freedom which always remains external to me. Jesus as the Christ also presents me with the content of freedom; that is to say, he is not only a form shaping the contents of his world but also an external reality for me, and unconditional as that reality. To acknowledge the freedom of another person requires only that I let him shape his world as I shape mine and that I interact with him as a subject (a thou) instead of objectifying him as part of my world. To acknowledge the freedom of Jesus as the Christ requires not only that I let him be the subject of his world, but also that I see in *his* shaping of himself and his world the real content of *my own* freedom and world. My relation to this reality is not simply one of acknowledging its right to be a free subject; it is also one of appropriating my world in the way he appropriates his. He is not only the form of human freedom but also the content of finite human being.

This is one way of explicating a relation that Tillich leaves unexplicated. A second way of explicating it is based on the difference between the structure of myth or cult and the structure of reason or morality, instead of on the difference between the form and the form-and-content of human freedom. The purpose of myth, like that of all religious expressions, is to bring to mind what is present everywhere as the depth of historical and natural reality. There is also a religious depth in every moral act, but without some direct expression of that depth, we are unable to recognize it. Hence, the religious symbol of this one man, Jesus as the Christ, serves to make us see what is present in every man. Without the symbol we cannot see it; with the symbol we can. Thus, the relation between the symbol and normal reality is that the symbol enables us to see something which is present but which would not be perceptible without the symbol. If we ask, "What *is* the depth of humanity in any other person?" We cannot answer by pointing to the subjectivity of his freedom. That is imperceptible. We can answer only by pointing to the religious symbol which awakens in us a knowledge of the dimension of depth otherwise hidden under the forms of cultural life, including moral acts.

The religious symbol is permanently necessary; it can never be supplanted or discarded, because without it we lose sight of the depth of reality. At the same time, the purpose of the symbol is always to point away from itself as a single reality to the depth which it is manifesting in a localized way. What is perceptible in a religious symbol is the very thing that we should, but do not, see everywhere. Our failure to see it is part of the estrangement from our essential being. Tillich says that there "should be" no myth or ritual (*ST, 1,* 80). By this, of course, he is not announcing a program to do away with them. What he means is that under the conditions of fallen existence things are necessary which essentially "should not" be at all. Essentially we should be able to see the depth of reality without special symbols; actually we cannot, because of our fallenness. On these terms, the relation between the moral unconditional and the religious unconditional is but one instance of the general relation between religion and culture, or myth and reason, or cultic and moral behavior.

In the foregoing cases we were concerned with points at which Tillich's exposition needed clarification and further development. In the second group of cases we discover contradictory motifs in Tillich's thought, which cannot be eliminated by clarification. Here we must choose one or the other of two themes, not both.

The first such instance is the question of how Jesus as an object of historical study is related to Jesus as an object of faith. There is a contradiction between two lines of thought in Tillich which cannot be reconciled by clarification. On one hand, he distinguishes the historical from the religious object correctly by calling attention to the different methodological procedures involved in our relation to the two. Historical research is a phase of critical reflection; faith is an act of response. Moreover, Tillich has seen this distinction more clearly than any of his critics, and his insistence that an act of faith cannot be based on the result of historical research is systematically more justifiable than is the claim of some biblical scholars that faith must rest upon historical study.

On the other hand, this very distinction rules out the second line of thought, according to which the picture of Jesus as the Christ can guarantee the factual existence of a person "behind" the picture. It cannot guarantee any particular detail about the person, nor can it guarantee that all of the details even come close to being an accurate representation of him. But it can guarantee that there was *some* actual, single person, in response to whom the picture was created by the first believers. How can that be? If faith originates only as a response to the symbol which elicits the believer's response, it follows that the only guarantee contained in the religious picture of Jesus as the Christ is that it is a picture which can sustain faith and that, because of its content, it anticipates and draws into its truth both affirmative and negative responses.[12] The first point follows from the systematic account of the nature of faith; the second point follows from the particular content of this religious symbol.

If, for example, historical research made it most improbable that there ever was a person named Jesus, or that there was a single person behind the New Testament picture, this would not undercut the faith any more than would the discovery that particular details of the person were not correct. It would, of course, alter many theoretical and theological explanations of the faith. But so long as the picture is the picture of a real person, even though fictionally created, it can theoretically continue to elicit a response of faith from men; and so long as it actually elicits such a response, the question whether where was a single person behind the portrait is irrelevant to the existence of faith, however relevant it might be for the theoretical explications of the content of that faith.

12. Above, pp. 106, 177, 180. Cf. pp. 57, 112. See also Tillich, *Dynamics of Faith,* p. 98. Bo Nylund, "Korsets plats i Paul Tillichs kristologiska tänkande," *Svensk teologisk kvartalskrift, 42* (1966), 214–36, esp. pp. 235f. A. J. McKelway, *The Systematic Theology of Paul Tillich* (Richmond, Va., John Knox Press, 1964), p. 100, is misleading on this point.

In other words, if one accepts Tillich's basic account of the nature and act of faith—and I think one must do so on systematic grounds—it follows that one must reject the claim that faith can guarantee the factual existence of the person portrayed by the picture. Such an existence cannot be guaranteed. It can be ascertained only by historical research into the records of the nearest witnesses and into the tradition which contains the collective memory of the church. Such research has concluded that the existence of Jesus is most probable. But even when it so concludes, we have to insist that an opposite conclusion would not of itself destroy the power of the picture to elicit a response, just as we insist that the present conclusion is not sufficient to found a response to the picture. The picture elicits a response if it has power to do so; when it loses that power, it no longer elicits a response, regardless of how much we wish to maintain that it *should* not lose that power. This is precisely the freedom of the picture as a religious symbol.

We can ascertain that a symbol is a symbol; we can even theoretically explain why one thing is a more adequate symbol than another—why, for example, a person is a better religious symbol than a stone, or why the cross is a better symbol of finality than an incarnation; but we cannot draw any guaranteed conclusions about what may be behind the picture. The only thing behind it as a symbol is the depth it expresses, not another reality, not even the person of Jesus as a historical man embodying the divine depth. Accordingly, on this issue we conclude that there are two contradictory themes in Tillich's thought, one of which must be given up for the sake of the other.

There is a second question on which one must make a similar choice between conflicting themes, although it is less central than the christological discussion. We noted that, somewhat surprisingly, Tillich excludes the basic self–world ontological structure from the material that symbolizes the divine life.[13] One can use the ontological elements, such as freedom and destiny or individ-

---

13. Above, pp. 120–122.

uality and participation, but not the basic structure of self and world. For example, one can say that God is freedom and destiny, but one cannot say that he is the self and the world. We suggested several reasons for Tillich's decision on this matter, none of which was intrinsic to the structure of his systematics. Here again, one must choose between the two lines of thought.

If God is really the depth of the self–world structure, then there is no systematic reason why we cannot say God is the self and the world when we can say that God is freedom and destiny or individuality and participation. There may be historical reasons why we do not in fact so speak of God, but there is no systematic reason why we should not. On the contrary, the systematic consideration could well correct the historical deficiency. Indeed, we do find material in Tillich where he himself does so. He speaks of God as being closer to the *I* than I am to myself and more encompassing than the universe. Is this not saying that he is the depth of the self and the world?

Predicating ontological terms of God is the technique Tillich uses for "deepening" these concepts in order to have them express the divine depth. Saying that God *is* freedom and destiny is a means of turning the concepts of freedom and destiny into expressions of depth.[14] Normally they articulate the structure of being. When they are predicated of God, however, they point beyond their polarity to their depth. By this very same technique we can "deepen" the concepts of self and world by predicating them of God. "God *is* the self and the world" would allow these ontological terms to express the depth that is beyond their polarity. If this kind of statement is actually absent from our religious vocabulary, in contrast to others of a similar kind, such as "God is the beginning and end" or "God is freedom and destiny," then the task of the systematic theologian is to introduce them rather than acquiesce to their omission.

In other words, if the technique of predicating ontological concepts of "God" is a legitimate device for theologizing ontologi-

14. Above, pp. 56, 125f.

cal terms—and there is no reason to deny that it is—then it is inconsistent to maintain that the basic ontological terms of "self" and "world" cannot be used for symbolical material. Tillich says they cannot be so used because they refer to "kinds" of being rather than to polarities of being. This cannot be the case, however. If they really grasp the ontological structure, they cannot refer to kinds of being, since kinds are "ontic," not "ontological" (*ST*, *1*, 164). On this whole point some accidental factors of the history of idealist thought seem to have determined a decision which Tillich should have made on systematic theological grounds. Here again is an instance where one of two contradictory themes needs to be given up for the sake of the other.

Finally, there is one conflict of motifs in Tillich's thought which suggests a new systematic structure entirely, a bursting out, as it were, from the structure which Tillich gave to systematics. Specifically, it suggests that a two-term analysis of the structure of being and thought (self-and-world, or subject-and-object) cannot handle a set of problems in which the real difference between a subject as "I" and a subject as "he" is of decisive significance.

We noticed with regard to the symbol of the cross[15] that Tillich's definition of its finality contains two conflicting themes. On one hand, he attributes its finality to the circularity of theological thought. Any actual revelation is a final revelation for those who receive it as revelation. Since the cross is the revelation upon which Christian faith rests, it is final for Christian faith. On the other hand, Tillich attributes the finality of this symbol to the fact that it includes its own negation. This self-negation contains two aspects. In the first place, it means that the material which expresses the depth of self and world becomes transparent to that depth by denying its own ultimacy. The symbol of the cross makes an ultimate claim—it is a reality eliciting ultimate concern—but it does so in such a way as to make it impossible for a believer to be ultimately concerned about the concrete material through which the claim is made. "Jesus sacrifices himself as Jesus to himself

15. Above, p. 196.

as the Christ" is the statement in which Tillich formulates this self-negating character of the material part of the final symbol. On these terms the cross is the final symbol because it can include all possible expressions of ultimacy. It excludes only the idolatrous attachment to some reality, itself included, as though that reality were in itself the ultimate.

A second aspect of the self-negation, however, turns our attention away from the material and depth of the symbol to the two possible positions that people can take toward it. We noticed in Tillich's discussion of the role of Judas and the leaders of the Jews in the crucifixion of Jesus[16] that even those who deny that Jesus is the Christ, the revelation of God, are affirming the substance of the revelation. To put it differently, the deepest meaning of the symbol of the cross of Jesus is that it reconciles those who affirm and those who deny that it is the very presence of God himself. A believer who says that Jesus is the Christ is not denying what an unbeliever asserts when he says that Jesus is not the Christ. The depth of this final revelation is expressed only by both sides of that issue. Here is a case where one person's affirmation of a definite content does not necessarily deny another person's denial of the selfsame content. On the contrary, if Jesus is the Christ, the final revelation, then the truth he reveals is unconditionally valid; that is to say, it is confirmed not only when he is affirmed to be the Christ but also when he is denied to be the Christ. His finality lies precisely in the fact that he includes those who deny and those who affirm. There is no way of *not* attesting the depth of truth revealed there.

Thus, on the one hand, Tillich treats finality in a circular way; on the other hand, he treats it in a noncircular way. The fact that he did not resolve this obvious conflict is attributable, I believe, to the inadequacy of his basic structural analysis. What is decisive in this analysis of the symbol of the cross is that it allows affirmers and deniers to be what they freely choose to be. It does not demand that everyone affirm the same thing. It says only that

16. Above, p. 105.

whether one affirms or denies that Jesus is the Christ one is con-
firming the truth he embodies.

This leads now to the critical issue. The situation determined
by the cross in this way cannot actually exist unless there is a real
difference between the "I" and the other subject "he"—that is,
between the subjectival and objectival subjects. If there is no real
difference between them, then it is impossible for "my" affirmation and "his" denial both to be truth. We are not saying that
each of the two has only half of the truth and that the two together make up the whole. We are saying, rather, that each of
them is a finite assertion of the whole truth, or, more exactly,
of the final truth, the depth of truth itself. They cannot be added
together, but in their dialectical interaction, as well as in their
independent statements, they can let the depth of truth itself be
known. To any thinker for whom there is no real difference between an "I" and a "he" as subjects, the notion that one person's
denial and another person's affirmation of the same content could
be equally true is absurd.[17] It is only when one recognizes a real
difference between a subjectival subject and an objectival subject
that this absurdity is removed.

Now, the state of affairs in Tillich's systematics is that its
analysis of the basic ontological structure does *not* allow this real
difference between subjects, whereas his analysis of the symbol of
the cross demands it. His basic ontological structure is constituted
by the two terms of "self" and "world"; his analysis of the cross
implies a polarity, equally basic, between the freedom of an I-
subject and that of a he-subject. This discrepancy can be reme-
died, I think, only by an analysis of the ontological structure
which has three basic terms rather than two. The structure is
constituted not by the self–world polarity but by a self–world–
other-self triad; the basic structure is not subject and object only,
but subject, object, and parasubject.[18]

If this analysis of the conflict of motifs in Tillich's christology

17. This point is stated at greater length in my "Pluralism in Theology,"
Journal of Ecumenical Studies, 5, no. 4 (Fall 1968), 676–96.
18. The term "parasubject" comes from Günther, *Idee und Grundriss.*

is correct, as I think I have shown it to be, we have reached a point where a "constructive analysis" of his thought must give way to a different systematic construction, based upon a three-term structure of thought and being. I have conducted this investigation within the limits imposed by the aim to provide a constructive analysis. This meant accepting as a starting point the analysis of the structure of being and thought as self and world, or subject and object, which accords with Tillich's own analysis of the basic structure. That analysis was modified, however, by further distinctions in the polarity which are derived from the possible relations implied in it. This permitted us to see dimensions of Tillich's thought which are otherwise not visible, and it uncovered a number of problems which are otherwise hidden. Now, however, we have arrived at the place where a treatment of the problem uncovered would require a different analysis of the basic structure. Instead of accepting the two-term ontological structure, we need to begin with a three-term structure, in which the difference between an "I" and another subject, which is the very difference that is never eradicable in the *act* of being or thinking, is acknowledged at the very start. This would be the beginning of a new systematics; it would no longer be a discussion of Paul Tillich, and it cannot, therefore, be part of the present book.

Tillich stood in the tradition of speculative idealism. He provided a solution to the problem of nihilism and atheism which that tradition, in its nineteenth-century form, spawned. And at the end this solution breaks away from the tradition, opening upon something new.

Bibliography

Works by Tillich

GW refers to the *Gesammelte Werke*, published by Evangelisches Verlagswerk, Stuttgart, Germany, of which the following volumes have already appeared:

1. *Frühe Hauptwerke*, 1959.
2. *Christentum und Soziale Gestaltung*, 1962.
3. *Das religiöse Fundament des moralischen Handelns*, 1965.
4. *Philosophie und Schicksal*, 1961.
5. *Die Frage nach dem Unbedingten*, 1964.
6. *Der Widerstreit von Raum und Zeit*, 1963.
7. *Der Protestantismus als Kritik und Gestaltung*, 1962.
9. *Die religiöse Substanz der Kultur*, 1967.
10. *Die religiöse Deutung der Gegenwart*, 1968.

Auf der Grenze, Stuttgart, Evangelisches Verlagswerk, 1962. (English translation: *On the Boundary*.)

Biblical Religion and the Search for Ultimate Reality, Chicago, University of Chicago Press, 1955.

Christianity and the Encounter of the World Religions, New York, Columbia University Press, 1963.

The Courage To Be, New Haven, Yale University Press, 1952.

Dynamics of Faith, New York, Harper & Row, 1957.

"Existential Aspects of Modern Art," in *Christianity and the Existentialists*, ed. Carl Michalson (New York, Charles Scribner's Sons, 1956), pp. 128–47.

The Future of Religions, ed. Jerald C. Brauer, New York, Harper & Row, 1966.

"Gläubiger Realismus I" (1927), *GW*, *4*, 77–87.

"Gläubiger Realismus II" (1928), *GW*, *4*, 88–106.

"Honesty and Consecration," *Response*, 8 (1967), 203–10.

The Interpretation of History, New York, Charles Scribner's Sons, 1936.

"Kairos I" (1922), *GW*, *6*, 9–28.

"Kairos II" (1926), *GW*, *6*, 29–41.

"Kairos III" (1958), *GW, 6,* 137–39.

"Kairos und Logos" (1926), *GW, 4,* 43–76.

"Kirche und Kultur" (1924), *GW, 9,* 32–46.

"Kritisches und Positives Paradox" (1923), *GW, 7,* 216–25.

"The Lost Dimension in Religion," *Saturday Evening Post, 230* (June 14, 1958), 29ff.

Love, Power, and Justice, New York, Oxford University Press, 1954.

"Masse und Geist" (1922), *GW, 2,* 35–90.

"The Meaning and Justification of Religious Symbols," in *Religious Experience and Truth,* ed. Sidney Hook (New York, New York University Press, 1961), pp. 3–11.

Morality and Beyond, New York, Harper & Row, 1963.

On the Boundary, New York, Charles Scribner's Sons, 1966.

The Protestant Era, tr. James Luther Adams, Chicago, University of Chicago Press, 1948.

Rechtfertigung und Zweifel, Giessen, Alfred Töpelmann, 1924.

"Rejoinder," *Journal of Religion, 46* (January 1966), Pt. 2, 184–96.

"Religionsphilosophie" (1919), *GW, 1,* 295–364.

The Religious Situation, tr. H. Richard Niebuhr, New York, Meridian Books, 1956.

"The Religious Symbol," *Journal of Liberal Religion, 2* (Summer 1940), 13–33. This is a translation of "Das religiöse Symbol," which first appeared in *Blätter für deutsche Philosophie, 1* (1928). It also appears in *Religiöse Verwirklichung* (Berlin, Furche Verlag, 1930), pp. 88–109, and in *GW, 5,* 196–212. The English translation appears also in *Daedalus, 87* (Summer 1958), 3–21, and in *Religious Experience and Truth,* ed. Sidney Hook (New York, New York University Press, 1961), pp. 301–21.

"Das System der Wissenschaften nach Gegenständen und Methoden" (1923), *GW, 1,* 109–293.

Systematic Theology, Chicago, University of Chicago Press, 1951, 1957, 1963, Vols. 1, 2, and 3.

"Die technische Stadt als Symbol" (1928), *GW, 9,* 307–11.

Theology of Culture, ed. Robert C. Kimball, New York, Oxford University Press, 1959.

"The Theology of Missions," in *Witness to a Generation: Significant Writings from Christianity and Crisis 1941–1966,* ed. Wayne H. Cowen (Indianapolis, Bobbs-Merrill Co., 1966), pp. 83–90.

"Über die Idee einer Theologie der Kultur" (1919), *GW, 9,* 13–31.

"Die Überwindung des Religionsbegriffes in der Religionsphilosophie" (1922), *GW, 1,* 365–88.
Ultimate Concern: Tillich in Dialogue, ed. D. Mackenzie Brown, New York, Harper & Row, 1965.
"The Word of God," in *Language: An Enquiry into Its Meaning and Function,* ed. Ruth Nanda Anshen, New York, Harper & Brothers, 1957.

OTHER WORKS

Adams, James Luther, *Paul Tillich's Philosophy of Culture, Science, and Religion,* New York, Harper & Row, 1965.
Alston, William P., "Tillich's Conception of a Religious Symbol," in *Religious Experience and Truth,* ed. Sidney Hook (New York, New York University Press, 1961), pp. 12–26.
Armbruster, Carl J., S. J., *The Vision of Paul Tillich,* New York, Sheed & Ward, 1967.
Barth, Karl, *Christ and Adam: Man and Humanity in Romans 5,* tr. T. A. Smail, New York, Harper & Brothers, 1956.
———, *Kirchliche Dogmatik,* Zollikon-Zürich, Evangelischer Verlag, 1955⁷ (1932), *1,* Pt. 1, Sec. 1–7; 1959⁴ (1942), 2, Pt. 2, Sec. 35.
———, *Die protestantische Theologie im 19. Jahrhundert,* Zollikon-Zürich, Evangelischer Verlag, 1952.
Bloch, Ernst, *Subjekt und Objekt: Erläuterungen zu Hegel,* rev. and exp. ed., Frankfurt am Main, Suhrkamp Verlag, 1962.
Brunner, Emil, *Die Mystik und das Wort,* Tübingen, J. C. B. Mohr, 1924.
———, *Wahrheit als Begegnung,* Zürich & Stuttgart, Zwingli-Verlag, 1938, 1963.
Buri, Fritz, *Dogmatik als Selbstverständnis des christlichen Glaubens,* *1,* Bern, Paul Haupt, 1956.
———, "Das Problem des ungegenständlichen Denkens und Redens in der heutigen Theologie," *Zeitschrift für Theologie und Kirche,* *61* (November 1964), 353–71.
———, "Zur Grundlegung einer Theologie der Existenz bei Paul Tillich," *Schweiz. Theol. Umschau,* 23 (1953), 40–57.
Cassirer, Ernst, *Individuum und Kosmos in der Philosophie der Renaissance,* Darmstadt, Wissenschaftliche Buchgesellschaft, 1963.

————, *Philosophie der symbolischen Formen,* Darmstadt, Wissenschaftliche Buchgesellschaft, 1964.

Cobb, John B., Jr., *Living Options in Protestant Theology,* Philadelphia, Westminster Press, 1962.

Dupré, Louis, *Kierkegaard as Theologian,* New York, Sheed & Ward, 1963.

Ebeling, Gerhard, *Luther: Einführung in sein Denken,* Tübingen, J. C. B. Mohr, 1964.

Emmet, Dorothy, "Epistemology and the Idea of Revelation," in *The Theology of Paul Tillich,* ed. Charles W. Kegley and Robert W. Bretall, New York, Macmillan, 1952.

————, " 'The Ground of Being,' " *Journal of Theological Studies,* N.S. 15 (October 1964), Pt. 2, 280–92.

Ford, Lewis S., Review of J. Heywood Thomas, *Paul Tillich: An Appraisal,* and Kenneth Hamilton, *The System and the Gospel: A Critique of Paul Tillich,* in *Journal of Bible and Religion,* 32 (July 1964), 279–81.

————, "The Three Strands of Tillich's Theory of Religious Symbols," *Journal of Religion,* 46 (January 1966), Pt. 2, 104–30.

————, "Tillich and Thomas: The Analogy of Being," *Journal of Religion,* 46 (April 1966), 229–45.

Frei, Hans, "Niebuhr's Theological Background," in *Faith and Ethics,* ed. Paul Ramsey (New York, Harper & Row, 1957, 1965), Chap. 1.

Gadamer, Hans Georg, "Martin Heidegger und die MarburgerTheologie," in *Zeit und Geschichte: Rudolf Bultmann zum 80. Geburtstag,* ed. Erich Dinkler (Tübingen, J. C. B. Mohr, 1964), pp. 479–90.

————, *Wahrheit und Methode,* 2d ed. Tübingen, J. C. B. Mohr, 1965.

Gilkey, Langdon, *Maker of Heaven and Earth: The Christian Doctrine of Creation in the Light of Modern Knowledge,* Garden City, N.Y., Doubleday Anchor, 1965.

Gogarten, Friedrich, *The Reality of Faith,* tr. Carl Michalson and others, Philadelphia, Westminster Press, 1959.

Goichon, A. M., *La philosophie d'Avicenne et son influence en Europe médiévale,* Paris, 1944.

Günther, Gotthard, *Idee und Grundriss einer nicht-aristotelischen Logik, 1,* Hamburg, Felix Meiner, 1959.

Hammond, Guyton B., *Man in Estrangement: Paul Tillich and Erich*

Fromm Compared, Nashville, Tenn., Vanderbilt University Press, 1965.

Hartmann, W., *Die Methode der Korrelation von philosophischen Fragen und theologischen Antworten bei Paul Tillich,* Göttingen, 1954.

Hegyi, Johannes, *Die Bedeutung des Seins bei den klassischen Kommentatoren des heiligen Thomas von Aquin: Capreolus—Silvester von Ferrara—Cajetan,* Pullach bei München, Verlag Berchmannskolleg, 1959.

Heidegger, Martin, *Sein und Zeit,* Tübingen, Niemeyer, 1963[10].

Heiss, Robert, *Die grossen Dialektiker des 19. Jahrhunderts: Hegel, Kierkegaard, Marx,* Köln & Berlin, Kiepenhauer & Witsch, 1963.

Kegley, Charles, ed., *The Theology of Emil Brunner,* New York, Macmillan, 1962.

Kelsey, David, *The Fabric of Paul Tillich's Theology,* New Haven, Yale University Press, 1967.

Kierkegaard, Sören, *Fear and Trembling,* and *The Sickness unto Death,* New York, Doubleday Anchor, 1954.

Krüger, Gerhard, *Die Herkunft des philosophischen Selbstbewusstseins,* Darmstadt, Wissenschaftliche Buchgesellschaft, 1962.

———, *Einsicht und Leidenschaft,* Frankfurt am Main, Vittorio Klostermann, 1963[3].

Looff, W., *Der Symbolbegriff in der neueren Theologie und Philosophie, Kant-Studien,* Supplement No. 69, Köln, 1953.

Loomer, Bernard M., "Tillich's Theology of Correlation," *Journal of Religion,* 36 (July 1956), 150–56.

McClean, George F., O.M.I., "Symbol and Analogy: Tillich and Thomas," in *Paul Tillich in Catholic Thought,* ed. Thomas A. O'Meara, O.P., and Celestin D. Weisser, O.P. (Dubuque, Priory Press, 1964), pp. 145–83.

McKelway, A. J., *The Systematic Theology of Paul Tillich,* Richmond, Va., John Knox Press, 1964.

Marsch, Wolf-Dieter, "Logik des Kreuzes," *Evangelische Theologie,* 28 (February–March 1968), 57–82.

Niebuhr, Richard R., *Schleiermacher on Christ and Religion,* New York, Charles Scribner's Sons, 1964.

Nörenberg, Klaus-Dieter, *Analogia Imaginis: Der Symbolbegriff in der Theologie Paul Tillichs,* Gütersloher Verlagshaus Gerd Mohn, 1966.

Noller, Gerhard, *Sein und Existenz: Die Überwindung des Subjekt-*

Objekt-Schemas in der Philosophie Heideggers und in der Theologie der Entmythologisierung, München, Chr. Kaiser Verlag, 1962.

Nylund, B., "Korsets plats i Paul Tillichs kristologiska tänkande," *Svensk teologisk kvartalskrift, 42* (1966), 214–36.

Oehler, Klaus, "Subjekt und Objekt" in *Religion in Geschichte und Gegenwart* (3d ed. Tübingen, J. C. B. Mohr, 1962), 6, cols. 448–51.

O'Meara, Thomas A., O.P., and Celestin D. Weisser, O.P., eds., *Paul Tillich in Catholic Thought,* Dubuque, Priory Press, 1964.

Pannenberg, Wolfhart, "Akt und Sein im Mittelalter," *Kerygma und Dogma, 7* (1961), 202–11.

Randall, John H., "The Ontology of Paul Tillich," in *The Theology of Paul Tillich,* ed. Charles W. Kegley and Robert W. Bretall, New York, Macmillan, 1952.

Rhein, Christoph, *Paul Tillich: Philosoph und Theologe,* Stuttgart, Evangelisches Verlagswerk, 1957.

Ricoeur, Paul, *Fallible Man,* tr. Charles Kelbley, Chicago, Henry Regnery, n.d.

Rowe, William L., "The Meaning of 'God' in Tillich's Theology," *Journal of Religion, 42* (Oct. 19, 1962), 274–86.

———, *Religious Symbols and God: A Philosophical Study of Tillich's Theology,* Chicago, University of Chicago Press, 1968.

Scharlemann, R., "Der Begriff der Systematik bei Paul Tillich," *Neue Zeitschrift für systematische Theologie und Religionsphilosophie,* 8 (1966), 242–54.

———, "The Scope of Systematics: An Analysis of Tillich's Two Systems," *Journal of Religion, 48* (April 1968), 136–49. (An English version of the previous listing.)

———, "Seinsstruktur und Seinstiefe in der Tillichschen Methode der Korrelation," *Kerygma und Dogma, 11* (October 1965), 245–55.

———, "Tillich's Method of Correlation: Two Proposed Revisions," *Journal of Religion, 16* (January 1966), Pt. 2, 92–103. (An English version of the previous listing.)

Schröer, Henning, *Die Denkform der Paradoxalität als theologisches Problem,* Göttingen, Vandenhoeck & Ruprecht, 1960.

Schulz, Walter, "Der Gott der modernen Metaphysik," in *Der Gottesgedanke im Abendland,* ed. Albert Schaefer, Stuttgart, Kohlhammer Verlag, 1964.

————, "Hegel und das Problem der Aufhebung der Metaphysik," in *Martin Heidegger zum 70. Geburtstag,* ed. Günther Neske, Pfullingen, Verlag Günther Neske, 1959.

————, "Das Problem der absoluten Reflexion," in *Einsichten: Gerhard Krüger zum 60. Geburtstag,* ed. Klaus Oehler and Richard Schaeffler, Frankfurt am Main, Vittorio Klostermann, 1962.

————, *Die Vollendung des deutschen Idealismus in der Spätphilosophie Schellings,* Stuttgart, W. Kohlhammer Verlag, 1955.

Schweitzer, Carl G., "Geist bei Hegel und Heiliger Geist," *Neue Zeitschrift für systematische Theologie und Religionsphilosophie,* 6 (1964), 318–28.

Smith, Huston, Review of Paul Tillich, *The Future of Religions,* in *Journal of Religion,* 47 (April 1967), 184–85.

Tanabe, Hajime, "Todesdialektik," in *Martin Heidegger zum 70. Geburtstag,* ed. Günther Neske (Pfullingen, Verlag Günther Neske, 1959), pp. 93–133.

Tavard, George, *Paul Tillich and the Christian Message,* New York, Charles Scribner's Sons, 1962.

Troeltsch, Ernst, *Die Absolutheit des Christentums und die Religionsgeschichte,* Tübingen, J. C. B. Mohr, 1929³ (1901).

Volkmann-Schluck, Karl Heinz, "Der Satz vom Widerspruch als Anfang der Philosophie," in *Martin Heidegger zum 70. Geburtstag,* ed. Günther Neske, Pfullingen, Verlag Günther Neske, 1959, pp. 134ff.

Wagner, Hans, *Philosophie und Reflexion,* München and Basel, Ernst Reinhardt Verlag, 1959.

Wernsdörfer, Thietmar, *Die entfremdete Welt: Eine Untersuchung zur Theologie Paul Tillichs,* Zürich, Zwingli Verlag, 1968.

Index